THE NEW CHRISTIAN RIGHT 1981—1988

Prospects for the Post-Reagan Decade

ERLING JORSTAD

Volume 25
Studies in American Religion

BIP-90
The Edwin Mellen Press
Lewiston/Queenston
Lampeter

Library of Congress Cataloging-in-Publication Data

Jorstad, Erling, 1930—
  The New Christian Right, 1981—1988

  (Studies in American religion ; v. 25)
  Includes bibliographies and index.
  1. Fundamentalism 2. Evangelicalism--United States. 3. Christianity and politics--History--20th century. 4. Church and state--United States--History--20th century. 5. Church and social problems--United States--Election--1984. I. Title. II. Series.
  BT82.2.J66   1987   322'.1'0973   87-1636
  ISBN 0-88946-669-6

This is volume 25 in the continuing series
Studies in American Religion
Volume 25 ISBN 0-88946-669-6
SAR Series ISBN 0-88946-992-X

For information contact: **The Edwin Mellen Press**
Box 450   Box 67
Lewiston, New York   Queenston, Ontario
U.S.A. 14092   CANADA L0S 1L0
                        Mellen House
                  Lampeter, Dyfed, Wales
                UNITED KINGDOM SA48 7DY

Printed in the United States of America

*To Henry, Richard, and Robert
in the memory of Bob Crossley*

TABLE OF CONTENTS

ACKNOWLEDGEMENTS

Once again, a number of friends have contributed to whatever merits this book may possess; brother Curtis, son Eric, Karen Petersen, Marvin Dulaney, James Johnson, and the Staff at Rølvaag memorial Library at St. Olaf College. Thanks also to the college for several Faculty Development grants. Thanks always to Lois Wilkens for whose talents in preparing my manuscripts I have run out of words.

PART ONE. 1981-1984
New Life

The resurgence and intertwined growth of religious fundamentalism and political conservatism in the United States in the 1980s stands as the dominant theme in American religious history of this decade. To some observers, however, it should never have happened at all. To them this society was supposedly moving rapidly toward total secularization, towards "man come of age" standing liberated from the crutches of supernatural religion, and moving towards the death of the local parish, among other solemn predictions. Yet by mid-decade those observers acknowledge the presence of some unprecedented developments; the impressive victories of Ronald Reagan, the immense new wealth and influence of right-wing televangelists, and the demise of the New Deal/Great Society welfare state agenda. Added to that were the persistent demands of the New Christian Right for ending the current legal protections of abortion, of restoring religious exercises in public schools, for curtailing proposed civil law protections of homosexuals, for keeping the Equal Rights Amendment dead, and for a host of other so-called family issues.

This legislative offensive, cast by its sponsors as a moral crusade to save America, led the populace to reconsider some fundamental national values and commitments. How far should organized religion extend its influence into political concerns? How high was the "wall of separation" between church and state? What should be done about religion in the public schools? In short, what was "the American way" in solving the issues created by these conflicts? Was there, indeed, such a way?

By the late 1980s one conclusion stood clear: no agreement, no consensus on what constituted the American way had been reached. The escalating trend in the opposite direction, called "Balkanization" (by Kevin Phillips) or

"Tribalization" (by Martin E. Marty) continued to go un-
checked. So pervasive was the power of each group seeking to protect and advance its own interests (geographic,
generational, gender, class, race, religion) that politics clearly lost much of its capability of being the
art of the possible. In sum, the "American way" of
blending politics and religion had turned into a major
dilemma bordering on crisis proportions.

It has such proportions because at this time the
emergence in this century of the all-pervasive nationstate
has forced people of faith to define again what belongs
to Caesar and what to God.[1] The totalitarian governments
of the 20th Century have demanded an obedience that seekers have found to be idolatrous. Hence the resistance
by the Bonhoeffers, the Soviet Jewish dissidents, and
the Roman Catholics in Poland, to name but three.

But obviously the battles in the United States fall
short of such epic proportions. Here no forms of resistance by church people lead to banishment or irreparable
harrassment of their organizations. The longstanding
protections of the free exercise clause of the First
Amendment, upheld by the scrupulously attentive decisions
of the Supreme Court, stand today as the primary barriers
to totalitarian usurpations.

Yet the historical record shows Americans are increasing both the number of battles and the level of emotional
intensity over resolving the tensions between church and
state, between religion and politics. For decades the
agenda of church/state issues facing the Supreme Court
remained virtually empty. Most Americans willy nilly
simply acceded to prevailing Protestant recipes for
blending religion and politics. Today citizens battle
over the whole range of "social agenda" issues (defined
below, ch. 2) and a score of other related matters. The
Tribalization continues to deepen.

Specifically, in this decade the battles have moved into an arena heretofore left unoccupied by many of today's contestants, that of elective politicking and public policy making. There, as conventional wisdom teaches, the citizenry should attempt to direct the policies of the government to accomplish their particular objectives.

Those are best achieved when the participants draw on such resources as goodwill, compromise, adroit bargaining, and a shared vision of the common good to sustain their politicking. And, acknowledging some monumental failures such as those over slavery, prohibition, and protection of minority group rights, that vision has arguably served the public well. By contrast to Dietrich Bonhoeffer's Germany, to Anatoly B. Shcharansky's Russia, and to Jerzy Popieluszko's Poland, in the United States the means for using political persuasion by political means to achieve one's objectives are still accessible.

So why then does the controversy over the American way rage? This book addresses itself to that question. It attempts to identify and track the source of the movement whose appearance has altered the traditional ground rules of blending religion and politics, namely the New Christian Right (NCR). This study, further, is an update of this writer's first assessment made of that movement: Evangelicals in The White House: The Cultural Maturation of Born Again Christianity, 1960-1981 (The Edwin Mellen Press, 1981). Since that work was published, the NCR has become a major force in American religious and political life. Its leaders, for instance, command multimillion dollar annual budgets; the names of Falwell, Robertson, and Swaggart are household words. Never before had a celebrity preacher, without prior political experience, attempted to run for the most powerful

position in the world, the Presidency, and been taken
seriously by voters. Never before as Martin E. Marty
suggests, have fundamentalists been in such positions
of privilege, having the ear of or a voice in the White
House, coming from nowhere to "hold the most visible
and assertive position in American politics."[2]

II

Readers may ask at this point what is so new about
this movement. They can trace fundamentalist preachers
mixing it up in the political realm as far back as the
1960s with the likes of Carl McIntire and Billy James
Hargis.[3] Today's programs, however, have moved far
beyond that activity. Today's politicking attracts
participation by ordained clergy in the hurlyburly, day
by day process of electioneering; voter registration,
education of the citizens on the issues, and stump-
speaking. Second, it is new because of its massive use
of television, a medium not available before this generation. Third, it annually generates tens of millions
of dollars of revenue through fundraising programs, revenue never remotely accessible to earlier Rightists.
Fourth, these fundamentalists are not the pure separationists so characteristic of the earlier leaders.

The newness extends further than that. A careful
NCR watcher, Robert C. Liebman, suggests it is original
because of "its scope, its scale, and its size."[4] In
scope, it promulgates a very broad socio-moral agenda
of crusades, rather than, as in earlier days, focusing
on single issue reforms. Its itinerary stretches from
"abortion to Zimbabwe." It is new because it offers a
carefully crafted, highly appealing new catchall conspiracy on which to blame America's woes, that of secular humanism. Its scale also makes it new. No longer
limited to the heartland of fundamentalism, the American

South, it moves easily across the fifty states, its
chief television markets being New York, Chicago, and
Los Angeles. Finally, its size differentiates it from
earlier movements. It commands a national constituency,
support from all regions and, apparently from the full
spectrum of socio-economic groups. This is something
new on the national scene.[5]

Other factors also contribute to its newness. Its
appearance caught the headlines because conventional
scholarly wisdom had been pointing out that America
was becoming a secular society. Organized religion,
the specialists were saying, was clearly in decline.
Then, suddenly, a subculture supposedly antiquated and
out of touch with the real world showed remarkable
energy, political savvy and direct access to the Oval
Office.[6]

The New Christian Right capitalized strongly on the
American penchant for public relations image building.
Its leaders knew the public would be intrigued, if also
angered, over having traditionally redneck, hillbilly,
freewheeling preachers now claim front page attention
as spokesmen for Christianity, commanding huge budgets
and, in classic fundamentalist style, being very pugna-
cious, very polemical as they called America back to
recapture a heritage saturated with patriotism, pride
and piety. The NCR had become, like so much of American
political life a media event, a photo opportunity.[7]

Unquestionably, the greatest appeal of this religious Right in the 1980s has been its final new ingredient, its social agenda stating what must be done immediately to save America. Through specific organizations such as Moral Majority, Liberty Federation,
Christian Voice, The Roundtable, the Freedom Council,
the Jimmy Swaggart Ministries, and the Christian Inquirer

alongside state and local lobbies and pressure groups,
it offers concrete, identifiable programs to turn America
back to God. All New Christian Rightists would support
what has come to be the "short list" of demands, the
minimal number of objectives to be achieved within the
domain of politics and policy making. Most Rightists
would also, with varying degrees of enthusiasm, support
a "long list" of objectives, basically those of religious and political conservatism of this decade.
     The short list includes:
     1, a constitutional amendment prohibiting abor-
         tion
     2, a constitutional amendment permitting reli-
         gious exercises in public schools, such as
         spoken prayers
     3, continued resistance to support for the
         Equal Rights Amendment
     4, opposition to legal guarantees of civil
         liberties for homosexuals
     5, full support for the budgetary priorities
         proposed by the Department of Defense.
     These are, of course, also the basic agenda of the
Moral Majority. The long list, while not supportable
by a comparable number of Rightists, would clearly receive the endorsement of most of them. Drawing up such
a list is bound to create controversy largely because
conservatives so vigorously and determinedly argue among
themselves over matters such as this; recall their internal battles leading to serious divisions at the time
of the candidacy in 1964 of Senator Barry Goldwater for
the Presidency. Today, the battles still rage over
traditionalists vs. libertarians, cultural vs. economic
conservatism. But, this writer suggests, the New
Christian Right would endorse these planks.

1, continued military support for Taiwan, the
    Republic of China

2, constitutional guarantees protecting the teach-
    ing of creationism in the public schools

3, continued American military and technological
    support for all developing countries understood
    to be 'anti-communist'

4, constitutional guarantees that local law offi-
    cials can shut down adult bookstores and the
    distribution of pornographic materials

5, gradual elimination of such governmental wel-
    fare state programs as Head Start, food stamps,
    AFDC, and school lunches

6, Tax vouchers and other forms of public financial
    support for parents sending their K-12 children
    to private schools

7, some form of consumer boycott for those sponsors
    who pay for objectionable television programs

8, support for the legislative proposals of the
    National Rifle Association for protection of
    citizen rights to bear arms

9, resistance to any federal, state, or local pro-
    grams for mandatory busing of pupils to achieve
    greater racial balance

10, opposition to those environmental groups who
    inhibit technological expansion

11, opposition to those churches extending sanctuary
    to refugees

12, opposition to proponents of the nuclear freeze
    agenda

13, opposition to those seeking to abolish capital
    punishment

14, opposition to those groups seeking to convince
    American stockholders to divest their invest-
    ments in the Republic of South Africa

15, support for religious day schools to utilize
     teachers not necessarily certified by state
     boards of education

16, opposition to extending full ownership controls
     to the Republic of Panama over the Panama Canal

17, opposition to proposals to extend federal credits
     to financially distressed cities such as New
     York City.[8]

To be sure, these issues attract considerable support from
voters outside New Christian Right circles. Their endorsement by the NCR, however, commands our attention for two
reasons. The supporters claim absolute moral legitimacy
in the name of the "Judeo-Christian" tradition for their
proposals and, second, they are organizing to "turn the
tide on humanism" by giving "their votes only to orthodox Christian candidates at every level."[9]

                          III

     Although the speed of New Christian Right growth
surprised observers, its roots extended well back into the
1970s. Some four or five identifiable and verifiable
sources help explain its expansion. First, it was deeply
influenced by a parallel upsurge in political dissent
of that decade known as "the New Right". Gillian Peale
defines this as "a loose movement of conservative politicians and a collection of general-purpose political organizations which have developed independently of the
political parties."[10] Led by Howard Phillips and his
Conservative Caucus, Terry Dolan and his National Conservative Political Action Committee, and Paul Weyrich with
his Committee for the Survival of a Free Congress, and
computer/fund-raising wizard Richard Vigurie, plus old
Goldwater dissidents along with some new, well-heeled
intellectuals in think tanks, all started calling for a
restoration of traditional and conservative economic and

moral values. Their ideology rested on the charge that
America was being mortally threatened by the secular
humanists, by its denial of the authority of moral
absolutes, and by a glorification of hedonism and moral
drift.[11] The New Right became something of a clearing
house for leadership and information on what sympathetic
supporters could do about the perils of the nation.

Secondly, the religious Right erupted with special
vehemence and anger because of its intensive emotional
reaction to specific rulings of the Supreme Court. Chief
among these were the legalizing of abortion, the restrictions on religious exercises in public schools, and the
rulings against introducing creationism into biology
curricula. Interpreted by Rightists as direct threats
against family values, the Court's rulings would have to
be overturned through the political process.[12]

Thirdly, the New Christian Right needed and at the
appropriate moment found effective leadership. Filling
in the vacuum left by the demise of the McIntires and
the Hargises of an earlier day, energetic and articulate
direction was now furnished by a new generation, glamorized
by their national television status and presenting a
clean slate unsullied by previous political involvement.
In American history, religio-moral crusades had always
found new energy with the emergence of new leadership
(as exemplified by Billy Sunday, Father Charles E.
Coughlin, or Billy Graham). In the late 1970s the same
situation emerged. The new televangelists offered
direction, momentum, inspiration and assurance to budding
New Christian Right supporters that they were on the way
to repelling the humanists as well as the Communists to
restore God's will for America. They offered nationally
focused crusades, nationally televised religious services, and nationally supported legislative agenda

for action among the rank and file. They were able to
connect their national programs with the existing power
bases of state and local fundamentalist clergy.[13]

In sum, the New Christian Right burst into the
political arena in a manner quite unique. Its source
of strength and legitimacy was its theology and its
political ideology, discussed in the next chapter. To
prove that its claim to being the American way was
correct, it would also need an enemy who was at work
destroying the foundations. This they found in secular
humanism, discussed in chapter 3.

Notes

1. Much of this is drawn from James E. Wood, Jr.,
    Nationhood and the Kingdom (Nashville, Broadman
    Press, 1977), and my Being Religious in America:
    The Deepening Crises over Public Faith(Minnea-
    polis, Augsburg Publishing House, 1986).

2. Martin E. Marty, "Transpositions: American Reli-
    gion in the 1980s", Wade Clark Roof, ed., Religion
    in American Today, vol. 480 of The Annals of the
    American Academy of Political and Social Science,
    (Beverly Hills, Sage Publications, 1985), p.14.

3. See my The Politics of Doomsday: Fundamentalists
    of the Far Right (Nashville, Abingdon Press, 1970).

4. Robert C. Liebman, "A New Christian Right?", R. C.
    Liebman and Robert Wuthnow, eds., The New Christian
    Right: Mobilization and Legitimation (New York,
    Aldine Publishing Company, 1983), p. 229.

5. Ibid., pp. 229-31, and Alan Geyer, "Religion, Poli-
    tical Culture and the New Right", a Shalom Paper
    #10 for the Center for Theology and Public Policy,
    Washington, D.C., April, 1981.

6. George M. Marsden, "Preachers of Paradox: The Reli-
    gious New Right in Historical Perspective", Mary
    Douglas and Steven Tipton, eds., Religion and
    American: Spiritual Life in a Secular Age
    (Boston, Beacon Press, 1982), pp.150-58.

7. Jeffrey K. Hadden, "Televangelism and the Future
    of American Politics," David G. Bromley and Anson
    Shupe, eds., New Christian Politics (Macon, Mercer
    University Press, 1984), pp. 151-65.

8. Robert Zwier, Born-Again Politics: The New
    Christian Right in America(Downers Grove, Il.,
    Inter-Varsity Press, 1982), pp. 37-57; Gillian
    Peele, Revival and Reaction: The Right in
    Contemporary America (Oxford, Clarendon Press,
    1984), pp. 91-101; H. Paul Chalfant, ed.,
    Religion in Contemporary Society(N.Y., Alfred
    Publishing Company, 1984), pp. 248-50; Colonel
    V. Doner, "Why Christians Must be Involved in
    Politics", a Christian Voice pamphlet, n.d.,
    p.12.

9. This is from one of the most widely quoted critics
    of secular humanism, Homer Duncan, Secular Humanism:
    The Most Dangerous Religion in America(Lubbock,
    Texas, Missionary Crusader Press, 1979), p.69.

10. Peele, Revival and Reaction; pp.91 ff., Jeffrey K. Hadden
    and Charles E. Swann, Prime Time Preachers: The
    Rising Power of Televangelism(Reading, Ma.,
    Addison-Wesley Publishing Co., 1981), pp. 141-44.

11. See the several articles on this in The Humanist,
    Sept/Oct,1976, 36:5, pp. 4-14; Richard V. Pierard,
    "Religion and the 1984 Election Campaign", Review
    of Religious Research, December, 1985, 27:2; pp.98-
    100; an excellent survey is Zwier, Born-Again
    Politics, ch.8.

12. Richard John Neuhaus, "What the Fundamentalists
    Want", Commentary, May, 1985, pp.45-46; Catholics
    were warned to stay clear of such ideological
    attraction; see George C. Higgins, "The Prolife
    Movement and the New Right:, America, September
    13, 1980, 107-110; Peele, pp. 96-98.

13. Peele, pp. 101-06; Liebman, "Mobilizing the Moral
    Majority", R.C. Liebman and Robert Wuthnow, eds.,
    The New Christian Right, pp.49-73; John S. Saloma
    III, Ominous Politics: The New Conservative
    Labyrinth (N.Y., Hill and Wang, 1984), pp.69 ff;
    Carol Flake, Redemptorama: Culture, Politics,
    and the New Evangelicalism(Garden City, N.Y.,
    Doubleday and Company, 1984), pp.225-31.

The Foundations

To promulgate its legislative agenda, the New Christian Right constructs the rationale for its policy on the
foundations of explicit theological doctrine. Its leaders recognize that to attract the support of those standing outside its doctrinal tradition (such as Mormons,
Roman Catholics, Orthodox), they must refrain from demanding uniform consent to their dogmas. Yet they affirm
their commitment to their teachings, they find their
identity in elevating it to the level of absolute truth.
Edward Dobson states it succinctly, "When we talk about
the fundamentals of Christianity, we are talking about
the essential doctrines without which our religion would
not be Christian at all."[1] What the leaders tell their
non-fundamentalist colleagues is that although people of
faith may differ over doctrines or forms of expression,
absolute truth expressed in absolute theological dogma
does exist and seekers avoid it at their mortal peril.
On that basis, fundamentalists can have fellowship
theologically and politically outside their carefully
defined ground. That position obviously separates this
generation from the total separationists such as Carl
McIntire and Bob Jones University.

Thus, absolute truth does exist; people of faith
can in verbal fashion express that truth. The soundness
of one's faith depends on "the basis of one's doctrines
of Christ", according to Dobson. "Correct doctrine is
the dividing line between truth and error. Since light
and darkness cannot have communion (2 Cor.6:14) there
can be no agreement between truth and error or God and
idols. To tolerate or compromise with error (heresy)
will eventually lead to embracing it. Thus, doctrine
becomes the basis for our fellowship."[2]

Although critics point to that commitment as being
unnecessarily divisive and hostile, fundamentalists find

in pure doctrine the only basis for unity among Christians.
Unity is that which they see their position will achieve.
To be specific, that means unity in doctrine will guard
the truth against the heretics. Unity in purpose which
leads to evangelizing the world is achieved by rejecting
false doctrine. Unity in action means, in classic fundamentalist style, being "confrontational and divides the
saved from the lost--the believer from the unbeliever."
This leads its adherents to realize their "spiritual and
moral influence upon our nation is essential in holding
back on all-out onslaught by Satan."[3]

It is in their role as the custodians of the true
faith and preservers of the nation from Satan that
fundamentalists come into sharp, often bitter disputation
with other believers. Having rejected the total separationists (those Dobson calls "the lunatic fringe"), they
also reject believers on what they call the "evangelical
left."[4] That coterie takes its inspiration from the
secular world, moving towards radical positions on feminism,
homosexuality worldly entertainment, and secular morality.
It fails to maintain total fidelity to biblical absolutes,
as exemplified to Dobson by the works of such evangelicals
as Lewis Smedes, Bruce Larson, Keith Miller, and Charles
Shedd.[5]

What is absolute truth to the NCR are the traditional
five "fundamentals of the faith, first codified in the
early 20th century in the publication of a series of
volumes, The Fundamentals. Anything less than allegiance
to these would be "not another form of Christianity, but
...not Christian at all."[6]

> 1, The inspiration and infallibility of Scrip-
> ture
>
> 2, The deity of Christ (including His virgin
> birth)

3,   The substitutionary atonement of Christ's
     death

4,   The literal resurrection of Christ from
     the dead

5,   The literal return of Christ in the Second
     Advent

These teachings, of course, are affirmed by people
of faith representing a very wide spectrum of denominational loyalties. Further, they do not necessarily demand
that their adherents will be directed to a specific set
of legislative agenda . Nothing in this quintet would
necessarily lead an American to take the stand she or he
does on religio-political issues. Yet to the New Christian
Right, these doctrines are fundamental because they demonstrate that God has revealed His will fully in rational,
verbal propositions to people of faith; thus certain absolute truths do exist in doctrine. Then NCR spokesmen go on
to affirm that the same kind of absolutes exist and must
be obeyed in matters of government, family, education,
and morality.

Obviously that affirmation attracts enormous criticism and hostility from a wide variety of observers. How,
for instance, can transcendent, eternal truth be en-
capsulated by human beings? How can the permanent
mysteries of God's actions in this universe be summed
up by admittedly fallible people? Is it not the height
of human arrogance to think that its definitions of the
essentials of truth are one and the same with that of
the all-knowing God?

New Christian Rightists reply by affirming in the
strongest terms the first of the five fundamentals: the
inspiration and infallibility of the scriptures. No
doctrine for them is of greater importance, both for
its doctrinal rationality and for its direct applicability

to the social agenda for saving America. Indeed, it and
the fifth fundamental, the premillennial return of Christ,
are the quintessential theological underpinnings for
the movement and, as such, are given extended consideration in this chapter.

The term "inerrancy" as well as "infallibility" are
the cornerstones for this position. The believer can
have total confidence in the teachings of the Scripture
because of the fully, verbally inspired manner in which
God revealed the very words to the authors of scripture.
It becomes "a document free from error in all of its
statements and affirmations. This meant that the Bible
was without error not only in theology but also in matters of science, history, geography, and the cosmos."[7]

The inerrancy/infallibility position has become in
the last decade the battleground for an all-out war among
fundamentalists and evangelicals. After years of combat,
the struggle continues over the extent to which inerrancy and infallibility, for instance, clarifies and
convinces believers about long-standing questions of
biblical interpretation: of Genesis 1-11, the authorship of Isaiah and Daniel, the historicity of the Chroni-
cler, the harmonization of the synoptic Gospels, the
authorship of the pastoral and Petrine epistles, and
the meaning of Revelation 20 as leading examples.[8] The
battles penetrate into the everyday lives of major denomi-
nations. They have, for instance, deeply divided the
nation's largest Protestant body, the Southern Baptist
Convention, they created a permanent rupture among
Missouri Synod Lutherans. They have cost tenured seminary
professors their jobs, they have used up enormous
energy and resources with no resolution in sight.

The obvious paradox, even a contradiction among NCR
adherents, is that they fail to agree on what they

understand to be the infallibility, inerrancy and
authority of the Scriptures. Yet when it comes time to
use the Bible for identifying the scriptural blend of
religion and politics, the religious Right presents
to the public a unified and cohesive consensus. That
unity, such as it is, offers us a very important clue.
It suggests that when all the academic battles are seen
in the context of the larger issue at stake--the survival of a God-fearing America--then the Bible is indeed
clear and normative in its message to this nation.

II

Much the same kind of unity within diversity char-
acterizes the second policy-shaping doctrine of the
movement, that of eschatology. All believers agree
on "the literal return of Christ in the Second Advent",
the historical intervention of Christ into human history
to reign bodily on earth until the final judgment and
the destruction of this planet and the departure into
heaven or hell.[9]

New Christian Right adherents espouse the premillennial position. To them it is verified daily in what
they interpret to be the rapidly increasing degree of
sin, evil, vice and corruption--the work of Satan--
throughout the world. As natural disasters seem also
to be increasing, as wars continue to break out and,
as people turn farther from religious faith, so too
does God's plan for saving this planet through the
militant return of Christ with his armies to defeat
Satan's legions.

In his study, "Nuclear War and the Second Coming
of Jesus Christ", Jerry Falwell presents a traditional
fundamentalist scenario of the last days. Writing
in 1980, he hinted that the world may end around 1985.
Since then he has avoided more direct timetable pre-

dictions. The decisive events proving that these were
the end times were understandable and classifiable into several categories; an increase in wars and rumors
of wars; extreme materialism; lawlessness; overpopula-
tion; an increase in speed and knowledge; a departure
from the Christian faith; intensive demonic activity;
the unification of the Systems of this world; recent
developments in Russia and in Israel and "the absence
of dynamic leadership."[10]

Those insights lead religious Rightists to reach
certain specific political conclusions. Many see the
Palestine Liberation Organization and Syria as representatives of the Antichrist's Gog and Magog; others
argue that the Trilateral Commission represents a part
of the seven years of Tribulation as promised in the Book
of Revelation. Falwell once preached sermons from what
he believed to be the location of the impending site
of the Battle of Armageddon. Further, so clearly was
the Soviet Union and its communism linked with the
Antichrist that Falwell called on the United States to
support the existing regime in South Africa against
Russian penetration (see below, ch. 10). Finally, end
times theology gives to the United States the licence
to rid the world of Satan and his socialist-communist
forces. Falwell writes, "Our government has the right
to use its armaments to bring wrath upon those who would
do evil by hurting other people." "If God is on our
side, no matter how militarily superior the Soviet
Union is, they could never touch us. God would miracu-
lously protect America."[11]

Within this school of eschatology, a subdivision
known as "Dispensationalism" attracts considerable
support. This teaches that the Bible refers to specific historical eras or dispensations. Some religious

Rightists argue the world is now in the last or at
least the next to the last era before the end times;
we are moments away from Armageddon (this is the position of the best selling author Hal Lindsay). Falwell,
Robertson, and Swaggart, among others apply this
teaching directly to the state of Israel. Biblical prophecies about that state will soon come true; it will
be the focus of the battles between Christ and Satan;
in other words, Israel has a totally unique place in
God's providential rule over history; hence its place
in this world must be defended at all costs. Falwell's
biographer writes, "For Mr. Falwell, nothing that
Israel does can be wrong. This realization came to
Menachem Begin, the former prime minister of Israel,
who is a close friend of Mr. Falwell's and awarded
him the prestigious Jabotinsky award for distinguished
service to Israel."[12]

III

Such concrete manifestations of New Christian
Right eschatology reflect one of its most significant
qualities for the 1980s--its determination to inject
directly its doctrines into the arena of public policy
making. Since God has given humankind theological and
moral absolutes, so in response believers by obeying
them bring society closer to him. The course of world
history indicates, however, that individuals and nations
have ignored or rejected such obedience. In fact, the
religious Right argues that the United States has come
perilously close to becoming a totally secular or
godless society. The case is well argued by Professor
G. S. Smith:

> In short, those who believe that secularization
> has substantially diminished the influence of
> the Judeo-Christian worldview in American

culture see three forces as primarily responsible. The differentiation of public life
into several spheres, each having its own
independent authority, has led people to
separate social, political, economic, and
educational institutions and issues from
religious control and jurisdiction. Plural-
ization (the development of competing world-
views) has given people many systems of
religious commitment and belief from which
to choose and has increased their tolerance
of diversity and ambiguity. And these two
processes have promoted privatization, where-
by many individuals confine their religious
beliefs to the private dimensions of their
lives."[13]

Religious Right thought affirms in general terms
that these three forces are directly preventing their
vision of a nation under God from being achieved.
Thus, in the concluding portion of this chapter, we
summarize that political ideology, which is in essence
their statement on the true American blend of religion
and politics. Obviously, no single voice or single
dominant school fully represents the totality of this
outlook. But by the mid 1980s, a reasonably clear expo-
sition of political doctrine by this movement became
visible and is offered here as such.[14]

Professor George Marsden reminds us of an important
point; fundamentalists "are among those contemporary
Americans who take ideas most seriously." Their abol-
lutes are of the utmost importance. They strike observers as being more "truth-oriented" than most other
groups. Despite their tendency to divide the universe
and all its people into only two categories--the moral

and the immoral, or the forces of light versus those
of darkness-the NCR spokesmen insist that rational,
demonstrable logic must underline the searchings for
true doctrine. The searching, for all practical
purposes, is complete because of their belief that the
Bible is "essentially a collection of true and precise propositions." "Truth is a matter of true and
precise propositions that, when properly classified
and organized, will work."[15]

Such propositions need verification, and to the
religious Right such verification is discovered con-
vincingly in the historical record of God's involvement in the history of the United States. There one
finds the hand of God, the clear indication of a people
being called out to restore righteousness on this earth;
the facts are totally convincing. The Puritan forefathers reflected both the Christian's yearning to be
free from secular governmental control, and yet establish public norms of righteousness. God endorsed the
aspirations of those early forefathers who sought to
make this a biblical commonwealth.

This same enthusiasm for righteousness so informed
the writers of the Declaration of Independence and the
Constitution of 1787. In the words of a major inter-
preter, Francis Schaeffer

> These men really knew what they were doing.
> We are not reading back into history what
> was not there. We cannot say too strongly
> that they really understood the basis of
> the government which they were founding.
> Think of this great flaming phrase "certain
> inalienable rights". Who gives the rights?
> The state? Then they are not inalienable

because the state can change them and
take them away.
Where do the rights come from? They understood that they were founding the country
upon the concept that goes back into the
Judeo-Christian thinking that there is
Someone there who gave the inalienable rights.
Another phrase also stood there "In God we
trust." With this there is no confusion
of what they were talking about. They
publically recognized that law could be
king because there was a Law Giver, a Person
to give the inalienable rights.[16]

That same faith in God's providential hand guided
American expansion westward in the 19th century. Professor Michael Leinisch writes that in the NCR belief
that as they believed in the long lines of women and
men moving westward to make the continent fruitful,
the NCR leaders ignore the shameful treatment of the
American Indian and other costs of geographical expansion. But to the religious Right America was expanding because it was God's will. The same kind of optimism infuses religious Right explanations of the remaind-
er of American history up through the Civil War and into
World War I and the New Deal. Leinisch concludes that
such interpretations suggest these are really 19th
century people living in a 20th century world wanting
to reclaim the past as they see God's will for the
future. Hence American history becomes something of a
sacred text, documentable proof that when this people
did adhere to God's absolute will, they indeed prospered.[17]

Throughout this unfolding, Americans in NCR judgment, prevailed over the forces of nature because they
recognized they had been the recipients of a national

covenant, inheritors of the promise once given Abraham
and the Hebrew people, and now renewed for believing
Americans. Known today as the "civil religion", this
interpretation for NCR adherents is further proof
of God's providential care for America, care that must
be preserved against the forces of secularism. A leading spokesman, Harold O. J. Brown, stated it; "Law
and public policy in our country should be in harmony
with the fundamental Biblical principles of Judeo-
Christian civilization."[18] By his reading of the
American past, its people had prospered because they
had accepted their role as people of a redeemer-nation,
a nation obedient to the will of God and a force for
good in an evil world. What has happened is that in
today's world this covenant has been broken. Those
who have done so have broken not only American law,
but the moral absolutes and imperatives on which
this society has flourished. Such disobedience will
not go unpunished; American must return to God or
perish.[19]

Notes

1. Edward Dobson, "Fundamentalism Today", The
    Fundamentalist Journal, June, 1985, p.12.

2. Dobson, "Fundamentalism Today", The Fundamentalist
    Journal, May,1984, p.10.

3. Emphasis mine; ibid., p. 11.

4. Ibid., April, 1984, p. 11.

5. Ibid,; see also Dobson's book,In Search of Unity: An
    Appeal to Fundamentalist and Evangelicals (Nashville,
    Thomas Nelson Publishers, 1985); see also Dobson
    and Ed Hindson, "Fundamentalism Today", The
    Fundamentalist Journal, January, 1984, pp. 10-11;
    a responsible critique of this position is James
    Barr, Beyond Fundamentalism: Biblical Foundations
    for Evangelical Christianity (Philadelphia, West-
    minster Press, 1984).

6. Dobson, "Fundamentalism: Its Roots", New Catholic
    World, January/February, 1985, vol.228, no.1363,
    pp.4-9; for a conservative who espouses these
    doctrines but repudiates the NCR legislative agenda
    see James M. Dunn, Executive Director, Baptist
    Joint Committee on Public Affairs, Report from
    the Capital, July/August,1985,p.15.

7. Dobson, "Fundamentalism", New Catholic World, p.7;
    Dobson, "Fundamentalism Today", The Fundamentalist
    Journal, October, 1984, pp.10-11.

8. Mark A. Noll, "Evangelicals and the Study of the
    Bible", The Reformed Journal, April, 1984, p.14;
    news story, Christianity Today, January 22, 1982,
    pp.36-37; ibid., Dec.17, 1982, pp. 45-47; James
    Davison Hunter, American Evangelicalism: Conserva-
    tive Religion and the Quandry of Modernity(New
    Brunswick, Rutgers State University Press, 1983),
    ch.6; Timothy L. Smith, "The Evangelical Kalaeido-
    scope and the Call to Christian Unity", Christian
    Scholar's Review, 1986, XV:2, pp. 125-40.

9. Dobson, "Fundamentalism", New Catholic World,
    January/February, 1985,p.8; Perry C. Cothan,
    "The Electronic Church", Allene Stuart Phy, ed.,
    The Bible and Popular Culture in America(Phila-
    delphia, Fortress Press, 1985), pp.130-32.

10. Falwell, "Nuclear War and the Second Coming of
    Christ", (Lynchburg, The Old-Time Gospel Hour,
    1983), pp. 27-31; Falwell, Listen, America!
    (Garden City, Doubleday and Company, 1980),
    pp.99-104.

11. See the documentation in Michael Leinesch, "The
    Paradoxical Politics of the Religious Right",
    Soundings, Spring, 1983, LXVI:1, pp.91-99.

12. Dinesh D'Souza, "Jerry Falwell's Renaissance",
    Policy Review, Winter, 1984, no.27, p.40; see also
    a full discussion in the journal Catalyst: A
    Forum of Jewish and Christian Thought, 1:1,1985;
    it has the endorsements of Jimmy Swaggert, Hal
    Lindsay, Congressman Jack Kemp and Ed McAteer;
    P.O. Box 24152, Denver, Co.80222.

13. G.S. Smith, "The Great Secularization Debate in
    America", The Reformed Journal, July, 1985, p.17.

14. For a superb introductory historical perspective,
    see George Marsden, "Preachers of Paradox: The
    Religious New Right in Historical Perspective",
    Mary Douglas and Steven M. Tipton, eds., Religion
    and America(Boston, Beacon Press, 1982), pp.159 ff.

15. Ibid., pp.162-64.

16. From A Christian Manifesto, 1981, quoted in Charles
    W. Dunn,ed., American Political Theology (New York,
    Prager Special Studies,1984), pp.133-34; Ralph
    Clark Chandler, "The Wicked Shall Not Bear Rule:
    The Fundamentalist Heritage of the New Christian
    Right", David G. Bromley and Anson Shupe, eds.,
    New Christian Politics(Macon, Mercer University
    Press, 1984), pp.440-50; Mark A.Noll, et al., eds.,
    The Search for a Christian America (Westchester,
    Il., Crossways Books, 1984),pp.141-42; footnote 10
    has excellent documentation.

17. Leinesch, "The Paradoxical Politics", pp.81-85.

18. Quoted in Paul D. Simmons, "Fundamentalism: Court-
    ing Civil Religion", Report from the Capital, June,
    1981, p. 6; Angela Elwell Hunt, "Lady Liberty: Her
    Lamp of Freedom Shines Again", The Fundamentalist
    Journal, July/August,1986,pp. 32-36.

19. Ibid;, Dick Anthony and Thomas Robbins, "Spiritual
     Innovation and the Crisis of American Civil
     Religion" in Douglas and Tipton, pp.229-48;
     see the brilliant interpretation by Grant
     Wacker, "Searching for Norman Rockwell: Popular
     Evangelicalism in America", Leonard I. Sweet, ed.,
     The Evangelical Tradition in America(Macon, Mercer
     University Press, 1981), pp.297 ff.

Secular Humanism

For a broadly based and zealous social crusade such
as the New Christian Right to attract sustaining support,
its leaders needed to create a reason for its existence.
That reason, characteristic of such crusades, would be
the presence of an enemy, clearly identifiable and
documentably destructive to the values espoused by the
crusade itself. That enemy must needs be more ominous
than simply erroneous theology or social philosophy;
such had flourished for centuries in academe and could
safely be resisted. But that enemy must be presenting
an enticing but fatal program of activities which
threatened the crusade and the society which it represented.

During the 1960s and 1970s, potential New Christian
Rightists watched with growing alarm the emergence of
such a movement, that of "secular humanism". This was
not a threat from the Soviet Union as such, a theme made
popular by the fundamentalists of the far right in the
1950s. This threat was far more insidious because it
came from within, an internal conspiracy. Americans
especially had long been prone to accept conservative
Protestants conspiratorial allegations about alleged
enemies to the Republic. Fears of Romanism, Judaism,
Mormonism, British bankers, thirdworlders, Bilder-
bergers, Trilateralists and ..one-worlders have thrived
throughout United States history. They have represented
a mindset which needed to find the explanations for
America's shortcomings in persons outside the domain
of the true citizens.[1]

Perhaps the entire story of what follows in this
chapter would never have occured, or would at least
have taken a far different direction had it not been
for a single sentence in a decision of the Supreme Court
Justice Hugo Black in the celebrated Torcaso v. Watkins
case of 1961. A citizen of Maryland, Roy Torcaso had

been appointed as a state employee, a notary public, by
the Governor. He refused the job when he was told he
was required to swear in a formal oath of office or
affirm that he believed in the existence of God. Torcaso brought suit, claiming the state had ignored the
First Amendment by preferring theistic religions over
those which were not theistic. The Supreme Court unanimously struck down the Maryland requirement, holding
that it invaded freedom of religion. Justice Black wrote

> We repeat and again reaffirm that neither a
> State nor the Federal Government can con-
> stitutionally force a person to profess a
> belief or disbelief in any religion. Neither
> can constitutionally pass laws nor impose
> requirements which aid those religions based
> on a belief in the existence of God as
> against those religions founded on different
> beliefs. Among religions in this country
> which do not teach what would generally be
> considered a belief in the existence of God
> are Buddhism, Taoism, Ethical Culture, Secu-
> lar Humanism, and others....[2]

That last phrase, clearly the opinion of one justice,
has come to dominate the New Christian Right offensive
of the 1980s. As Martin E. Marty suggests, "a new
name for a nonexistent denomination was born full-blown
from the mind of one justice."[3] Later Joseph L. Blau
discovered that the term showed up in an amicus curiae
brief submitted by the American Humanist Association.
He commented, "It is perhaps unfortunate that a term
originally used by one group of humanists to distinguish
itself from other groups of humanists should have become a term of political reproach to be used widely as a
condemnation of those Americans who do not share the

religious view of a minority that seeks to be a
majority." Marty suggests that a fundamentalist
spokesmen discovered the term and was able to convince like-minded believers that "non-Judeo Christian
values, teachings, etc., were '"secular humanism'."[4]

Those conclusions were endorsed by the attorney
who pleaded Torcaso's case before the Supreme Court,
Leo Pfeffer. Clearly from Black's opinions came a
greatly expanded idea of what constituted a religion
when it is considered to be protected by the Constitution. Pfeffer wrote it "evoked a reaction that I am
sure Justice Black never intended. Protagonists of
religion in the public school and governmental aid to
religious schools have since demanded that either their
claims be accepted or that the public schools cease
teaching subjects such as biology, history, and others
that, to them, clearly were predicated upon the religion
of "'Secular Humanism'".[5]

As this chapter will survey, the conspiracy took
form in NCR judgment under the rubric of "secular humanism". Since a justice of the Supreme Court, the nation's
highest authority, had so deemed it as a religion, then
it was clearly a religion. As such it was to religious
Rightists recognized as having legal status and the
protection of the law. But that recognition violated
their understanding of the state remaining neutral in
endorsing any one religion. Hence, since secular humanism
was being taught in the schools, and promulgated in all
areas of American life (as this chapter will examine)
then it directly violated the First Amendment; it was to
become "the most dangerous religion in America," "the
source of all the sins of America, the multiformed beast
of modern liberalism: the brazen serpent of pornography and homosexuality: the unpainted temptress of

women's liberation: the meddling giant of big government."[6] In the eyes of its leading popularizer, Tim
LaHaye, the internal conspiracy leaders, the humanists
"are the mortal enemy of all pro-moral Americans,
and the most serious threat to our nation in its entire
history."[7]

Throughout the 1970s that interpretation found ready
believers but no single organizing focus to give it
political clout. Some efforts led by Senator Orrin Hatch
(R.--Utah) to eliminate possible secularism in public
schools appeared in 1978 (see ch.11). Then, in 1979
religious and political leaders announced the formation
of what would be the first major New Christian Right
organization, Moral Majority. Its leaders fully
accepted the internal conspiracy interpretation of
America's woes and pledged to drive it from the nation's
shores (see below, chs. 7,8).

Within a few months, religious Rightists started
to build their indictment of the power of secular humanism.
Using a variety of news media, as well as sympathetic
pulpits, they promulgated their explanation of the
nation's crisis. Drawing on their theology, political
ideology and interpretation of the sacred character of
American history, NCR leaders also reached out to attract
support from non-fundamentalist groups such as some
Roman Catholics and Mormons and Eastern Orthodox. Such
sympathy for the indictment appeared quickly in, for
example, the study by Dr. James Hitchcock, a historian
at St. Louis University. In his book of 1982, What is
Secular Humanism? Hitchcock looked back as far as the
Renaissance in western Europe to locate the roots for
the current crisis. To demonstrate just how vast, wide
and heterogenous that movement really was, thus adding
to its allure, Hitchcock in his book included photographs

of the contributors to secular humanism. These included
(in the order presented), John Dewey, Betty Friedan,
Desiderius Erasmus, Voltaire, Charles Darwin, Sigmund
Freud, Friedrich Nietzsche, Thomas Jefferson, John F.
Kennedy, Harvey Cox, Eric Fromm, Elvis Presley, The
Rolling Stones, Archie Bunker (Caroll O'Connor),
William O. Douglas, Harry Blackmun, Rudolph Bultmann,
Jean-Paul Sartre, Hans Küng, Karl Marx, and B. F.
Skinner.[8]

In concrete terms, Hitchcock detected a conspiracy
at work among entertainment celebrities, "situated in
strategic places in society", among those advocating
the "me generation" philosophy of enjoying life here
and now, from those advocating divorce and abortion,
users of drugs, and "the increasingly open and bitter
antagonism to traditional values expressed in the
media."[9] Further evidence was the breakdown of the
American family through the soaring numbers of those
practicing cohabitation and sexual promiscuity. Further evidence was found in the most powerful institutions of the land, the Supreme Court, the public
schools, and mainline churches.[10]

More explicitly, fundamentalist spokesmen made the
same case. Homer Duncan found secular humanism rampant
in the colleges and universities, and also in the
"United States Government", "by far the most powerful
and effective means for promoting humanism through
its various agencies, primarily through controlling
education. I repeat, American taxpayers are paying
for their own destruction."[11] Falwell stated it directly: "Humanism challenges every principle on which
America was founded. It advocates abortion on demand,
recognition of homosexuals, free use of pornography,
legalizing of prostitution and gambling, and free use

of drugs, among other things." Pat Robertson during the
early 1980s focused frequently on the conspiracy, discussing homosexuality, the AIDS epidemic, specific
American Humanist Associations publications, high-
school textbooks, abortion, sexual promiscuity, and the
morally permissive tone of the national television
broadcast programs.[12]

III

The most influential and controversial spokesmen
among religious Rightists for the conspiracy interpretation has been from the beginning the Rev. Tim LaHaye.
His credentials were extensive: founder and Vice President of Moral Majority, a member of the board of
directors for Christian Voice, a prolific author, the
organizer of an informal alliance of wealthy conservatives and right-wing legislators in Washington entitled
the Council for National Policy, a longtime minister in
San Diego where he headed the San Diego Christian Unified
School System and Christian Heritage College and in 1984
the chief officer of the American Coalition for Traditional Values (see ch.9).

LaHaye's first major appearance on the national
scene came with the publication in 1980 (including
sending 75,000 gratis copies to ministers and church
leaders) of his book, The Battle for the Mind. There
he built his indictment. Some 275,000 humanists in positions of the highest power were speeding America towards
internal destruction by promulgating the tenets of
secular humanism. That meant the glorification of atheism,
evolution, amorality, self-centered personalities,
socialistic one-world loyalties, and hostility to the
Bible. The humanist leaders, he found, controlled
broadcast television, radio, the largest newspapers,
Hollywood movies, most magazines, the Supreme Court,

many state governments, public education, and most
college and universities. Specific institutions within
the conspiracy included the American Civil Liberties
Union, the American Humanist Society, the National
Education Association, National Organization of Women,
most labor unions and foundations such as those of Ford,
Rockefeller and Carnegie.[13]

LaHaye's book received widespread attention among
the growing New Christian Right movement. He became
something of a celebrity. In 1983 he made his next full
length contribution, a book entitled The Battle for the
Public Schools, documenting how the conspiracy was
destroying the public schools. "Public education today
is a self-serving institution controlled by elitists
of an atheistic, humanistic viewpoint." Obviously, such
conclusions brought on considerable criticism. LaHaye
responded to them by suggesting that "I do not know
if the conspiracy theory has any validity." But then,
as Marty detected, LaHaye proceded in this book to
"treating your children as victims of a conspiracy he
says he is not even sure exists."[14]

Yet America was not yet fully in the power of the
enemy. There remained the political arena, the public
policy making source of reform to take back this nation.
LaHaye thought that had already occurred with the results
of the 1980 Presidential election. "Our Heavenly Father
looked down and saw our plight. He saw thousands of
us working diligently to awaken his sleeping church to
its political responsibilities and He gave us four more
years to perpetuate religious freedom." He added that
if "liberals" gained control of the White House and Congress, "it will be all over for free elections by 1988".[15]
His social agenda harmonized with that of full New
Christian Right. Continuing criticism by opponents

seemed only to help strengthen his credibility among
the religious Right.[16]

IV

Ironically, since it was the Supreme Court, or at
least Justice Black, who had recognized the presence
of secular humanism as a major force in American life,
the NCR found that same institution as the most
threatening power to implement its goals and thus to
destroy this nation. Working through legislative
allies in Congress, its leaders had introduced some 40
bills and proposed amendments to the Constitution all
with one specific aim: to overturn unpopular Supreme
Court decisions (for example, school prayer, abortion,
Bible reading in schools) and to place the independent
authority of that court under the control of the legislative branch of government. The leading spokesmen
informed their supporters of the power of the conspiracy
at work. Robertson said, of the Constitution, "the
minute you turn the document into the hands of non-
Christian people and atheist people, they can use it to
destroy the very foundations of our society--and that's
what been happening." Federal judges, he explained,
constitute "a deliberate attempt to bring the United
States into line with the Constitution, not of the U.S.,
but of the U.S.S.R." An early New Christian Right lobby,
The Religious Roundtable (later "the Roundtable")
stated in 1981

> The born-again Ayatollahs of Paganism, enrobed
> as federal judges, with unchecked power, in
> violation of the Constitution, have established
> their religion of Paganism upon us, imposing
> its barbarism and corruptions, demanding the
> modern materialist gods of consumerism and
> careerism be sated with children's blood."[17]

Jimmy Swaggart preached, "I'm concerned that the U.S.
Supreme Court is an institution damned by God." Falwell stated, "the fact is, one day Jesus is going to
come and strike down all the Supreme Court rulings
in one fell swoop."[18]

Thus, during the early 1980s the final issue came
down to being more than the internal conspiracy. It
rested on the authority of the Constitution, and who
was entitled to interpret it correctly. The NCR leaders
put forward their position. The justices were to carry
out the intentions of the Founding Fathers, those who
wrote the Constitution itself. Justices were to discern the true motives of the Framers and implement those
motives in their decisions. Schaeffer wrote, "if the
Founding Fathers could come back and see what's being
made of the First Amendment, they would consider it
nothing but tyranny." To a prominent religious Right
attorney and author, John W. Whitehead, the religion
of this nation at its founding was Judeo-Christian
theism; that was the glue that held together both
society and liberty. Rightist historian C. Gregg
Singer argued that the Framers accepted "a Christian
world and life view... which furnished the basis
for this nation's political ideology."[19]

During these same years other scholars argued that
no such consensus existed; that the Founding Fathers
were a motley assortment of deists, skeptics, evangelicals and others with religious commitments too complicated to identify. These observers pointed out
just how carefully the author of the First Amendment,
James Madison, had been when he had written the "no
establishment" and "free exercise" clauses, justifying
them on the basis of his and Jefferson's earlier writings explaining their personal commitments to these
principles.[20]

In summary, the appearance to the New Christian
Right of the enemy with its ideology and its power
gave its leaders the reason to launch their crusade.
Drawing on their theology, and political ideology
they put together an indictment which in their judgment
must be sound because it attracted so much criticism
from those with whom they disagreed. Still, there were
those millions of unmotivated voters and like-minded
believers out there in America who needed to be
brought into the camp. They might not be energized
for the crusade by theology or ideology. But perhaps
they could be energized when they could be shown
with facts how the enemy had permeated two areas of
their lives which they experienced every day; public
schools and public morality.

Notes

1. George Johnson, Architects of Fear: Conspiracy Theories and Paranoia in American Politics (Los Angeles, Jeremy P. Tarcher, Inc., 1983); Erling Jorstad, The Politics of Doomsday: Fundamentalists of the Far Right (Nashville, Abingdon Press, 1970).

2. Torcaso vs. Watkins, 367 U.S.468, 1961.

3. Quoted in Marty's newsletter, Context, November 1, 1985(17:19), p. 1.

4. Ibid.

5. Milton R. Konvitz, "The Problem of a Constitutional Definition of Religion", James E. Wood, Jr., ed., Religion and the State: Essays in Honor of Leo Pfeffer(Waco, Baylor University Press, 1985), pp. 149-50, and Leo Pfeffer, "An Autobiographical Sketch", ibid., pp.511-12.

6. See Homer Duncan, Secular Humanism: The Most Dangerous Religion in America(Lubbock, Texas, Missionary Crusader Press, 1979); Carol Flake, Redemptorama: Culture, Politics, and the New Evangelicalism (Garden City, Doubleday and Company, 1984), p.218; Onalee McGraw, "Secularism and the Schools: The Issue Whose Time Has Come" (Washington,D.C., The Heritage Foundation,1976), passim.

7. Tim LaHaye, The Battle for the Mind (Old Tappan, N.J., Fleming Revell, 1980), p. 187.

8. James Hitchcock, What Is Secular Humanism? (Ann Arbor, Servant Books, 1982), passim.

9. Ibid., p.59.

10. Ibid., pp.69,71, 72-88, chs. 7-8.

11. Duncan, Secular Humanism, p.17.

12. Falwell, quoted by Robert E. Webber, Secular Humanism: Threat and Challenge (Grand Rapids, Zondervan Publishing House, 1982), p. 19; 700 Club for Nov. 1-21, 1982; also Robertson in The Freedom Report of the Freedom Council, December, 1984, 10:2, passim; also James T. Draper and

Forrest E. Watson, If the Foundations Be
Destroyed (Nashville,   Thomas Nelson Publishers,
1984).

13. See The Battle for the Mind, pp.27,74,97,141-79.

14. "MEMO", Christian Century, January 26, 1983,
     p. 79.

15. News story, Christianity Today, October 5, 1984,
     p.56.

16. LaHaye's leadership is discussed in Sidney Blumen-
     thal, "The Righteous Empire", The New Republic,
     October 22, 1984, pp.18-24; The Battle for the
     Mind, pp.14, 137-38; interview, Christianity
     Today, February 17, 1984, pp. 18-19; see also
     George Marsden, "The New Fundamentalism", The
     Reformed Journal, February, 1982, pp.7-9;
     Kenneth Woodward on LaHaye in Newsweek, July 6,
     1981, pp.49-50.

17. See the publication from People for the American
     Way, "Special Report: The Crusade Against the
     Courts", (Washington, D.C., 1982), pp.1-2; David
     Bollier, Liberty and Justice for Some (New York,
     Frederick Ungar Publishing Co., 1982), p. 258;
     Richard V. Pierard, Religion and the New Right
     in Contemporary American Politics", James W. Wood,
     Jr., ed., Religion and Politics (Waco, Baylor
     University Press, 1983), pp.59-81.

18. The Jimmy Swaggart television program, December
     16, 1984; Falwell, The Old-Time Gospel Hour, March
     11, 1983; The PTL endorsed this interpretation al-
     so; see Vice President Vernon K. McKellen, The
     Great American Arena! Positive Strategies for
     Twentieth Century Patriots (Charlotte, Associates
     Press, 1984), passim.

19. Robertson and Schaeffer on The 700 Club, March 3,
     1982; Jack R. Van Der Slik, "Respecting an
     Establishment of Religion in America", Christian
     Scholar's Review, 1984, XIII:3, pp.217-35;
     Richard V. Pierard, "Standing the Founding
     Fathers on their Heads", Christian Century,
     April 20, 1983, pp.368-72; see ch. 13.

20.   Robert P. Hay, "The Faith of the Founding
      Fathers", USA Today, May, 1986, pp.80-83;
      Sharon L. Worthing, "Religion and Religious
      Institutions Under the First Amendment,"
      Pepperdine Law Review, 1980, vol.7,,pp.313-
      53; William Lee Miller, The First Liberty:
      Religion and the American Republic (New
      York, Alfred A. Knopf, 1986), pp.77-150;
      Robert S. Alley, ed., James Madison on
      Religous Liberty (Buffalo, Prometheus
      Books, 1986), passim.; Peggy Thomson, "The
      Four Gospels According to Thomas Jefferson",
      The Smithsonian Magazine, May, 1984, pp.139-
      48;Peter L. Berger, "Religion in Post-
      Protestant America", Commentary, May, 1986,
      pp.41-42; A.James Reichley, Religion in
      American Public Life (Washington, The
      Brookings Institution, 1985), pp.53-114.

Public Education

Armed with their theology, political ideology and
conspiracy interpretation the New Christian Rightists
in the early 1980s launched several powerful counter-
attacks. The enemy was everywhere; in the abortion controversy, in the women's movement, in assaults on
family values, on sexual deviance, in the media, and
courts and in both public and private education.[1]
The next three chapters explore the rise of the NCR
from obscurity into a powerful political movement
strengthened by their organizational skills, their
expanding multi-million dollar war chests and from
knowing their interpretation of the American way had
the endorsement of President Ronald Reagan. In the
1980 Presidential campaign, they recalled, he had
made a pledge, "I want you to know that I endorse
you and what you are doing."[2]

Nowhere did that support make itself known more
clearly than in the combined efforts of the White House
and the New Christian Right to change the direction of
public education. To the crusaders, those schools
represented America's future; the society could be no
better than its informed citizenry. Further, local
schools still maintained some autonomy for parents
and residents rather than turning over the children's
lives to outside elitists. Here was grassroots
governance at its best--the American way. As Charles
Krauthammer suggested, the battle for the schools turned
into a major offensive in America's new "holy war"
against the humanists.3

By contrast to many other nations, the United
States had long held public education in the highest
esteem. In Justice Felix Frankfurter's celebrated
dictum, "The public school is at once the symbol of
our democracy and the most pervasive means for

promoting our common destiny", a very tall order.[4] For
much of the course of American history, a loosely defined but pervasive evangelical Protestant morality
informed the educational ethos, well exemplified in
the McGuffy Readers. Then, around World War II, the
Supreme Court recognized the obvious impact of a more
religiously pluralistic society as that affected public
schools. Within a few years, the Court ruled as unconstitutional such religious practices as spoken prayers
and the reading of the Bible as a regular feature of
the curriculum. That trend, as much as any other
single feature, helped mobilize large numbers of citizens into joining in loose coalitions denouncing what
they believed to be anti-religious decisions by the
Court. Now, to them, the secularists were dictating
the curricula, installing such controversial programs
as affective learning, values clarification, and moral
relativism.[5] Beyond that, they charged, the public
schools were failing to teach the basics, the three Rs.
In the name of social relevance they were abdicating,
in religious Rightist judgment, their responsiblities
and their mandate from the taxpayers.[6]

Defenders of public education would, in turn, interpret that criticism as scapegoating, blaming the social
woes of the nation on the public schools and unwilling
to respect the academic freedom and integrity of those
institutions. The process of tribalization became evident. Americans, one observer noted, could no longer
"agree as a people about what beliefs and fundamental
commitments make sense of the world. What we do not
agree about for ourselves, we are unable to agree about
for our children...."[7] In concrete terms, the battles
which the New Christian Right would focus on, among
the several swirling about among educators and parents

were those of private versus public education, religious
versus secular education, and the extent of parental
control over school administration and teaching.[8]

In classical fundamentalist style, NCR leaders
presented a combative, legalistic, no middleground
kind of indictment against the public schools. They
charged the humanists had turned the public schools into
social laboratories, into clinics "whose purpose is to
provide individualist psycho-social treatment for the
student, and teachers will become psycho-social thera-
pists." They charged that the teaching of morality,
such as considering the Ten Commandments, had long
been discarded as relics of an earlier, superstitious
religiosity. They found schools offering explicit sex
education, glorifying the hedonistic lifestyle of
materialistic America, teaching homosexuality as a viable
alternative lifestyle, and minimizing parental input
into their children's education. The NCR's case was
well summarized by Jimmy Swaggart, "The public school
system...gutted by secular humanism, is literally
attacking the home, the family structure in this
country."[9]

II

The stridency and gusto of this indictment drew
considerable inspiration from religious Rightists knowing that President Reagan supported their cause. Starting as far back as his Presidential bid in 1976, he
had actively courted the support of fundamentalists
and evangelicals, transforming that grouping "from
an almost irrelevant fringe into a centerpiece of the
conservative moment." The President had shown himself, in Sidney Blumenthal's judgment, "unwilling
to distance himself from them...he briefed them, encouraged them, deployed White House resources to

coordinate them, and thereby magnified them." Such
recognition gave the New Christian Right "a legitimacy it had previously lacked."[10] The best known
groups--Moral Majority, Christian Voice, the Freedom Council, the Roundtable and related subsidiaries--
all identified their case against public education
with the position of the President.[11]

The adherents for this cause agreed that the first
priority must be the passage as quickly as possible
of a constitutional amendment to restore prayers in
the public schools.[12] The issue quickly took on
immense symbolic importance for everyone, critics
and supporters alike, because of the centrality of
the larger issue at stake--the role of religion in public education. Professor Robert Webber asked: "Should
government protect freedom from religion or freedom of
religion in the public schools?"[13] That issue, plus
the one of states rights rather than national controls
over the schools engaged the support of the Oval Office.
After some planning, and certain internal squabbling
among Rightists over the best course of action, the
President in May, 1982 presented through the Senate a
proposal

> Nothing in this Constitution should be
> construed to prohibit individual or group
> prayer in public schools or other public
> institutions. No person shall be required
> by the United States or any State to parti-
> cipate in prayer.

That proposal, Leo Pfeffer suggested, filled a need
of Reagan "to pay back the debt owed to far right conservatives as well as religious fundamentalists."[14]
However, the conservative movement failed to unite behind it. Writers such as George Will and James J.

Kilpatrick called the amendment "a mistake" serving
not authentic religion but "mere attitudinizing, a
thin gruel of vague religious vocabulary..." leading
to trivialization of religion and the coercion of
children who take their own religious traditions
seriously."[15]

Robertson and Falwell, however, hailed the proposal as a returning of God to the nation's public
schools. They, along with many other observers, were
caught by surprise when the Administration turned its
major attention and persuasion powers with Congress
away from the amendment to the enactment of its economic
and foreign policy proposals. By August, the Moral
Majority concluded that the President had, in fact,
given the cause only symbolic support.[16]

Then, after considerable private negotiations,
several Senators brought out a revised proposal. Aware
that several Christian and Jewish groups had mounted
considerable opposition to the May proposal, Senator
Jesse Helms (R.--N.C.) proposed an alternative. This
would bar the Supreme Court from ruling on the con-
stitutionality of school prayer, a measure on which
Reagan soon said he would take "no position." Although
supportive of voluntary school prayer, the President
had come under considerable criticism from conservative
Senators for remarks made critical of school prayer
by his Attorney General, William French Smith. He
had stated Congress should not make "exceptions" to
Court jurisdictions in the "core functions" of the
court "as an independent and equal branch in our system
of separation of powers." Reagan had been asked, in
essence, to choose between that position and that of
his vocal support for prayer; hence, the "no position"
stance.[17]

The Senate, late in the summer, had locked itself in
a filibuster over the Helms proposal as well as a proposed amendment overturning legal abortion. That dead-
lock, together with widespread public confusion over
the implications of the Helms Amendment gave the anti-
school prayer forces time enough to mobilize support for
pressuring wavering Senators. The filibuster continued
on well into September, each vote on the prayer amendment falling just short of the required two-thirds
needed for endorsement of a constitutional amendment.

By late September the battle simply stopped. The
White House ceased its lobbying for any kind of prayer
amendment and Senator Helms lost control of his strength
on the floor of the Senate. Apparently, enough Senators
decided his amendment was not only unsound by unconstitutional. Senator Max Baucus (D.--Mont.) suggested that
voters said "this is not perceived as a court-stripping
bill, it's perceived as a school prayer bill." Voters
were not yet ready for that kind of measure.[18]

Hardly noticed at the time was a proposal by Senator Mark Hatfield (R.--Ore.) to allow public secondary
school students to meet voluntarily for religious purposes, just as they would meet for other extracurricular
activities. This was based on a recent Supreme Court
decision, Widmar v. Vincent, holding that college students could meet for such purposes on campus if the
college also generally made its facilities available
to students for non-religious activities. The Hatfield
proposal would, in a short time, become another major
item on the religion/politics agenda, that of "equal
access."[19]

The failure of the 1982 amendment stemmed from the
failure of its proponents to convince enough Senators
of the power of the secular humanist conspiracy. The

same general measure had been proposed already in 1974
and in 1980. Each time, including 1982, it had met
with very strong opposition by many Jewish and Christian
communities. In sum, it had not convinced those groups
nor the Senate that its position was the American way.[20]

During 1983 Senator Orrin G. Hatch (R.--Utah)
proposed an alternative which would allow silent devotions
rather than vocalized prayer. The Administration renewed
its call for its 1982 prayer amendment, reworded somewhat to read now, "Nothing in this Constitution shall
be construed to prohibit individual or group prayer in
public schools or other institutions. Neither the
United States nor any State shall compose the words of
prayers to be said in public schools." Two weeks later
the proposal failed. Although the Senate voted 56 to 44
for passage, it lacked the required two-thirds margin.[21]

In that brief period of debate, however, the nation
witnessed some of the most intensely religious and
bitterly denunciatory lobbying seen for years in the
Senate. New Christian Right leaders had turned out their
full forces, attempting to show the world their new
political clout. Their strategists had argued, such
as did Pat Boone, head of "SAVE OUR SCHOOLS," (SOS)
that school prayer would reduce illegitimate births and
pregnancies in the schools, violence and teen age suicide, drug and alcohol abuse by school children and
vandalism in the schools.[22] Using computer printouts
and direct mailings with great efficiency, NCR leaders
sent to their supporters printed petitions, already
addressed to the specific two Senators and the one House
of Representatives lawmaker of the supporter; these
called for passage. The users had only to put check
marks on the appropriate lines, affix a stamp and mail
it in. The rhetoric used was pitched at the highest

level of intensity; Falwell's sympathetic biographer,
for instance, wrote about the battle, "we may have the
Supreme Court to thank for the destruction of our
public school system". The thinktank, Heritage
Foundation, a close ally of the NCR claimed the nay-
saying Senators failed to represent the voters of
their states. Those voting against the Amendment
would face the wrath of the voters in November.[23]

During the Senate debate, supporters held all night
vigils on the steps of the Capitol, with participants
holding signs with wording such as "Return God to our
Schools. And Live as A Nation Under Christ." Professional football celebrities gave personal testimonials for the amendment to a special House of
Representatives hearing. The White House orchestrated
"a sweeping Christian Media Blitz" co-sponsored by
Robertson. Falwell's promotional material had printed
on the envelopes, "Voluntary Prayer in Public Schools.
America's Last Chance!"[24]

The brief debate served to illuminate the larger
issues at stake. The religious Right had failed to
explain to any wavering Senators why such strong
opposition to the prayer amendment came from such
respected organized religious bodies, groups not in
the clutches of secular humanism. Perhaps the most
searching criticism of the voluntary prayer amendment came from Roger Rosenblatt in a column in Time.
He asked why it was wrong, and then gave four reasons.
"First, the voluntary nature of school prayer would
be compromised by the fact that a public institution
was handling it. Second, no matter how earnestly
school officials would protest that the God referred
to is anybody's God, it is almost inevitable that God

in a public institution will appear to take on the
religion of the majority. Third, school prayer does
not allow full freedom of choice because it deals
with children and in an educatoinal situation; if a
school says, 'Pray (or do what you feel like),' a
child assumes that prayer is part of learning.
Finally, school prayer violates a fundamental assump-
tion of American life, one that has something to do
with privacy, something with freedom of speech, and
something less codified and explicit; that one
ought to be able to retain one's humanity without
being made to feel a pariah in one's own country."[25]

The year 1984 was one for a Presidential election,
a time for the American version of a referendum on
the record of the officeholders, especially the
President seeking re-election. Pragmatic politics,
"the art of the possible", slowly came to prevail
in that year over two substitute measures for the
prayer amendment, that of "equal access" and "the
moment of silence". The national lawmakers wanted to
enact some symbolic, but politically acceptable form
of recognition of the place of religion in the public
schools. Many found that these proposals demonstrated how volatile but also how pervasive the
religion/politics struggle continued to remain on
the national scene.

By way of background, in 1981 the Supreme Court
ordered the University of Missouri to allow a student religious group the right to use its physical
facilities. Already that school had allowed some
100 other non-curricular groups to use its premises.
No university sponsorship of such organizations was
allowed; the student groups were not scheduled by
university authorities for a period that elsewise

would have been devoted to classroom teaching. No
faculty or administration presence was involved,
no one would take attendance, and students would
make their own choices about inviting speakers.

When the Senate realized in March, 1984, that
the school prayer amendment would fail, some of their
number led by Hatfield brought back the "equal access"
proposal. Its major thrust was it would allow students in secondary level schools, (adding to that of
the public university level) who were interested in
exploring religious issues to have equal access to
public school property as did other extracurricular
groups. A bill including those principles came
before the House in May, 1984, supported with some
enthusiasm by the New Christian Right as well as
other evangelicals. However it quickly ran into
extreme opposition.[26] Critics stated it left the door
open for outsiders to participate and proselytize
among vulnerable youth; it sounded too much like public endorsement, or establishment, of religion; it
seemed too close to being approval by the officials.
Under its terms, critics noted, school children could
be addressed by the likes of Ku Klux Klan, the
Unificationist Church, or the Posse Comitatus.[27]

Those criticisms received the careful attention
of the bill's sponsors. By August, 1984, just prior
to Congressional adjournment for the re-election battles, the lawmakers produced a proposal which
attracted commanding support in both Houses. That
enthusiasm came from support for specific revisions of
the original proposal. The act, as amended, did not
authorize the federal government to withhold any
federal financial support to schools that did not comply, a provision of the first bill. The new measure

more clearly defined "noninstructional time"--that
in which extracurricular groups could meet as occur-
ing before or after the school day. The new bill
explicitly stated that non-school personnel would
not start, lead, control or regularly attend such
student meetings; attendance at all meetings was
voluntary and would not be recorded. The lawmakers
also attached to it a very popular bill of some $1
billion, funding various mathematics, science and
foreign language programs.[28]

To the surprise of many, given the contentious-
ness of recent battles, the equal access measure
attracted support from all points on the political/
religious spectrum. Being embarrassed or perhaps
weary over the long wrangling over the Helms amendment,
and determined to show voters back home they did not
reject religion in public life, and delighted to draw
support from everyone from Falwell and Robertson
to the National Association of Evangelicals to the
National Council of Churches, the lawmakers concluded
that act's passage "was itself something of a political miracle". A bill so controversial and so easily
misunderstood received a solid endorsement by a
convincing majority of lawmakers. No talk was made
in equal access of an internal conspiracy.[29]

In the same general realm, that of public recognition of religion in the public schools, lawmakers
in the early 1980s also gave careful attention to
what became known as "moment of silence" proposals.
These generally included a minute or so of quiet for
pupils just at the formal start of the school day.
Everyone could smile over the quip that such a proposal should be favored by teachers especially because that would be the only silent moment for the

entire school day. However, close observers noted that
in some demonstrable manner, moments of silence constituted a form of prayer in the schools. By 1984
some 23 states had placed such measures into their
statute books, allowing for reflection, meditation or
silent prayer within school property on school time.
This issue, supported strongly by the New Christian
Right among other interest groups, reached the
floor of the House that summer. Again, as with the
Helms Amendment, the debate was cast over how far
the legislative branch could extend its authority
over the powers of the courts which had been taking
a very strict separationist position on such issues.[30]
In NCR judgment, could the courts, who were the tools
of the secular humanists, forbid something so harm-
less and voluntary as a moment of silence?

The answer to that question quickly became a strong
yes. Clear constitutional issues came into the debate,
based on the three fold test of the Supreme Court of
Lemon v. Kurtzman, 403 U.S.602(1971). Was the activity in dispute, here the moment of silence, religious
and was it supported and sponsored by the school?
Was there a clearly secular purpose involved in the
intentions of the state's endorsing such activities?
Would the intention of the law have the primary effect
that would neither advance nor inhibit religion?
Finally, would such legislation avoid excessive government entanglement with organized religion?[31]

Faced with such a formidable obstacle as those
criteria, pro-voluntary prayer lawmakers in Washington decided to press for a national law favoring such
moments. If nothing else, in an election year, the
voters back home would know they had at least tried to
find some constitutional means to bring prayer back

into the schools. Robertson and other NCR leaders
strongly endorsed the proposals. After considerable
debate, the House 307-85 passed a measure requiring
schools to allow silent prayer in the classroom. But
the Senate failed to take up the measure. Apparently
they saw the proposal as being primarily ceremonial
a "fall-back position for members who opposed allowing
vocal school prayer but did not want to appear to be
hostile to religion." Critics in the Senate stated
the proposal would "simply ratify current policies
because...nothing now bars voluntary silent prayers
in schools."[32]

Perhaps of greater weight working against the House
bill was the knowledge that the Supreme Court had already announced it would rule in 1985 on the consti-
tutionality of one of the most controversial of the
states' bills, that of Alabama. To aid the cause,
groups such as Moral Majority sent friend-of-the-court
briefs to the Supreme Court urging it to approve
the Alabama statute despite numerous lower court rulings against it. As their justification, the supporters
of the Moral Majority position argued the Alabama
provision would accommodate religious freedom and
hence prevent the religion of secular humanism from
being imposed on the students. To exclude religion
from the public schools would be to impose a "man-
centered religion that denies God's existence and
emphasizes the self-sufficiency of mankind".[33] The
White House added its support to the Alabama law. In
its printout letters asking supporters for their help,
Moral Majority included the statement, "I understand
Jerry Falwell will be speaking for me when he files
a 'Friend of the Court' brief in the United States
Supreme Court".

The matter rested until the Court ruled in July,
1985. The justices voted 6-3 against the Alabama
law. Using the Lemon v. Kurtzman test, they stated
that the law had a religious, not a secular legislative purpose because it was intended to "characterize
prayer as a favored practice." That is, the Alabama law clearly meant to allow students the right
to pray, not simply to meditate or reflect. The law
had no secular purpose; hence it was unconstitutional.
Those states who had such moments of silence laws
which were not intended to be endorsing of prayer
would have such measures upheld by the Court. That
was the key point; meditation or reflection as such
was constitutional; school administration endorsement
of prayer was not.[34]

To Falwell, the decision was one more blow to
religious freedom in the name of secular humanism.
"Surely the United States of America, which presents
itself as a nation under God, can only be viewed as
hypocritical when it refuses to tell its children
that they may pray to that God."[35] By late 1984,
and then confirmed by the late 1985 Alabama decision,
New Christian Rightists could make a tally. Legal
abortion was still the law of the land, voluntary
school prayer had failed, the moment of silence
bill was about to be rejected; equal access had been
approved because of broad and ecumenical support from
groups anathema to religious Rightists. But their
battle over the schools embraced more than those
measures; it aimed at the control over the curriculum
as well.

V

The public schools, staffed by specialists and
dominated by teacher organizations, posed to the New

Christian Right a mortal threat through the subjects
being taught. So perilous did that threat appear as
to lead religious Rightists to believe that were they
to fail here in their warfare against the humanists,
they would have failed their religious calling. But
despite their eschatology which informed them of the
necessary rapid increase of evil and sin in the world,
they still had the opportunity to organize, become involved in public policy making, and save the nation.

    Nowhere did this take more vivid and bitter form
than in the battle with the public schools over
the teaching of creationism, the claim that the
literal Biblical accounts of the creation of the universe and the life on it were documentably scientific.
As their numbers increased during the 1970s and their
organizational skills improved for binding together
like minded citizens, they chose in several states to
make a stand against the teaching of evolution as fact-
ual science in the schools. Then, their morale could
not help but be boosted when President Reagan stated,
"I have a great many questions about it [evolution].
I think that recent discoveries down through the years
have pointed up great flaws in it."[36] New Christian
Rightists for the most part came to agree with a body
of thought, not always tightly unified, known as
"creationism" which claimed its interpretations had
as much if not more scientific credibility as evolution
and should be presented as such in the public classrooms. Evolution, they claimed, was atheistic but
still a religious viewpoint; should not creationism
be presented as a viable alternative?

    Creationism, as an organized body of information
and interpretation, came into prominence in the 1970s,
flourishing among anti-evolutionist supporters

following the Epperson v. Arkansas(393 U.S.97,1968) decision. Unanimously the Supreme Court ruled unconstitutional an Arkansas statute which made it unlawful for
any teacher in a state-supported school or university
"to teach the theory or doctrine that mankind ascended
or descended from a lower order of animals", or "to adopt
or use in any such institution a textbook that teaches
this theory." The Arkansas State Supreme Court had ruled
that this evolution law was a proper function in the
state's power to regulate the school curriculum. The
Supreme Court rejected that, holding that the law violated both the no establishment and free exercise
clauses of the First Amendment. The state legislature
lacked constitutional authority to dictate specific
religious teachings such as were embodied in the Arkansas statute.

Having been started some years earlier, the
creationist movement took on increased momentum following that ruling. With several important variations,
its central core claimed that its positions were sci-
entifically verifiable through some six teachings
"where through observation and a knowledge of the
principles of science, creationists are able to see
the handiwork of God." First, the creationist believes that the universe and the solar system were
suddenly created; 2, the creationist believes that
life was suddenly created; 3, the creationist believes
that all living kinds or types of animals and plants
have remained fixed since creation, other than those
that are extinct, and genetic variation (within the
limits of the created genetic information) has remained
constant since the beginning; 4, the creationist
believes that man and apes have a separate ancestry;
5, the creationist believes that the earth's geological

features were fashioned largely by rapid, catastrophic
processes that affected the earth on a global and
regional scale; 6, the creationist believes that the
creation of the earth and of life was probably rela-
tively recent.[37]

By the 1980s at least some five major groups, es-
pousing somewhat different detailed interpretations,
were on the scene.[38] Yet when it came down to insisting that creationism was scientific and that evolutionism was largely theoretical, the five stood firmly
together. Their position came to be fully endorsed
by the New Christian Right. Its leaders encouraged
supporters to support the bills, in some 18 states
by the early 1970s, to allow creationist materials to
be taught in high school science classes. But by that
time only in Arkansas and Louisiana had such measures
been signed into law.[39]

The creationists, with religious Rightist endorsement, had staked out a legitimate claim for credibility,
in the eyes of Professor Max L. Stackhouse. He acknowledged, first, that their science was "wrong" to insist that the data must be forced into patterns which
accord with their particular interpretation of scripture; and wrong in trying to have sectarian views
propagated in the public schools by law. But, Stackhouse argued, they had struck on a valid issue; whether
there is "divine order, design, or intention govern-
ing the universe...any higher law for guiding life
other than that" purely naturalistic. "The Creationists know that there is another, more ultimate reference point...one by which we can discipline our
instincts, tame our passions, assess our civilizations,
guide our patterns of interaction, and structure our
lives together."[40]

However, within the courts, the creationists found
their case dealt a devastating blow with the 1982 McLean
v. Arkansas Board of Education case, that delivered by
U.S. District Judge William R. Overton, 529 Supp.1255
(E.D.Ark 1982). Drawing from a wide array of sources,
utilizing the three-fold test of Lemon, and the testimony
of a large number of specialists, Overton ruled the
Arkansas law violated the constitutional provisions
separating church and state. The law failed to protect religious neutrality, it was rooted in fundamentalist interpretations of Genesis, and "there can be
no doubt that Arkansas has sought to prevent its teachers
from discussing the theory of evolution because it is
contrary to the belief of some that the Book of Genesis
must be the exclusive source of doctrine as to the
origin of man...It is clear that fundamentalist
sectarian conviction was and is the law's reason for
existence." In a thirty-eight page decision Overton
found the law had failed the three tests of the Establishment clause: secular purpose, primary effect, and
excessive entanglement. "Since creation-science is
not science, the conclusion is inescapable that the
only real effect of Act 590 is the advancement of religion, the unconstitutionality of which there can be
no doubt."[41]

Throughout the trial, which received extensive
national publicity promising to be the major event it
turned out to be, New Christian Right leaders gave
full support to the Arkansas law. Robertson frequently spoke in favor of divine creationism; Falwell
sponsored at his Liberty Baptist College (now University) debates on the issues. Asked why he supported
creationism, he stated "How can I believe in anything
but creation." His biographer suggested that Falwell's

hermeneutics forbade him from seeing metaphor: am-
biguities "in the biblical account that might ren-
der the positions of evolution and divine creation
compatible."[42]

In summation, the warfare waged by the New
Christian Right in the early 1980s over the public
schools helped give full financial and public relations expression to its theology and ideology.
For those supporters who might not have understood the
full nuances of inerrancy or apocalyptic premillennial-
ism, or internal conspiracy machinations, the evidence
from NCR leaders about the battles for the lives of
the children was often compelling enough to attract
new members into the ranks. It was all beginning to
take clear form; the schools must be saved. That conclusion, as we see in the next chapter, made itself
evident also among those working to save the country
against the humanists' warfare against the private
sector, the smaller but indispensable world of church-
related education.

Notes

1.   Tim LaHaye, The Battle for the Mind (Old Tappan,
     N.J., Fleming H. Revell, 1980), p. 142.

2.   Christianity Today, September 19, 1980, p.1071;
     Christian Century, September 24, 1980, p.872.

3.   Krauthammer, "America's Holy War", The New
     Republic, April 9, 1984, pp. 15-19.

4.   McCullom v. Board of Education of Champaign,
     Illinois 333 U.S. 203(1948).

5.   Franklin Parker, "Moral Education USA: Back-
     grounds and Trends", The College Board Review,
     Fall, 1985, vol.137, pp.10-15,30; editorial,
     Christianity Today, April 10, 1981, pp.16-18.

6.   The indictment against the public schools is
     summarized in my Being Religious in America
     Minneapolis, Augsburg Publishing House, 1986),
     ch.6; and Burton Yale Pines, Back To Basics
     (New York, William Morrow and Company, 1982),
     ch.4; Leo Pfeffer, Religion, State and the
     Burger Court (Buffalo, Prometheus Books, 1984),
     ch.3.

7.   See the news story in U.S.A. Today, December,
     1984, p.14 based on an address by James E.
     Wood, Jr. to the B'nai B'rith, May 31, 1984;
     Charles L. Glenn, Jr., "Religious and Public
     Education: Can We Stop the Fighting?",
     The Reformed Journal, June, 1984, p.8.

8.   See the complete agenda discussed in John M.
     Swomley, Jr., "The American Education Debate",
     Christian Century, Sept. 7, 1983, pp.778-80;
     Robert L. Van Dale, "Religious Values and
     Secular Humanism in the Schools", Religious
     Education, 1985, 80:1,pp.12-28.

9.   The Jimmy Swaggart Program, January 6, 1985;
     the earlier quote is from Carl Horn, "How Free-
     dom of Thought is Being Smothered in America",
     Christianity Today, April 6, 1984, p.14; CBN,
     "The Freedom Report", January, 1985, passim;
     David G. Bromley and Anson Shupe, eds., New
     Christian Politics (Macon, Mercer University
     Press, 1984), "Introduction", p.6; a flyer
     from Christian Inquirer (Niagara Falls, N.Y.),

"God Help America", n.d. 4 pages; news story,
Time, September 2, 1985, p.44; The Moral Majority
Report, April, 1984, p.14; Analee McGraw,
"Family Choice in Education: The New Imperatives"
(Washington,D.C., The Heritage Foundation, 1978),
passim.

10.   Sidney Blumenthal, "The Righteous Empire", The
      New Republic, October 22, 1984, pp.18-22; two
      articles by Richard V. Pierard, "Reagan and the
      Evangelicals: The Making of a Love Affair",
      Christian Century, December 21-28, 1983, pp.1182-85,
      and "Religion and the New Right in the 1980s",
      James E. Wood, Jr., ed., Religion and the State:
      Essays in Honor of Leo Pfeffer (Waco, Baylor
      University Press, 1985),pp.393-417; Dinesh D'Souza,
      Falwell Before the Millennium: A Critical Bio-
      graphy (Chicago, Regnery Gateway, 1984), p.132.

11.   An excellent, if slightly dated, guide to these
      and related groups is David Bollier, Liberty and
      Justice for Some (New York, Frederic Ungar
      Publishing Co., Washington, D.C., People for
      the American Way,1982), pp.15-38.

12.   For an extended reading list see Albert J.
      Menendez, ed., School Prayer and Other Religious
      Issues in American Public Education: A
      Bibliography (New York, Garland Publishing Inc.,
      1985).

13.   Homer Duncan, Secular Humanism (Lubbock, Texas,
      Missionary Crusader Press, 1979), p.90.

14.   Pfeffer, Religion, State and the Burger Court,
      p.94; Minneapolis Star, February 22, 1982, pp.1A,
      4A; New York Times, May 18, 1982, p.11.

15.   Newsweek, June 7, 1982, p.84; Kilpatrick quoted
      in an editorial, Christianity and Crisis, April
      16, 1984, p.123 referring to 1982.

16.   Old-Time Gospel Hour, August 8, 1982; 700 Club,
      August 5, 1982; ibid., August 8, 1982; Moral
      Majority Report, August, 1982, p.3.

17.   News story, New York Times, September 9, 1982,
      p.1.

18. Minneapolis Star, August 21, 1982, p.10A; Cleve-
     land Plain Dealer, August 22, 1982, p.18A; New
     York Times, September 23, 1982, p.15; see the
     public opinion polls on prayer compiled in Richard
     John Neuhaus, ed., Unsecular America (Grand
     Rapids., Wm.B.Eerdmans Co., 1986), pp.149-51.

19. News story, Christianity Today, October 22, 1982,
     p.58.

20. Phillip E. Hammond, "The Courts and Secular
     Humanism", Society, May/June, 1984, p.16; see
     the general interpretation of the religion
     factor in Congressional votes in Peter L. Benson
     and Dorothy L. Williams, Religion on Capitol
     Hill: Myths and Realities (San Francisco, Harper
     and Row, Publishers, 1982), passim.

21. Norman Redlich, "Religion and Schools: The New
     Political Establishment", James E. Wood, Jr.,
     ed., Religion and the State, pp.283-84.

22. Pamphlet in 1984, "Save Our Schools", p.3; in it
     is an endorsement by President Reagan. Boone also
     included in the mailing several order blanks for
     some of his recent recordings.

23. D'Souza, Falwell, p.197; Robertson and Falwell
     discussed the issue intensely during these weeks
     and shortly thereafter; Minneapolis Star and
     Tribune March 21, 1984, pp.1A,16A; news item,
     Journal of Church and State, Spring, 1984, 26,
     pp.374-75; The Heritage Foundation, "Education
     Update", Spring,1984, 7:4, p.5; Moral Majority
     Report, May, 1984, p.1.

24. News story, Christianity Today, April 6, 1984,
     pp.60-61; Time, March 19, 1984, pp.12-13; "The
     School Prayer Controversy", Congressional
     Digest, May, 1984, 63:5, pp.131-60.

25. John W. Baker, "Views of the Wall", Baptist
     Joint Committee on Public Affairs, Report from
     the Capital, May, 1984, p.10; Rosenblatt,
     "Whose Country Is It Anyway"?, Time, March 19,
     1984, p.94; see also the letters exchanged
     between Norman Lear and President Reagan in
     Harper's, October, 1984, pp.15-19.

26.   John W. Swomley, Jr., "A Toehold for Religion
      in Public Education", Christian Century, February
      15, 1984,p.171; news items, Christianity
      Today, January 1,1982, p.46, and ibid., April 20,
      1984, p.37; Baker, "Views from the Wall",
      February, 1984, p.6.

27.   News item, Minneapolis Star and Tribune, May 16,
      1984, p.3A; Lutheran Perspectives, May 14, 1984,
      p.4; news item, Christianity Today, June 15, 1984,
      pp.58-59; editorial, Christian Century, May 9,
      1984, pp.477-78.

28.   Public Law No.98-337 effective August 11, 1984;
      news item, Christianity Today, September 7, 1984,
      p.77; Seattle Times, July 26, 1984, p.A12;
      Redlech, "Religion and Schools", pp.286-89.

29.   Editorial, James E. Wood, Jr., Journal of Church
      and State, 1985, 27:1, p.8; passim, pp.5-16;
      Pfeffer, Burger Court, pp.99-101.

30.   A clear analysis made before the House debate
      is that of Donald Drakeman, "Religion's Place in
      Public Schools", Christian Century, May 2, 1984,
      pp.462-63; news item, New York Times, October 19,
      1982, p.1; Time, March 19, 1984, p.14; Pfeffer,
      Burger Court, p.107; news story, Journal of
      Church and State, Spring, 1983, 25:2,p.388.

31.   Ibid; and Minneapolis Star and Tribune, April 3,
      1984, p.8A.

32.   News story in Congressional Quarterly, July 28,
      1984, pp.1809-10.

33.   News story, The Moral Majority Report, September,
      1984, p.3.

34.   See reports in New York Times, July 10, 1984,
      p.12; Minneapolis Star and Tribune, July 15, 1985,
      p.3C; Christian Century, jUne 19-26, 1985, pp.604-05;
      Detroit Free Press, June 5, 1985, p.1; U.S. News
      and World Report, July 15, 1985, p.43.

35.   Our Sunday Visitor, June 23, 1985, p.17; editorial,
      The Fundamentalist Journal, July/August, 1985,
      p.10.

36. See the documentation in Robert Webber, Secular
     Humanism: Threat and Challenge(Grand Rapids,
     Zondervan Publishing House, 1982),p.88.

37. An article, "Evolution vs. Science", Christian
     Herald, July/August, 1985, pp.40-42.

38. Richard Stempien and Sarah Coleman, "Processes
     of Persuasion: The Case of Creation Science",
     Review of Religious Research, December, 1985,
     27:2, p.169.

39. Samuel Rabinowitz, "The Fourth 'R': Religion
     in the Public Schools", American Jewish Congress
     booklet, New York, 1982,p.7.

40. Stackhouse, "An Ecumenist's Plea for a Public
     Theology", This World, Spring/Summer, 1984,
     no.8, p.59; similar arguments are William H.
     Becker, "Creationism: New Dimensions of the
     Religion--Democracy Relation", Journal of
     Church and State, Spring, 1985, 27:2, pp.323-27;
     and Richard A. Baer, J., "They Are Teaching
     Religion in the Public Schools", Christianity
     Today, February 17, 1984, pp.12-15.

41. See the full text in Society, January/February,
     1983, pp.3 ff., and other background stories
     in that issue; ibid. at 126A,1261,1272; James
     E. Wood, Jr., "Religion and Education in Ameri-
     can Church-State Relations", Wood, ed., Religion,
     The State and Education (Waco, Baylor University
     Press, 1984), pp.37-40.

42. D'Souza, Falwell, 142; for examples of Robert-
     son, view his 700 Club program for January 30,
     1983, April 13, 1982, July 8, 1982.

The Penetration of Private Education

Both the New Christian Right and the Reagan
administration understood how crucial to their
causes the battles in public schools were. That
same sense of crisis also pervaded their concerns
for private education, especially church-related
secondary schools throughout the early 1980s. That
battle, however, attracted far less media attention
than had been given the public domain. Lacking
the large numbers of parents and teachers involved in
public schools, and considered by many to be religious fanatics, fundamentalists failed to win extensive coverage by the media for their particular
causes. That, however, as this chapter will explore,
did not diminish their conviction that they were engaged in a holy war.[1]

The religious Right faced a highly complicated
and sensitive problem in its indictment of public
secondary education. Since, as its charge stated,
the secular humanists had wrecked such havoc, showing
no signs of letting up, should parents then send
their children to private, church-related schools?
If none existed in the nearby vicinity, should they
then start their own? What though of the obviously very high financial costs connected with sending
children to either the existing or such new schools?
Should the government, which had expressed its support
for the teaching of religion and morality in schools,
in fact show some measurable support for those willing
to reject the secularist schools? Those questions,
in essence, were all a part of the larger issue:
what is the proper, the American way, of blending
religion into formal education?

By way of background, the matter of tax-exempt
status and federal control of church schools, and

the possibility of public finance of such schools,
reached back into the 1970s. As parental and
fundamentalist dissatisfaction with public education
increased during those years so too did the number
of so-called "Christian day schools" appear, often
rapidly in most sections of the nation. Often un-
accredited by state department or education agencies,
and most often committed to the doctrines and the
ideology of what would become the New Christian Right,
they were a clear indication of the new energies
building within the anti-liberal citizenry. Jerry
Falwell claimed as much when in 1980 he stated that
some 14,000 "conservative Christian schools in America"
were flourishing, growing at the rate of three per
day.[2]

Such a phenomenon obviously attracted the direct
attention of government officials at all levels. In
1978, in a decision which would strongly energize
support for the embryonic NCR, the Internal Revenue
Service attempted to carry out a newly stated policy
requiring all schools which started after 1953 to obey
public policy guidelines on matters of racial integration.
Those schools who refused would be denied their tax-
exempt status, a potentially fatal blow to their survival.

As historian Gillian Peele suggests, the IRS decision was based on its well founded belief that "many,
if not most, of the Protestant Christian schools
existed to circumvent the desegregation process that
the courts had imposed on the public schools, especially in the South." Granted that some day school
founders espoused more noble motives, they also in their
suspicion of government interference from any level had
shown themselves to be highly reluctant to allow any

public regulatory supervision of their programs. In
their own schools, prayers would be built into the
daily schedule, the teachers would not need "equal
access" or "moments of silence", and creationism
would be indigenous to the curricula.[3]

The IRS decision helped galvanize the larger
issue of secular humanism in the schools. Concerned
parents looked for elective office seekers who would
promise to take seriously their demands for reform.
The Reagan campaign identified early with their
aspirations, listening to the suggestions of leaders
such as Robert Billings, an early activist against
the IRS ruling. Billings went on to be the Executive
Director of Moral Majority and, following the taking
of power in 1981 by the Reagan administration, the
Presidential liaison to the Protestant community.
Since in his judgment the IRS had chosen to play
political hardball with the fundamentalists, so that
group could play the same game just as well if not
better.[4]

During the 1980 Presidential campaign, Governor
Reagan promised to give direct attention to this
general issue, with special emphasis on a tax voucher
system which would give tax relief to parents with
children in parochial and private schools. The
original plan would allow parents to subtract from
their tax charges a specified portion of the tuition
they paid for enrolling their children in nonpublic
schools. This would, in fact, be using public revenue
to support private education. As such, the proposal
was highly controversial. Immediate and strong
opposition emerged from several evangelical Protestant
groups, especially the Southern Baptist Convention
and the Americans United for Separation of Church and

State.[5] That response indicated that the New Christian
Right support for tax vouchers fell short of widespread
conservative Protestant endorsement. No consensus
among this family of believers could be reached.

Faithful to his campaign pledge, President Reagan
helped supporting Senators introduce the tuition tax
credit proposal, first appearing in extensive hearings
in the summer of 1981. Led by Senator Robert Pack-
wood (R.--Ore.) and Daniel Patrick Moynihan (D.--N.Y.)
the measure would grant parents of children in primary
or secondary private schools up to $250 in income tax
credits in 1983 and $500 in 1984. The Treasury Depart-
ment estimated that the measure would cost the federal
government $2.7 billion in 1983 and nearly $7 billion
in 1984. The proposal drew strong support from
Moral Majority, Catholic clergy, and various Orthodox
Jewish bodies. Falwell argued that "rather than destroying public schools, the plan would strengthen
competition from the private sector and force public
schools to be more accountable." A large number of
mainline Protestant and Jewish groups, along with
labor and teacher unions and public school parents'
groups testified that the proposal would be a sub-
sidy to the non-needy and a violation of the Constitution.[6]

Their opposition was strong enough to keep the
proposal in Senate committee. It had attracted very
strong support among those for whom it would be a
benefit, but failed to win support outside its
own constituency. In 1983 the Administration proposed a revised plan. Parents with income below
$60,000 who sent their children to nonpublic schools,
could claim tax credits on a sliding scale: up to

$100 per child for 1983, $200 for 1984 and $300
thereafter. The plan was estimated to be of cost
of some $780 million by 1987 to the government.
Revisions were made in committee where it passed
11-7 but then the proposal met headon opposition
on the Senate floor. President Reagan stepped in
to argue that the bill would "allow financially
troubled parochial schools and other private
schools to remain open and thereby not place any
added financial burden on overcrowded public schools."
That, however, was not the rationale of the New
Christian Right which nonetheless supported the
proposal. After considerable debate, again attracting
support only within its own circles, the proposal
failed to reach a test vote in the Senate before the
1984 elections.[7]

II

The Reagan administration started another attack
on the 1978 IRS rulings on tax-exempt status for
schools practicing racial discrimination. In the
most celebrated case it chose to support the case
of the fundamentalist Bob Jones University. The
Administration opened by stating it would reverse
the 1978 ruling. But when an enormous amount of
criticism by church and civil liberties groups reached
the White House, its leaders stated in January,
1982 they would transfer the responsibility of tax
exemption to Congress by asking the legislative
branch to authorize the IRS policy. Congress refused, stating the IRS already held legal authority
for its policy. Ultimately, the case was taken
before the Supreme Court where it lost 8-1.[8]

The New Christian Right involved itself only in
a minor way. Falwell had for years been involved in
a no-holds barred, bare-knuckled theological and
ideological brawl with fellow fundamentalist Bob
Jones University; the latter had kept up a fulsome
attack against most of his many activities in the
early 1980s. Falwell did not involve himself in this
contest. Only one major religious Right figure, William
Billings, President of the National Christian Coalition,
supported the Administration on its proposals to
endorse programs of schools with "sincerely held
religious beliefs" such as Bob Jones.[9]

III

No such restraint, however, was made by NCR spokesmen towards one of the most celebrated and controversial of all parochial school cases of the early 1980s,
that of State ex rel. Douglas v. Faith Baptist
Church, 301 N.W. 2d 571 (Neb.1981). There, issues
of fundamentalist theology, secular humanism, fear
of government interference, and claims for free exercise of religion all came to bear in an astounding-
ly emotional, often seemingly out-of-control contest
between the state of Nebraska and New Christian Right
clergy and educators. The whole episode embraced
just about everything a news hungry media and the
defendents themselves could have wanted; arrests,
police padlocking churches and sending clergy to
jail, law officers searching for clergy and
families fleeing in exile to other states; and state
troopers preventing church members from entering
their churches. In brief, the secular humanist conspiracy in their minds had materialized in the imbroglio at Faith Baptist, Louisville.[10]

Before the religious Right had organized politically, Faith Baptist in 1977 had opened a day school
without receiving state board of education approval.
The ministers asserted that "the operation of the
school is simply an extension of the ministry of
the church, over which the State of Nebraska has
no authority to approve or accredit". The minister,
Everett Sileven, maintained that the state had "no
right to inspect God's property." He and Faith
Baptist officials then refused the state's requests
to (1) provide a roster of students enrolled there; (2)
ask endorsement of its educational program; (3) engage
certified instructors; (4) request approval to operate
the school.[11] Nebraska meanwhile responded by attempting to close the school for such refusal. The case
went to the Nebraska Supreme Court.

That tribunal gave major consideration to Sileven's
claim that the accreditation process violated the
constitutional right of free exercise of religion
and parental control--both classic anti-secular
humanist contentions. The justices focused also on
the state's claim to have a compelling interest in
secondary education. They ruled that Nebraska's requirements for teacher certification and curriculum
approval requirements were minimal, that the state
did have the power to impose "reasonable regulations
for the control and duration of basic education". In
their conclusion the high court justices made clear
their criteria: "The refusal of the defendents to
comply with the compulsory education laws of the
State of Nebraska as applied in this case is an
arbitrary and unreasonable attempt to thwart the
legitimate, reasonable, and compelling interests of
the State in carrying out its educational obligations,
under a claim of religious freedom'."[12]

Apparently, Faith Baptist lost largely because
its lawyers had failed to produce evidence supporting
their position, along with the near anarchistic, anti-
rule of law position they assumed. The Faith Baptist
leadership, however, decided to take their case to
the highest tribunal. In October, 1981, the Supreme
Court dismissed their case for want of a substantial
federal question; that is, the lack of its jurisdiction over a non-federal case.[13]

That, however, turned out to be only the beginning
of the battle. Sileven now reopened an "underground
church school" near Louisville, clearly an illegal
act. For that he was sentenced to four months in
jail. Then, after apparently winning an argument with
his school board which had wanted to close the school,
he had it reopened. He was again arrested and returned to jail.

The battle had attracted widespread support
from fundamentalists across the region. Many traveled
to Louisville in a show of support. During a prayer
service, state patrolmen entered the church and
evicted some 85 in attendance. The school was
padlocked. Then some parents decided to reopen the
school; seven men of their number were arrested for
truancy, while their wives and children left the
state to avoid prosecution. Sileven was declared
a fugitive from justice.

Taking a cue from the 1960s leftist civil disobedience demonstrations, utilizing the news media
for its cause, the Faith Baptist people decided now
was the opportunity to transform their case into a
demonstration to the world of what was wrong with
America, the churches, and Nebraska officialdom.
Led by Moral Majority officials such as the Reverend

Greg Dixon of Indianapolis, some several hundred
ministers (the exact headcount is impossible to
ascertain) visited Louisville to   ask for the re-
lease of the minister and the unpadlocking of the
church. Their request, made in the full glare of
the media hoopala, was rejected, and the state patrol
could not enforce the eviction notice, and notified
the presiding judge of the potential for violence
which existed there. The judge released Sileven,
and everyone concerned agreed to work for an ami-
cable settlement.[14]

All of this attracted the full attention and
eventually the support for Faith Baptist of the New
Christian Right. Pat Robertson frequently endorsed
the leaders' activities, interpreting the battle
as a classic test of religious freedom versus state
attempts at strangulation. Falwell in his national
Sunday television service and in Moral Majority
publications gave total endorsements to the efforts
of the congregation. So   did the new religious
Right monthly magazine, Christian Inquirer.[15]

It was obviously all just too much. Negative
national attention against the Nebraska government
increased over the months abetted by local spot
investigations by Falwell and Jesse Jackson. In
April, 1984, a compromise bill was approved by the
Nebraska legislature. It did not require schools
to provide any information to state officials.
Parents sending their children to a non-state
approved school were required to furnish the state
with information about the subjects being taught
there. Private schools in the state would be
allowed to hire non-certified teachers if they
agreed to have their teachers either take a competency

test prepared by the state education officials or
be evaluated by those officials. What Nebraska officials learned, among other things, was that the
costs required to enforce their extensive regulations of non-public education proved to be prohibit-
ively high. They found themselves in a no-win situation and moved towards accommodation to the realities
of the battle.

IV

Other states, such as Maine and Michigan, encountered
similar kinds of confrontations. The issue at bottom
remained: To what extent should the government expect obedience to its requirements for the teaching
of religion in primary and secondary schools? After
extensive litigation in Maine, and a transfer of jurisdiction from state to federal courts, a U.S. District
Court judge there in 1983 ruled that Maine could not
shut down church-related schools that had refused to
ask for state approval based on religious convictions.
That case later became a cause célèbre, reaching no
less than a spot on the CBS television program,
"Sixty Minutes" on Sept. 30, 1984.[17]

Other New Christian Right involvement in secondary
and college education programs turned up in locations
where dedicated leaders offered their supporters
the opportunity to express hostility towards the
humanists. Much, if not most of these activities
have been limited to specific local school situations
and thus are very difficult for the historian to
track. For the scope of this book, such activities
demonstrate both the intensity and precisely defined
enemy which the religious Right seek, activities

at the same time the extremely diverse, often un-
coordinated efforts by the believers to destroy
their enemies. As much as educators, parents,
historians and other concerned citizens might
want to have a central clearing house of information on such struggles, such does not exist.

Yet the zeal and effectiveness of New Christian
Right involvement in both public and private education controversies continued into the mid 1980s.
Battles were launched, victories and defeats were
experienced both within the redbrick walls of
academe and in the everyday life of every community
in the world of public morality.

Notes

1. See the excellent discussion of both the general and specific dimensions in private education in Alan Peshkin, God's Choice: The Total World of a Fundamentalist Christian School (Chicago, University of Chicago Press, 1986).

2. This section is based heavily on the concise discussion by Gillian Peele, Revival and Reaction: The Right in Contemporary America (Oxford, Clarendon Press, 1984), pp.96-98; see also Erling Jorstad, Evangelicals in the White House: The Cultural Maturation of Born Again Christianity, 1960-1981 (New York, The Edwin Mellen Press, 1981), ch.11.

3. Peele, Revival and Reaction, pp.97-98.

4. Ibid., pp.97-98; Carol Flake, Redemptorama: Culture, Politics, and the New Evangelicalism (Garden City, Doubleday and Company, 1985), p.37.

5. See the debate in Christianity Today, November 6, 1981, p.1499; ibid., July 16, 1982, pp.25-27. By 1982 the Tuition Tax Credits measure had the approval of Falwell, Phyllis Schlafly, and several pro-life groups; see the critical pamphlet by Americans for Religious Liberty, "Tuition Tax Credits", 1982, P.O. Box 6656, Silver Springs, Md. 20906.

6. News item, Journal of Church and State, 1981, 23:2, p.606.

7. Ibid., 1983, 25:2, p.589; news story, Christianity Today, June 17, 1983, pp.20-23; news story, Journal of Church and State, 1983,26:1, pp.158-61; ibid., 1984, 26:2, p.375; news story, Congressional Quarterly, July 6, 1985, p.1339.

8. Peele, Revival and Reaction, pp.164-65, 82 and appropriate foornotes.

9. Dinesh D'Souza, Falwell Before the Millennium: A Critical Biography (Chicago, Regnery Gateway, 1984), ch.13; news item, Journal of Church and State, 1982, 24:2, p.423.

10. Much of the following is from the excellent
    summary, James C. Carper and Neal E. Devins,
    "The State and the Christian Day School",
    James E. Wood, Jr., ed., Religion and the
    State: Essays in Honor of Leo Pfeffer
    (Waco, Baylor University Press, 1985), 223-26;
    the secular humanist charge is in a news item,
    Journal of Church and State, 1982, 24:1, p. 188.

11. Carper and Devins, "The State and the Christian
    Day School", p.223.

12. Ibid., p.223.

13. Ibid., see the documentation.

14. Ibid.,see the excellent parallel account in
    Richard V. Pierard, "Religion and the New
    Right in the 1980s", ibid., 403-07, which
    contains much of the storm and stress details.

15. For example, 700 Club for September 5, 1982;
    Old•Time Gospel Hour, October 21, 1982;
    Moral Majority Report, May, 1984, p.1;
    "Special Report" published by Moral Majority,
    January, 1983, p.1; The Fundamentalist
    Journal, September, 1983, p.55; Christian
    Inquirer, April, 1985, p.23; Moral Majority
    Report, April, 1985, p.6; news item,
    Christianity Today, July 13, 1984, pp.40-41;
    news story, Christian Century, January 26,
    1983, p.63; Christianity Today, October 19,
    1984, pp. 26-27; also the article by Edward
    Dobson and Ed Hindson in The Fundamentalist
    Journal, September, 1983, pp.10-14.

16. Carper and Devins, p.225; news item, Christian
    Herald, June, 1984, p.5.

17. Carper and Davis, pp.226-27; the Michigan
    case, still in litigation, is discussed there;
    see news story, U.S. News and World Report,
    August 19, 1985, p.59; Newsweek, March 25,
    1985, p.87; news story, Christianity Today,
    February 3, 1984, pp.58-60.

Warfare Over Public Morality

From its inception, the New Christian Right directed
a major portion of its energies to enacting its social
agenda, its family issues list of legislative items.
To accomplish that, it would inject itself forcefully and often abrasively into the already heated
national debates over these and other related issues.
In this chapter we explore religious Right involvement through 1984 over public morality as the debate
took shape over the women's movement, legalized abortion, and public sexual mores.

The dominant teaching controlling all NCR public
policy activity is its conviction that men and women
are totally, socially, and biologically separate
entities each with their own role in God's providence. Any human attempt to act as though the sexes
were equal would be to flaunt the authority of God's
teachings as found in the inerrant Bible, especially
Ephesians 5-6. The fact that throughout recorded
history, humankind has lived under a patriarchy where
males controlled the economy, the government and all
social institutions is proof of its validity. Those
who reject such a teaching are not only foolish, they
are nonbelievers.[1]

Yet in recent years, such traditional teaching
has been subjected, in NCR reckoning, to major on-
slaughts from liberals, secular humanists and their
allies. After blasting their specific groups such as
the ACLU, NOW, Planned Parenthood and the NEA, Falwell
sounded the alarm: "As we look at them attempting
to secularize society, purging society of God
and religious heritage, and others trying to eliminate all moral absolutes, you begin to realize what's
happening in this country... America is in serious
trouble. America must have revival now or we will

find ourselves in the grips of philosophies like those
espoused by the groups I've just mentioned. In my
opinion, that would spell the death knell for the
United States of America as a free, democratic
republic."[2]

Much of the blame for such decay could be traced,
in NCR leadership judgment, to those people of faith
who had failed to assert their political rights as
citizens to halt the moral decay now so evident. A
major NCR agency, Christian Voice, explained where
believers had failed: "Christian stewardship" had
failed on school prayer, voluntary abortion, religious observances on public property, secular humanism
in school curricula, public expressions of homosexuality, accessible pornography, sexual promiscuity,
easy access to liquor and drugs, corrupt public
leaders and rampant street crime. Public morality
was indeed in shambles.[3]

But, the leaders pointed out, God had not yet
given up on America. Its people were at the final
crossroads with one last chance for a restoration
of public morality available to them. That crusade must focus on saving the traditional family and
its attendant social values, of returning to traditional gender roles, of rebuilding the work
ethic of individual responsibility rather than
reliance on the welfare state, of restoration
of chastity before marriage, of restoring the dignity of women who choose to be full-time homemakers
and, among other things, of endorsing parental
responsibility for the discipline of their children.

Such solutions harmonized fully with the social
agenda and proposed legislation to protect the family
put forward by the Reagan administration. For

instance, in July, 1982, it sponsored "Family Forum
II" where these and related themes were pondered
by government officials and endorsed by Falwell,
Onalee McGraw, Pat Robertson, Phyllis Schlafly
and Don Wildmon (see below, ch. 11). The Forum
clearly represented the extent to which the White
House understood the importance of bringing the religious Rightists into its leaders' plans for implementing its agenda.[4]

The New Christian Right responded in kind
with full support of the Reagan proposals. Recognizing the attention given to women's issues,
the Old-Time Gospel Hour, for example, sponsored
"A Wonderful Weekend for Women" in October, 1984,
with workshops and speakers focusing on themes
such as the mid-life crisis, motherhood, marriage, and afflictions of womanhood. The LaHayes, Tim
and Bev, offered membership in a newly created
"Family Life Association" designed "to help
strengthen you morally, spiritually and financially...to stand up to the forces working against
your family." Membership included a subscription
to Family Living magazine; the first 1,000 who
enrolled would receive "a personally autographed
copy" of Tim's The Battle for the Family, plus
savings of up to 50 percent on name brand merchandise, vacations and travel, car rentals, Christian
books, vitamins, prescription drugs, group insurance, film processing, low interest loans "and
Much, More More!" On a different level, Religious
Roundtable offered pro-family seekers the opportunity
to sign a petition to be sent to the National Council
of Churches opposing that agency's program rewording
portions of the Bible to be placed in a new

lectionary which would harmonize more closely with
feminist theology.[5]

Such alternative courses of action indicated
how bold and innovative the New Christian Right
leadership had become to preserve its understanding of public morality. No longer, in their eyes,
should politics be limited to bread and butter
issues such as inflation, jobs, taxes and business
issues. Now the government, supported by New
Christian Right voters, was claiming it had a
constitutional right and duty to be the custodians,
or keepers or a specific moralistic worldview
and set of behaviors.[6]

This new momentum came together in 1981 in a
bill sponsored in the Senate by Roger W. Jepson (R.--
Iowa) and Paul Laxalt (R.--Nev.) and in the House
by Albert Lee Smith (R.--Ala.). It was a variation
on a similar bill proposed by Senator Laxalt in 1979.
Its preamble stated it was intended "to strengthen
the American family..to preserve [its] integrity,
to foster and protect [its] viability by emphasiz-
ing family responsibilities in education, tax
assistance, religion and other areas related to the
family and to promote the virtues of the family."
Briefly, the terms would require several responses
from the citizens involved: (1) it would require
parental notification when unmarried minors received
contraceptive devices or abortion-related services
from a federally funded organization; (2) it would
prohibit the federal government from pre-empting
or interfering with state statutes related to juve-
nile delinquency, child abuse, or spouse abuse;
(3) the definition of child abuse would be revised
to include corporal punishment or other forms of

discipline authorized by   parents; (4) parents could
sue if a federally funded educational   agency prohibited them from being involved in decisions regarding their child's enrollment in religion courses,
or prohibited them from visiting the child's classroom, or required forced payment of union dues
as a condition for the employment of the teachers;
(5) no federal funds could be used to promote
educational material that "denigrates the role of
women as it has been historically understood"; (6) the
right to the free exercise of religion is to be
guaranteed, including the right of voluntary school
prayer in the classroom; (7) federal agencies could
not regulate religious activities such as church
schools, religious activities, or ministries of
religious instruction; (8), religious organizations
would be exempt from the regulations of affirmative
action quotas, or actions designed to redress
racial imbalance.[7]

Briefly, almost every important NCR proposal
for combatting the secular humanists in the matters
of public morality and family issues found its
way into the bill. It created an almost instant
thunderous outbreak of criticism from teacher,
civil liberty and organized religious groups. The
Laxalt-Jepson-Smith measure never came to a final
vote in Congress, or even to either floor for a
vote. But it stands as a landmark piece of evidence in the early 1980s of the willingness of the
religious Right in the early 1980s to use the power
of government through its political representatives
to enforce its agenda.

II

Equally propitious before the end of 1984 as a
demonstration of the New Christian Right involvement
in politics was its offensive against the Equal
Rights Amendment. As was true with the legislation discussed above, the older lines of demarca-
tion between religion and politics, in the American
way, yielded to the direct participation of religious
Right leaders. But at this one point, the traditional patriarchal leadership of the NCR bowed to
the dazzling and ultimately triumphant power of a
woman campaigner, longtime radical Right activist,
Phyllis Schlafly.

Since her debut during the Senator Goldwater
campaign with her study, A Choice, Not an Echo,
Schlafly had maintained strong ties with the Right
through further books, frequent speaking engagements
and the development of her own lobby, Eagle Forum.
In 1972 she published her first major anti-ERA
article, this despite its having been endorsed by
President Richard Nixon and approved by Congress,
needing by that date ratification by two-thirds
of the states. Schlafly turned her small-scale
program into a highly efficient pressure group, mobilizing several hundred largely decentralized clubs
and associations to follow her strategy. Guy Sorman
described it well; "pressuring legislators who
are up for re-election in a process sometimes tanta-
mount to blackmail, and focusing the attention of
the media by the creation of an event". Such included locked arm demonstrations at state capitols
calling on God to restore decency, on telegram
blitzes to lawmakers and the media, on the delivery
of "a mountain of apple pies", symbol of family

cooking to a lawmaker.[8] Just as the feminist movement seemed to lose energy in the mid 1970s Schlafly's
highly mobilized forces took command and persuaded
enough states to halt ratification, the final
vote coming in 1982.

The supporters were not, as Carol Flake wrote,
"simply kill joys" out to restore old time morality,
but "were frightened wives who regarded their very way
of life as threatened." ERA, they believed, would
lead to unisex public toilets, to women being eligible for the military draft, for the loss of legal
rights they now enjoyed, for making masculine the
feminine instincts of women. Schlafly made something
of a definitive statement for her position during
Campaign '84. Women, she argued, were not really
interested in competing with men, but in homemaking,
raising children to be good patriots and were religiously inclined. Schlafly endorsed the conservative
principles of limited government and self help, and
sharply criticized programs of sex education in the
public schools, "liberal teachers" who taught or
discussed topics such as class conflict, poverty,
and sexual proclivities such as homosexuality. She
concluded with the belief that the Bible commanded
that women were subject to their husbands.

Her critics, and they were in attendance at this
particular speech, were labeled as "Yippies, hippies,
dykes on bikes, and other Democrats." Her critics
also were "Communist inspired", "misguided" and
"lesbian controlled."[9] Throughout the early
1980s her position was warmly endorsed by the major
NCR leaders, all determined to keep the lid on the
ERA casket. Robertson, Tim LaHaye, Jimmy Swaggart,
and Falwell zealously endorsed her diagnoses of the

women's movement being a common enemy, the product
of secular humanism. That in itself served as a
major force keeping united the several factions
of the American Right.[10]

III

Without question, however, the New Christian
Right took the form it did after the full legal
and medical implications of the Roe v. Wade abortion
decision of the Court became known. So strong and
so widespread was the ensuing denunciation of
legalized abortion by specific interest groups as
to make clear the United States here faced its
greatest internal division on a domestic issue since
the antebellum days of slavery. To these citizens
the abortion of a fetus was nothing less than the
killing of an unborn human being. An agency of
the government, the Supreme Court, had "decided that,
inter alia, a mother had an unconditional constitutional right to an abortion during the first tri-
menster (three months) of pregnancy; and that while
thereafter the state might intervene to place condi-
tions on the performance of an abortion, the initial
decision was a private one between the woman and
her medical adviser."[11] Thus, opponents of legal
abortion chose to make the political arena their
combat zone, working for repeal through proposed
constitutional amendments and attempting to
restrict federal funding for abortions. So ex-
cruciatingly complex and sensitive a moral issue
during these years was turned into a political
polemic.[12]

Virtually every organized religious body spoke
out on the issue; pro life versus pro choice drew

church members into the political realm in a manner
"more analogous to a crusade than to ordinary
politics." Those crusaders who became involved
soon learned, as they had not known before, how to
make their opinions known in the realm of politics.
That was a necessary and pragmatic means to introduce
them into the world where they would make so strong
an impact in the 1980s.[13]

The full New Christian Right took up the cause
of pro-life. They sent printed petitions and opinion
poll forms to supporters asking for the return of
them to their respective lawmakers in Washington.
As authority for their stance, they pointed to the
full support given their general position by President Reagan, and widespread endorsement from a variety
of organized religious bodies. Various attempts by
cooperating Congresspersons to stop federal funding,
or require minors to notify parents when seeking
birth control information from federally funded
agencies were ruled invalid by the higher courts.[14]
Several Senators introduced a variety of pro-life
constitutional amendments; Senators Jesse Helms,
Orrin Hatch and Mark Hatfield all attempted to find
the right kind of working for a measure which
would receive the necessary two-thirds endorsement
by their colleagues. The divisions among the
three helped contribute to the defeat of any such
measure. In a major Senatorial floor fight in September, 1982, including a long filibuster by Helms,
the lawmakers reached an impasse.[15] No comparably
organized effort in that assembly developed after
that point.

Every New Christian Right leader spoke out sharply and frequently about abortion, linking it directly

to the secular humanist conspiracy. Throughout 1982
Falwell and LaHaye devoted their heaviest attacks
of all on the issue. Pat Robertson accused the
"humanists" of trying to make the product of sexual
intercourse between a man and a woman something that
is not a human baby, but only "the product of conception, so you can kill it."[16] In what at first
seemed a startling change of direction, Jim and Tammy
Faye Bakker of the PTL club reversed an earlier policy
of avoiding issues as controversial as abortion.
In August, 1983, Bakker stated, "until now, no one
has ever gone on national television and said the
things that I am saying. No one has dared to speak
out as I have about the hideous crimes going on in
our country...I have exposed the mass murders of unborn babies and cried out against rulers in government who are trying to play God!" "I believe the
judgment of God will fall on America if we let
this wholesale slaughter continue."[17] Falwell stated
he did not personally favor abortion even in the case
of rape or incest, but believed that if such a
provision were included in a constitutional amendment, it would surely fail. During these years, Falwell also started a "Save-a-Baby" ministry, inviting
unwed pregnant women to come to a shelter home in
Lynchburg or other facilities funded by his program.
There they would live expense free and there deliver
the baby relieved of hometown or family pressures. At
those homes counselling and adoption assistance were
provided by the staffs.[18]

IV

     The third major area of religious Right crusading
within the public morality centered on homosexuality,

herpes and AIDS. For those citizens who might not
accept the internal conspiracy thesis being responsible for everything the NCR claimed, its leaders
introduced them to what they claimed was the internal plot to destroy this nation. In 1984 Falwell
stated, "militant homosexuals plan to take over both
political parties. Militant homosexuals plan to convince this generation and the next"..."the only sin is
to feel guilt or shame--that Jesus Christ was gay--that
the Bible endorsed lesbian and homosexual behavior--
that there are no values." He continued, "And it is
clear they are determined to recruit our young people
and, unless we educate the American people on this
issue, many of them will succeed!" He pledged to
launch a program to educate the populace about gay
rights ordinances, the Gay Rights Bill in Congress,
and to urge Americans at the grassroots level to turn
back this threat. "They have their eyes on our schools...
our churches...our government...and our precious
children."[19]

     Falwell's mention of a gay rights bill points
to the appearance in the political arena in the early
1980s of another ingredient of the New Christian
Right social agenda, opposition to "the efforts of
homosexuals to obtain special privileges as a 'bona-
fide minority'." Stating its members were committed
to guaranteeing the civil rights of homosexuals,
Moral Majority leaders stated their opposition to
any efforts by homosexuals "to flaunt their perversion
as an acceptable lifestyle and/or attempt to force
their lifestyle upon our children."[20] Comparable
statements came from Jimmy Swaggart; "homosexuality,
abortion, the terrible divorce rate...V.D....Satanism,
witchcraft, every type of filth that one can imagine

that would make Sodom and Gomorrah blush."[21] Christian
Voice, Christian Family Renewal and Summit Ministries
made the same general indictment.[22]

During the late 1970s some organized gay groups
started fighting back against the legal and sometimes
illegal restrictions against their rights to hold
certain jobs (especially teaching), own or rent property (especially housing). Such battles often created
enormous public criticism, such as in New York City
where the warfare continued for 14 years. Many
groups outside the religious Right, of course, also
opposed organized gay measures. Yet that movement,
especially as led by Falwell mounted an on-going
series of political and fundraising offensives against
such proposals. Supporters were sent petitions,
ballots, and opinion polls which they were informed
would be sent "to every congressman [sic], state legislator, and governor; to judges, many school board
members, P.T.A. presidents, TV networks, and major
newspapers--even President Reagan himself."[23]

National attention was focused, in part, by NCR
spokesmen who asked for support for leaders in Oklahoma who had atempted to purge schoolboards of their
programs to dismiss teachers advocating, encouraging,
or promoting homosexuality. They called for the
defeat of a proposal in Houston, Texas which would
have banned gay applications to the city police
department. As to the "Gay Rights Bill" in Congress,
its terms would have made illegal discrimination
against homosexuals in employment, education, public
accommodations and housing. The measure was debated
in both the House Judiciary Committee and its sub-
committee, the Civil and Constitutional Rights Committee. In religious Right judgment, the measure

would be a green light encouragement by the national
government to all that was reprehensible about gay
lifestyles.[24] The measure failed to reach a final
vote, but served (as did the ERA) as a demonstrable
piece of evidence to NCR donors of the presence of
the enemy in their midst.

The most compelling evidence to that effect of
all, that America was indeed threatened by homosexuals came with the beginnings of the herpes and
AIDS (Aquired Immune Deficiency Syndrome) crises in
the early 1980s. As medical evidence indicated,
during those years that these diseases were largely,
but not exclusively, rampant in homosexual groups,
the NCR leaders made their judgments. Robertson
said herpes was sent by God to end the sexual
revolution; Falwell called herpes the judgment of
God. A Moral Majority Vice President, Cal Thomas,
stated that political liberalism had contributed to
the herpes epidemic, the evidence being that they
both flourished at the same time. To that former
Senator George McGovern replied, "It also happened
while the Minnesota Vikings were playing football.
That doesn't necessarily mean the two are tied."[25]
Falwell asked his supporters to ask Congress to enact
a law quarantining or imprisoning homosexuals who
continued sexual activity after they had been diagnosed as having AIDS. That was, again, a political
remedy for a major, and by all acounts, frightening
matter of public morality. Most of the leaders
gave more extended consideration to AIDS, as it
spread more rapidly in the later 1980s; that discussion is in ch.11 below.

Thus before the elective battles at all levels came before the populace in 1984 in America's expression of a referendum, the "newness" of the New Christian Right stood out clearly on the religious landscape; its adherents had committed themselves to the political world of public policy making. Yet the story before Campaign '84 is not yet quite complete. Before exploring it, we trace how these specific leaders all came into such prominence and support in so short a time.

Notes

1.   Shirley Rogers Radl, The Invisible Woman: Targets
     of the Religious New Right (New York, Delta Books,
     1983), ch. 1 and p. 58.

2.   "Old-Time Gospel Hour", July 28, 1984; see Dinesh
     D'Souza, Falwell Before the Millennium: A Criti-
     cal Biography (Chicago, Gateway Regnery, 1984),
     pp.161-62; See Swaggart for similar views, for
     instance his writing in The Evangelist, November,
     1984, p.32.

3.   Colonel V. Doner, "Why Christians Must be Involved",
     American Christian Voice Foundation, n.d.,; Eve
     Pell, The Big Chill (Boston, Beacon Press, 1984),
     ch.2.

4.   Minneapolis Star and Tribune, July 28, 1982, p.6A;
     ibid., July 29, 1982, p.12A.

5.   Moral Majority Report, September, 1984, p.14;
     advertisement in ibid., June, 1983, p.15; letter
     signed by Edward McAteer, The Roundtable, "Stop
     the Liberals from Rewriting the Bible".

6.   Gillian Peele, Revival and Reaction: The Right
     in Contemporary America (Oxford: Clarendon Press,
     1984), pp.91-93; Grant Wacker, "Uneasy in Zion:
     Evangelicals in Postmodern Society", George
     Marsden, ed., Evangelicalism and Modern America
     (Grand Rapids, Wm.B.Eerdmans Co., 1984), pp.21-24.

7.   Summarized in The Hastings Center Report, August,
     1981, p.16; see David Bollier, Liberty and Justice
     for Some (New York, Frederick Ungar Publishing
     Co., 1982; People for the American Way), p.226;
     Radl, The Invisible Woman, see references in
     "Index", "Family Protection Act", p.193; Peele,
     Revival and Reaction, p.11; see the discussion by
     the National Education Association in The Right-
     to-Work Revival...Far Right and Dead Wrong
     (Washington, D.C.), n.d., pp.81-86.

8.   Guy Sorman, The Conservative Revolution in America
     (Chicago, Regnery Books, 1985), p.117.

9.   Carol Flake, Redemptorama: Culture, Politics,
     and the New Evangelicalism (Garden City, Double-
     day and Company, 1984),p.86; Arthur Frederick Ise,

Tomorrow's Tyrants: The Radical Right and the
Politics of Hate (Dallas, Monument Press, 1985),
pp.24-28.

10. D'Souza, Falwell, p.21; Radl, Invisible Woman,
     pp.136-41; another good summary is in Moral
     Majority Report, January, 1982, pp.9,14,15;
     Sorman, Conservative Revolution, p.111, ch.10;
     Andrea Dworkin, Right-Wing Women (New York,
     G.P. Putnam's Sons, 1983), pp.29-31; Mary Frances
     Berry, Why ERA Failed: Politics, Women's Rights,
     and the Amending Process of the Constitution
     (Bloomington, Indiana University Press, 1986); an
     excellent analysis of the ERA is Jerone L.
     Himmelstein, "The Social Basis of Antifeminism:
     Religious Networks and Cultures", Journal for
     the Scientific Study of Religion, 1986, 25:1,
     pp. 1-15.

11. Peele, Revival and Reaction, p.93.

12. Additional discussion is in Ide, Tomorrow's
     Tyrants, pp.143-83; the penetration of pro life
     forces into the Republican party is in Andrew
     H. Merton, Enemies of Choice: The Right-To-
     Life Movement and Its Threat to Abortion
     (Boston, Beacon Press, 1981),pp.151-72;
     Dworkin, Right-Wing Women, pp.71-105.

13. Peele, Revival and Reaction, p.94.

14. News item, Journal of Church and State, 1984,
     26:3, p.570,575-76; Christianity Today,
     June 17, 1983, p.42.

15. New York Times, September 17, 1982, p.12;
     Congressional Quarterly, September 18, 1982,
     p.2299; Ellen Goodman's column, Minneapolis
     Star and Tribune, May 7, 1982, p.16A; Moral
     Majority Report, October, 1982, p.2.

16. 700 Club, November 11, 1982; also ibid.,
     January 11, 1982, and January 16, 1983; The
     LaHaye television weekly program, February 7,
     1982.

17. Letter from Jim Bakker, PTL Club, August 10,
     1983.

18. D'Souza, Falwell, pp.167-68; Old-Time Gospel
     Hour, May 20, 1984; Brenda D. Hofman, "Politi-
     cal Theology: The Role of Organized Religion
     in the Anti-Abortion Movement", Journal for
     the Scientific Study of Religion, 1986,
     28:2, pp.240-47.

19. A monthly fundraiser letter reprinted in Ide,
     Tommorrow's Tyrants, pp.239-44, written in
     conjunction with Falwell's visit to the 1984
     Democratic National Convention; in a post-
     script he adds, "For those who send $25 or
     more, I will send you a "Photo Journal" of
     my San Francisco experience, featuring pages
     of pictures taken by my 17 year old son
     Jonathan, who went incognito into the streets
     with the demonstrators and obtained unbeliev-
     able pictures and information".

20. "What is the Moral Majority"?, an 8 page
     flyer, n.d.

21. Swaggart's television program, October 7, 1984;
     700 Club, May 6, 1982, and May 21, 1982.

22. Noble is from the old Billy James Hargis Ministry,
     see my Politics of Doomsday: Fundamentalists
     of the Far Right (Nashville, Abingdon Press,
     1970).

23. Letter to supporters from Falwell, Moral Majority,
     February 15, 1982; ibid., January 2, 1982; ibid,
     September 7, 1982; a note at the end of that
     letter reads, "Mr. Erling Jorstad, could you
     possibly send a special 'crisis' gift of $25.00
     today?".

24. News story, Minneapolis Star and Tribune, March
     27, 1985, p.3A; San Francisco Chronicle, December
     22, 1981, p.2; Bollier, Liberty and Justice for
     Some, p.333; see mailings by the Christian Family
     Renewal and Christian Voice; Colman McCarthy's
     column in Minneapolis Star and Tribune, October
     7, 1982, p.14A.

25. 700 Club, August 23, 1982; ibid., September 16, 1982;
     ibid., November 11, 1982; ibid., November 16, 1982;
     Old-Time Gospel Hour, March 20, 1983; Moral Major-
     ity Report, July, 1983, p.10 passim; Minneapolis
     Star and Tribune, December 7, 1982, p.38; Moral
     Majority Report, September, 1983, p.7; Ide,
     Tomorrow's Tyrant,   pp.279-80; Time, September 2,
     1982, p.55.

Television: The Accessway to Leadership

The single greatest source of influence in American
life by the New Christian Right from its beginnings has
been its enormously strong control over the television
media to promote its message. Its leaders are conservative Protestants, committed to use their chosen means
of communication for evangelism, spreading the good
news of the Gospel to those persons unconvinced or un-
aware of its validity. Every major religious Right
preacher has utilized several media--print, public
speaking, radio, the pulpit. But the leaders are where
they are because they have mastered the technology,
the fundraising and the programming of religious broadcasting. By the mid 1980s their programs could stand
as the definition by tens of millions of viewers as to
what constituted religious television.[1]

Yet television by its very nature stood out as
totally unique and as qualitatively different from
earlier forms of evangelism. Whereas Protestants
had identified it with great preachers such as George
Whitefield or Dwight L. Moody or Martin Luther King,
Jr., the opportunities for spreading the word through
television presented a totally different situation.
With its enormously heavy emphasis on personality--on
facial and body gestures, on pleasing personalities,
on keeping a program moving in an engaging but
simple to understand manner, television became unique.

Following the pioneer evangelism done during the
1950s and 1960s by Billy Graham and Oral Roberts and
Rex Humbard, the New Christian Right evangelists each
would make his own contribution to this new medium.
In so doing each became nothing less than a highly
specialized celebrity. Each had the task to provide

in Peter G. Horsfield's estimate, "an integrated symbolic world filling the socially functional role demanded of it both by its viewers and its advertisers.
Such integrated mythic structures provide the continuity and stability among the different types of
programs..."[2] That integration clustered around the
preachers' utilization of their theology, political
ideology, and conspiracy thesis. Claiming expertise
in that three-fold message gave them in their viewer's
eyes the legitimacy and authority to preach what they
believed God wanted America to hear at that time in
history.[3]

Yet, from the outset, that legitimating world view
has been subjected to strong criticism, not along
the old fundamentalism vs liberalism battle lines
but because, many charged, television simply could
not convey the essence of religious faith. Television
programmers found their audiences strongly preferred
productions that were very simple, easy to follow
and   soft on such doctrinal issues as sin and hell.
Religious television further was charged as isolating
viewers from one another rather than create body
community such as in a congregation. Critic Neil
Postman stated it forcefully: In television

Everything that makes religion an historic,
profound and sacred human activity is stripped
away; there is no ritual, no dogma, no theology
and above all, no sense of spiritual transcendence. On these shows, the preacher is tops.
God comes out as second banana." "There is
no way to consecrate the space on which a television show is experienced; the screen is so
saturated with our memories of profane events,
so deeply associated with the commercial and

entertainment worlds that it is difficult for
it to be recreated as a frame for sacred
events.[4]

In reply, the preachers by choice offer their
evangelism message not in the older "repetitive,
aesthetic pattern of religious ritual" but emphasize
instead the persuasive gifts of the leader. The setting they use, either a low church auditorium or a
television studio is by choice an attempt to change
that space, actually any space, into a sacred area
where conversion can occur. The NCR leaders accept
the opportunity presented by television for the en-
hancing of the spoken word with the accompanying
gestures and expressions of the preacher's arts, attempting to "establish a sense of presence and directly
engage the viewer."[5] For instance, Falwell's cameras
scan the congregation to present "sacred space"; the
sermon is often enhanced by taped interviews with experts
endorsing his viewpoints. Swaggart has mastered the
technique of stalking across the stage as he preaches,
"alternating between the roles of prophet, preacher,
and musician." Robertson consciously enhances his
spiritual authority by playing the role of an informed
anchorman "with news commentaries, prophecies, prayers,
biblical exegesis, and interviews with persons who
have had significant conversion experiences."[6]

This chapter explores the coming into national
leadership of the ministries of Falwell, Robertson,
Swaggart, and the Bakkers through 1984. Much has
already been written about the televangelists and
the electronic church; that will not be rehashed
here. Rather the focus is on (1) their utilization
of business techniques to carry out their evangelism;
(2) their similarities and their differences as

celebrities; (3), a summary of their leading critics.
The underlying question throughout is whether their
message and their enterprises constitute a harmony
with the earlier character of conservative Protestant
evangelists.

II

Since a major part of "the American way" is to respect size and growth, that "bigger is better", the New
Christian Right showed during these years it had
learned how to expand rapidly.   In its number of additional outlets, the size of staff and financial contributions, it became a multi-million dollar enterprise.
Although no single clearing house agency exists for
keeping the tallies, the following figures serve as
reliable indices for the pattern of growth.

For 1980 Time reported income of $51 million to
Bakker, $47 million to Robertson, $46 million to Falwell
and $20 million to Swaggart (along with comparable sums
to other televangelists).[7]   A. C. Neilson ratings for
later in 1981 indicated Swaggart had just under two
million viewers with 218 stations (all of these include
cable); Falwell had 1,260,000 viewers with 254 stations,
Bakker worked with 946,000 supporters and 178 stations,
and Robertson had 630,000 viewers and 133 stations (The
three leaders then were Oral Roberts, Robert Schuller
and Rex Humbard).[8]

The 700 Club of Robertson moved into the leadership
after it changed its programming to include old favorite
sitcoms, nostalgia movies and family fare, including
a "Christian soap opera."   By 1984 the 700 Club was fed
into 3,200 local cable systems claiming an access to 20
million homes.   By late 1985 Robertson's empire was
bringing in revenue of $233 million annually.   The total

evangelical broadcasting domain had moved up to some
200 local TV stations with religious formats. Swaggart
announced income of $140 million a year with 197 sta-
tions broadcasting his show. Bakker continued to grow
also, standing second only to Robertson in Christian
cable with 13 million households, with a 24-hour-a-day
all religion format. Falwell's Sunday services were
seen in 172 markets; his receipts in 1985 ranked at near
$100 million. Robertson was reaching with his daily
program 16.3 million households, Swaggart with a weekly
show reached some 9.3 million households, Bakker with
his daily program some 5.8 million viewers and Falwell,
with a weekly program 5.6 million watchers, according
to the Nielson surveys.[9]

These preachers obviously had convinced a growing
number of viewers that they spoke with authority, that
their exhortations if obeyed would turn America back
to God, that the righteous will indeed prevail. But
that assurance could never be taken for granted. The
religious life was explained by them as being a constant battle between God and the devil for individual
souls; conspiracies such as those of the secular
humanists or internal communism always were attempting
to lure believers away from full confidence in God's
providential care. In short, as Horsfield argues,
this competitive kind of theology exhibits itself
clearly also in the kind of high pressured, multi-
million dollar competitiveness for viewers, dollars,
and clout.[10]

To earn that support, the preachers would have to
convince their viewers of their mastery of the subject
matter and demonstrate through their on-camera expertise they could be trusted. Richard Quebedeaux argues
that they became "stars" in popular religion, depending

upon appeal and subliminal legitimization. They provided viewers with a compelling image of what the
knowledgeable, successful Christian leader should be.
When they appeared live in regional or local rallies,
they came to enjoy the status of superstars because
they epitomized the American ideal of success.[11]

Success is measured in numbers: dollars, stations,
cable systems, and that occurs when evangelism is
adaptable to the demands of the market and to the
requirements of media promotion inherent in the
highly competitive world of television broadcasting.
Evangelicals and fundamentalists in the 1960s and
1970s saw in television the potential for spreading
their message. They also learned the rules of television marketing and the demands of television financ-
ing. In contrast to mainline Protestantism which
failed to pursue an aggressive program of fundraising
to pay for their own programs, the budding New Christian
Right learned how to raise funds so they could pay
for as much air time as the commercial television
executives were willing to give them. Since the religious Right had the cash, they received the opportunity
to broadcast their message. That message, in contrast
to mainline Protestant programming, was adapted to
viewer expectations which meant they wanted to have
a quick, simple, entertaining message which made them
feel good about themselves.[12]

Beyond that, hardball business maneuvering contributed to NCR success in television. A critic, Franklin
B. Krohn, argued that its success could be traced
largely to its successful use of basic marketing
techniques, the satisfying of human needs and wants
in a sensitive manner. The televangelists were able
to live up to five demands of marketing: market

segmentation, product development, pricing, distribution, and advertising and sales promotion. Segmentation refers to the manner in which researchers isolated out demographic and psychographic variables to better define potential customers. This the NCR did very well in learning to identify where and who their supporters were, recognizing that the true market consisted of people already predisposed to believe their message.

Second, supporters need a product, some payoff for any contribution or sacrifice they are called on to make. This was understood by the Right when, in Jim Bakker's words, "We have a better product than soap or automobiles. We have eternal life." Third, as to pricing the NCR market specialists learned the value of brand loyalty. The more a consumer pays and the longer he buys the product the more likely he will be to stay brand loyal. Fourth, on distribution, the products (discussed below) were delivered directly to the living rooms of the requesters, an advantage local churches could not match. The viewer seemed to perceive the celebrity preacher was talking directly to him, guaranteeing that the products would be sent by him. Finally, through careful market analysis the religious Right learned to know how to promote their programs; market analysis showed them what was popular and what failed to win support. [13]

Horsefield elaborates on several of these themes, stating that NCR "success is also a result of a careful and determined marketing; the product of a unique blending of charisma with a personal drive and audacity, accurate social intuition, hard-nosed principles and techniques." [14] Their fundraising campaigns, while highly controversial and reprehensible to large numbers of other church leaders, accomplish the job; always

the emphasis was on the personal commitment of the
contributor and very rapid acknowledgement of the
support from the national office.   This mail became
a barometer of the celebrity's performance; when an
unpopular issue is broadcast, the mail will show
that quickly, telling the programmers what to avoid.
Using time-tested techniques such as direct on-air
solicitations, offering incentives such as gifts,
records, or books, presenting an 800 telephone number
where people with personal problems could call for help--
all these told the broadcaster what worked.

On the mail to the viewers, the NCR used the familiar
technique of having the recipient's name printed out one
or a few times to make the letter seem more personal.
With Moral Majority mailings, my name got on the computer as "Jorstad History", and I could never, after
several attempts, get that changed.   Another successful
program was to create several select groups, inside
supporters, who were given "exclusive privileges" in exchange for a pledge above the average.   Bakker promised
everyone at a gala fund raiser who would come forward
with a $1000 gift to take a cassette tape of the donor's
shaking hands with him as the negotiation was consumated.
A final technique popular to the New Christian Right
was to impress on potential donors the fact that the
national office was almost broke due to their expen-
sive battles against the enemy and unless the national
office received emergency gifts immediately, there may
not be any more letters.   Falwell and Christian Voice
relied extremely heavily on that approach.[15]

What became clear by late 1984 was that the religious
Right chose to use marketing and fundraising programs
eschewed by mainline and other traditional religious
groups (such as the Orthodox, and Roman Catholics).

Obviously, a potentially lucrative market already existed for evangelists such as the New Christian Right
to develop, and they learned how to develop it.   In
part, in this writer's judgment, their success was also due to the fact that many people of religious faith
chose to separate themselves from the more confessional
and liturgical churches and instead chose to support
the more culturally compatible expressions of faith
portrayed by the New Christian Right.   Its leaders
appealed to a different social strata, another level of
aesthetic appreciation of what being religious meant in
terms of music, liturgy, emotional expression, social
outreach, and theological sophistication.[16]

III

Given their celebrity status, their commission to
evangelize the world, and their adaptation of proven
marketing techniques, the four television preachers
considered in this chapter learned to present to the
nation their respective religious and moral convictions.
Not given to ecumenical fellowship with one another,
they came to find their own "integrated symbolic world",
their own identities which set them apart from one
another.   This section seeks briefly to identify those
features.

Falwell became at the beginning of his celebrity
status best known for his broadcast of the weekly
services of his congregation in Lynchburg.   Later he
became a regular one hour a week commentator on
Turner Broadcast System cable.   As a minister he
emphasized his identification with a thriving, enthusiastic Protestant parish with thousands of members, a large pastoral staff, an active social outreach
program, and a clear understanding of its place along

the Protestant spectrum.   The centerpiece of the weekly program was Falwell's sermon in which he talked
about his ministry and its trials, the opposition
he encountered, and the reasons for asking for continued support. Viewers could see this was a Sunday
morning church service, complete with organ, choir,
and Scripture reading. The worshippers understood
and sympathized with Falwell's burden of being a
celebrity and enthusiastically supported his agenda
for restoring righteousness to the nation.[17]

Jim and Tammy Faye Bakker broadcast to another level
of religious consciousness. On a daily basis, and drawing from the experiences they encountered from once working for Robertson, they chose to bring to their
audience a format originally developed by Jack Paar
on the "Tonight Show." That included having the host
seated behind a desk, celebrities brought in for con-
versation and, often, for testimonials, guest spots
for vocalists or instrumentalist musicians, and generally
throughout a very cheerful, upbeat mood. The accent was
always on the blessings available to believers who seek
to do God's will. No sustained effort was made at
consideration of doctrine, complex public moral issues,
or the demands of Christian discipleship. Considerable
time was spent on fundraising, with periodic scheduled
time given over to direct appeals using songs such as
"I Started Living when I Started Giving to the Lord."
By contrast to Falwell (but endorsed by Robertson and
Swaggart) the Bakkers often referred directly to the
importance of receiving the charismatic experience, the
"second baptism", the Pentecostal emphasis on the
spiritual gifts of 1 Cor.12:4-11. Viewers could see
the excitement and sense of the presence of the Holy
Spirit as people in the audience raised their hands

in the familiar charismatic expression of receiving
the power leading to manifestations such as speaking
in tongues or discernment of spirits. Throughout,
the Bakkers accented joy, triumph over evil, and
assuredness that the believers enjoyed the on-going,
providential care of God.[18]

Pat Robertson of the 700 Club and Christian Broadcast Network offered another alternative. On a
daily basis, using the "Tonight Show" format, he became through these years increasingly involved in
public policy issues. He brought in speakers he considered expert and sympathetic to his theology for
commenting on a very wide variety of issues: farm
prices, foreign policy, diet, exercise, the nuclear
freeze movement, terrorism, the gold standard, the
social agenda, parochial education, and the secular
humanist conspiracy. Robertson also contributed
articles to a variety of evangelical journals.

Most important, he decided to make his daily program an alternative news show to those of broadcast,
commercial television. To accomplish that, he em-
ployed a growing numbers of reporters and analyists
who broadcast from various parts of the world to
specialists back in the national office studies which
explained to the viewers through maps, graphs, charts
and other electronic apparatus what the importance of
this news was. As did the Bakkers, Robertson periodic-
ally held Pentecostal-charismatic gifts services,
demonstrating his belief in the power of the second
baptism to heal, to know more clearly the will of God
through tongues and to discern the presence of evil
spirits. Falwell, by contrast, had clearly repud-
iated any endorsement of such practice. The viewers,
in brief, were being given choices.[19]

Jimmy Swaggart of Baton Rouge, Louisiana, started
more slowly than the others to reach national visibi-
lity. By the early 1980s, however, he had clearly
carved out his own empire. His daily program regularly featured a Bible study in which he demonstrated
his considerable oratorical and exegetical skills by
delivering without notes an on-going interpretation
of the text for the day. He also presented a Sunday
service on national television clearly loyal to his
Baptist tradition. More than the other three preachers,
however, Swaggart offered for sale an extensive line
of merchandise: books, tapes, records, pamphlets,
overseas tourist trips, special studies for children
and teens, women and seniors and teaching packets. His
bookstore also offered for sale materials by like-minded
New Christian Rightists as Franky Schaeffer, Francis A.
Schaeffer and John W. Whitehead. His monthly magazine,
The Evangelist, offered considerable discussion of
biblical themes, exploration of the several world-wide
social outreach and evangelism programs of the Jimmy
Swaggart Ministries, and exhortations for financial
support. In this writer's estimate, more than any
of the others discussed here, Swaggart modeled himself
in the mold of the television celebrity whose entire
ministry, in essence, depended upon his (considerable)
talents.

    To visitors from abroad viewing these four preachers,
the messages they proclaimed may well have seemed very
similiar. To the evangelists themselves, however,
and to their loyal supporters, each had his own dis-
tinctive identity. It was that which gave them their
capacity to continue to grow into the mid-1980s.

IV

By the time of the Presidential election of November, 1984, an event which (as discussed below) many interpretated as a referendum on the New Christian Right, its programs and teachings had generated an enormous amount of criticism from observers located across the full political and religious spectrum. Varying in quality from hyperbole to penetrating scriptural and doctrinal exegesis,this body of thought serves as a superb insight into the new and increasingly bitter tensions over what did constitute the American way in religion and politics. For that reason we give it extended discussion here.

Criticism centered on a wide variety of topics, stretching from alleged anti-Semitism to excessive profit taking to dictatorial leaders to clergy having no constitutional right to mix religion and politics.[20] Gradually over the early 1980s the criticism took more recognizable form in categories such as theology, social ethics, constitutional law, politics, and educational practices. The critics represented a very wide variety of church, academic, journalistic and educational specialists, and observers from all along the liberal to conservative political and religious spectrums. The New Christian Right was being taken seriously.

Considerable attention to the NCR theology quickly appeared. One of the most important critics, the conservative Lutheran clergyman-editor Richard John Neuhaus devoted extended time to the task, using it as a basis for his influential book of 1984, The Naked Public Square. There, and in articles, he pointed to several areas in which the religious Right seemed hostile to the American way: (1) in its condemnation of

society, it failed to point out its excessively
materialistic and individualistic qualities; (2) its
political solutions failed to account for the needs
of a pluralistic society, being restless with compromise and hostile to those who approached dialogue
from different perspectives; (3) its social agenda
was not prophetically bold, focusing on issues not
threatening to the pocketbook or lifestyles of its
supporters; (4) it virtually ignored the victims of
poverty,   oppression and injustice; (5) it glorified
a parochial nationalism bordering on idolizing America
as the agent of God; (6) it failed to realize God's
purposes could not converge with any one or more
political agenda;   faith always demanded a critical
distancing from secular-based movements; (7) it treated
the democratic process more as warfare than as compromise of give and take; (8) its premillennial eschatology seemed ill-suited for democratic politics,
asserting that only a handful of believers would be
saved, and that all humankind's strivings on earth
would soon be destroyed.   Their doctrines were "de-
ductively authoritarian in their method.   They work
within a closed circle of supposedly revealed truth
that is neither accountable nor accessible to those
outside that circle....There is no way in which the
truth can be publicly weighted and tested."   They
refused to "engage the Christian message in conversa-
tion with public and universal discourse outside the
circle of true believers."[21]
     Among the criticisms levelled by specific public
policy and church related groups, only the briefest
summary can be made here.   Among the most determined
and wide-scaled was that of People For the American
Way founded in 1980 as "a nonprofit, nonpartisan

educational group to promote and defend citizens'
constitutional freedoms and traditional American
values." PAW used "public education programs, citizen action, training and the media" for its agenda,
along with pursuing research on anti-democratic
movements and providing printed resources for those
studying the NCR.[22] As matters unfolded this meant
most of its energy was spent on engaging the religious
Right in fullscale combat over religion and politics
(see below, ch. 15). Other incorporated activist
programs opposing the NCR have been Americans United
for Separation of Church and State, the American
Humanist Association, Americans for Religious Liberty,
the American Civil Liberties Union, the National Education Association, the Conference on Alternative State
and Local Politics, and Clergy and Laity Concerned.
Each criticizes the religious Right according to its
own range of interests--legal,educational, theological,
civil liberties. They kept alive through the early
1980s before the American public the fact that indeed
a major war was being fought over which very little
consensus existed at the grassroots level.

Frequently, educational leaders at denominational
national or regional headquarters gave extended consideration to the NCR. The Roman Catholic Church of
Cincinnati, for instance, published a carefully prepared study guide on Fundamentalism--What Every
Catholic Needs to Know. It presented a balanced account
of the history, scriptural interpretation and Catholic
response to fundamentalist teachings.[23] Regional
offices of groups such as the Minnesota Council of
Churches sponsored workshops on the political impact
of the New Christian Right. Mainline activist publications such as Engage/Social Action produced critical

analyses of the movement.   Others such as the evangeli-
cal activist Sojourners frequently published sharply
critical evaluations of most religious Right activities.
The Baptist Joint Committee for Public Affairs in
Washington included in many of its monthly publications,
Report from the Capital searching dissents from NCR
positions.   The scholarly Reformed   Journal from Calvin
College frequently included vigorous criticisms of
Falwell and Robertson.[24]   Another scholarly periodical,
The Journal of Church and State, having strong Baptist
underpinnings, became a frequent, precise and spirited
critic.   Its editorials pointed with alarm to the increasingly powerful alliance of fundamentalist preachers
and conservative politicians, a trend the editors saw
as laden with serious threats to the traditional separation of church and state.[25]

V

Finally, since this chapter opened with a consideration
of television it seems appropriate to conclude with the
same topic, relating it to critics of the New Christian
Right.   The kind of criticism discussed above helped
create interest among church leaders and scholars
alike as to whether NCR television broadcasting actually
had the pernicious or the faithbuilding effects the
critics or supporters were claiming.   A major empiri-
cal study was undertaken directed by the Gallup Poll,
the Office of Research of the National Council of
Churches, and the Annenberg School of Communications
of the University of Pennsylvania.   It was endorsed
and supported by some 38 religious agencies including
Falwell, Bakker, Robertson, and the Roman Catholic
Church as well as many mainline churches.   Among its
several findings were these; (1) religious televising,

including that of the fundamentalists, was not attracting an essentially new nor young nor varied audience.
Viewers were those who were already believers, church
goers and contributors to NCR preachers; (2) their view-
ing of religious programming was attracted by the
content not available anywhere else on television; (3)
their support of celebrity preachers did not keep them
from attending and supporting their local congregations.[26]

Obviously, such statistical studies, as media specialist
John W. Bachman suggested, are always open to varying
interpretations. But clearly both critics and supporters
found something in this report to support their own
positions. The charge made early in the 1980s that
local financial support would be siphoned off from
the parish and into the coffers of the televangelists
failed to be substantiated. But at the same time their
primary mission of evangelism, of winning the conver-
sions of the uninformed or the doubters failed to
materialize; their viewers were the 90 and 9 already
in the fold.[27]

Whatever final assessment is made of religious Right
televising during the early 1980s obviously will have
to be made at a later date. Suffice it to say at this
point that as a strictly evangelistic (non-profit, non-
political) form of broadcasting it probably would
have expanded during these years but at a much slower
rate. What gave the television segment so much energy,
in this writer's estimate, was the realization by the
supporters of one or more of the four luminaries that
these were now celebrities, commanding annual megabuck
budgets, household words, pictured in People, interviewed on talk shows, and frequenters of White House
consultations. That realization helped energize
supporter commitment to the televangelists because
they were so explicitly political.

Notes

1. Much of the following is based on Peter G. Horsfield, Religious Television: The American
   Experience (New York, Longman, Inc., 1984).

2. Ibid., p.47.

3. Jeffrey K. Hadden, "Televangelism and the Future
   of American Politics", David G. Bromley and Anson
   Shupe, New Christian Politics (Macon, Mercer
   University Press, 1984), pp.164-65; Burton Yale
   Pines, Back to Basics: The Traditionalist Move-
   ment That Is Sweeping Grass-Roots America (New
   York, William Morrow and Company, 1982), ch.7.

4. Quoted in Washington Post National Weekly
   Edition, November 25, 1985, p.35.

5. Gregor Goethels, "Religious Communication and
   Popular Piety", Journal of Communication, Winter,
   1985; 35:1, pp.151-52.

6. Ibid., p.152; see also the articles in the Review
   of Religious Research, June, 1984, 25:4, for
   additional discussion.

7. Christianity Today, February 6, 1981, p.150;
   Horsfield, Religious Television, p.59; more
   data is in Ralph Clark Chandler, "The Wicked
   Shall Not Rule: The Fundamentalist Heritage
   of the New Christian Right", Bromley and Shupe
   in   New Christian Politics, pp.41-58.

8. Summarized in David Bollier, Liberty and Justice
   for Some (New York, Frederick Ungar Publishing
   Co., People for the American Way, 1982), pp.110-11;
   John S. Saloma, III, Ominous Politics: The New
   Conservative Labyrinth (New York, Hill and Wang,
   1984), pp.51-52; news story, Christianity Today,
   August 6, 1982, pp..44,46.

9. Drawn from two accounts by Time religion editor
   Richard Ostling; "Evangelical Publishing and
   Broadcasting", George Marsden, ed., Evangelicalism
   and Modern America (Grand Rapids, Wm. B. Eerdmans
   Publishing Co., 1984),pp.46-55, and Time, February
   17, 1986, pp. 62-69.

10. Horsfield, Religious Television, p. 63.

11.   Richard Quebedeaux, By What Authority: The Rise
      of Personality Cults in American Christianity
      (San Francisco, Harper and Row, 1982), pp.7-8,
      113-15; Carol Flake, Redemptorama: Culture,
      Politics, and the New Evangelicalism (Garden
      City, Doubleday and Company, 1984), pp.55-56.

12.   Jeffrey K. Hadden and Charles E. Swann, Prime
      Time Preachers: The Rising Power of Televangelism
      (Reading, Ma., Addison-Wesley Publishing Company,
      1981), pp.10-13; Horsfield, Religious Television,
      pp.17-23; Perry C. Cotham, "The Electronic Church",
      A.S. Phy, ed., The Bible and Popular Culture in
      America (Philadelphia, Fortress Press, 1985),
      pp.115-16.

13.   Franklin B. Krohn, "The Sixty-Minute Commercial:
      Marketing Salvation", The Humanist, November/
      December, 1980, pp.26-31.

14.   Horsfield, Religious Television, p.26; see also
      Robert Abelman, et al., "How Religious is Reli-
      gious Television Programming?", Journal of
      Communication, Winter, 1985, 35:1, pp.98-110.

15.   Horsfield, Religious Television, pp.25-35.

16.   Preliminary social science research is in the
      Journal of Communication cited in ft. 14 and
      Donna Day-Lower, "Who Is the Moral Majority?",
      Union Seminary Quarterly Review, 1983, 37:4,
      pp.335-46; and Louise M. Bourgault, "The 'PTL
      Club' and Protestant Viewers: An Ethnographic
      Study, Journal of Communication, Winter, 1985,
      pp.132-48; see ibid., pp.89-156 for related
      articles.

17.   Among the many interpretations, see Frances
      FitzGerald, "A Reporter at Large: A Disciplined,
      Charging Army", The New Yorker, May 18, 1981,
      pp.53-141; Dinesh D'Souza, Falwell Before the
      Millennium: A Critical Biography (Chicago,
      Gateway Regnery Books, 1984).

18.   The best interpretation is Louise M. Bourgault,
      "The PTL Club", pp.132-48, and all issues of the
      PTL monthly, Together, 1981-84.

19.   Among the many interpretations see Flake,
      Redemptorama, ch. 6, and Cotham, "The Electronic
      Church", pp.108-16.

20. See, for instance, D'Souza, Falwell, pp.150-55.

21. Neuhaus, The Naked Public Square: Religion
     and Democracy in America (Grand Rapids, Wm.B.
     Eerdmans Publishing Co., 1984), ch.1; Neuhaus,
     undated article "Religion And...Addressing
     the Naked Public Square," pp.11-12, and ibid.,
     "What The Fundamentalists Want", Commentary,
     May, 1985, pp.41-46. See also the criticisms
     by Kenneth Woodward, Religion Editor for
     Newsweek, July 6, 1981, p.50, and by Robert
     McAfee Brown, "The Need for a Moral Minority"
     Herbert F. Better, ed., Speak Out Against the
     New Right (Boston, Beacon Press, 1982), pp.
     118-26.

22. Bollier, Liberty and Justice for Some, p.7.

23. Anthony E. Gilles, Fundamentalism--What Every
     Catholic Needs To Know (Cincinnati, St. Anthony
     Messenger Press, 1985); see also The Catholic
     Bulletin, May 27, 1982, p.19 of the St. Paul--
     Minneapolis Archdiocese, 72:22.

24. Brochure from the Minnesota Council of Churches;
     Engage/Social Action, January, 1981; Danny Collum,
     "The Big Picture", Sojourners, May, 1986,pp.14-16;
     editorial, The Reformed Journal, February, 1982,
     pp.9-11.

25. See the editorials in the Journal of Church
     and State by James E. Wood, Jr., for example,
     Autumn, 1984, 26:3, pp.401-11; see also the
     critique in Harvey Cox, Religion in the
     Secular City: Toward a Postmodern Theology
     (New York, Simon and Schuster, 1984), Part One.

26. Summaries in Gary D. Gaddy and David Pritchard,
     "When Watching Religious Television is Like
     Attending Church", Journal of Communication,
     Winter, 1985, pp.123-48; Peggy L. Shriver,
     "Guardians of Fundamentalism's Fortress",
     New Catholic World, January/February, 1985,
     vol.228,no.1363,pp.16-17; Shriver, "Cultivat-
     ing the Convinced", Constant H. Jacquet, ed.,
     Yearbook of American and Canadian Churches
     (Nashville, Abingdon Press, 1985), pp.259-66;
     news story, Christianity Today, May 18, 1984,
     pp.70-71; summary in Christian Century, July
     18-24, 1984, pp.710-13.

27. John W. Bachman, <u>Media</u>: <u>Wasteland</u> <u>or</u> <u>Wonderland</u>
     (Minneapolis, Augsburg Publishing House, 1984),
     chs. 5, 8.

1982: The First Test

For all their enthusiasm, resources, and organizational skills, New Christian Rightists would have to
have their programs judged, as would all politically-
minded Americans, by one standard: Did they win votes
for their cause? The first major test of their strength
would be in the Congressional elections of 1982. In
politicking as the leaders quickly learned, the winners
were those who knew where the power was located and
how it could be used. Their appearance on the electoral
scene in 1980 convinced the political operatives of
the Reagan forces that here they could find votes,
donations, and political carriers of water and hewers
of wood. From that date through the elections of
1982 the two groups would achieve a mutually attractive if not always fully harmonious alliance
     Starting back in 1980 with his nomination for
the Presidency, Ronald Reagan actively pursued the
religious Right vote and muscle. According to Sidney
Blumenthal, that movement was transformed from the
fringes "into a centerpiece of the conservative movement". "It commanded an extensive organizational and
communications network, a freshly minted ideology
and enough troops adequate to do battle". Reagan understood that and, despite advice from moderate Republicans, refused to distance himself from the Right. Instead he "briefed them, encouraged them, deployed
White House resources to coordinate them and thereby
magnified them." They became "an auxiliary force,
a division of Christian soldiers in the conservative
army".[1] The key figure, the liaison between them
and the White House, was a Presidential staff assistant
Morton C. Blackwell, the person assigned to coordinate
NCR and Presidential programs. He worked closely with

both the New Right and the New Christian Right,
bringing their leaders to the White House for conferences, making long range plans for implementing the
social agenda, and circulating rough drafts of pending
legislation to them.[2]

Blackwell's access to the Oval Office reflected
the major but not the only direct political link between the Administration and the religious Right. The
White House appointed to high level positions several
persons endorsed for those posts by NCR leaders. Such
was Dr. C. Everett Koop, a fundamentalist and anti-
abortionist who became the Surgeon General; another
powerful pro-life figure, Margery E. Mecklenburg became
director of the Office of Adolescent Pregnancy Programs.
The former executive director of Moral Majority, Robert
Billings was named "consultant and assistant" to the
Secretary of Education, and was later promoted to a
regional directorship. Blackwell, prior to his new
position, had been on the payroll as editor of the New
Right Report. And the most controversial appointment
of all from among fundamentalists was that of James
Watt to head the Department of the Interior.[3]

In the first months of the new administration, the
conservatives found themselves in positions of power
they had not known before. To advance the social
agenda they started finding means and ways by which
they could advance the specific items on their respective organizational timetables. There emerged a loose
but viable working alliance between the more prag-
matically minded New Right leaders such as Richard
Vigurie, Howard Phillips, Paul Weyrich and Terry Dolan
and the New Christian Right spokesmen (there were no
spokeswomen). They found common ground and common
interests on fundraising, voter education, and voter

registration programs. Falwell moved quickly, dis-
tributing early in 1982 a "Top Secret Battle Plan for
1982" which was sent to supporters of the Moral
Majority. There he described a campaign to combat
perceived homosexual influence in state and munici-
pal government and television; a master plan to enact
a constitutional amendment outlawing legal abortion;
tactics to counter the influence of the American Civil
Liberties Union; continuing anti-ERA activity led by
Phyllis Schlafly, and an all-out offensive to pass
the Family Protection proposal.[4]

Christian Voice utilized the support of Senator
Jesse Helms and Jim Bakker's PTL Club. The National
Christian Action Coalition attracted the help of
Weyrich, Helms, Senator Gordon Humphrey and other
Congressional leaders.[5] Inevitably, some overlap
and jurisdictional confusion emerged during the
early months. A strong effort to remedy that was
made in May when leaders announced the creation of
an umbrella organization, known as a "coordinating"
group of some 80 programs; it was entitled the
"Council for National Policy", and its President
was Tim LaHaye. All the major voices of the New
Right joined as did Blackwell, William Rusher of
National Review, Robert Billings (now of the Department of Education), Scott Stanley of the John Birch
Society, and representatives of several tax limita-
tion and anti-gun control programs. From the religious Right came Falwell, Ed McAteer, Robertson,
James Robison, Phyllis Schlafly, Bill Bright (of
Campus Crusade), John Whitehead and some spokesmen
for creationism.[6] With varying levels of effectiveness these leaders worked with the several political
action committees authorized a decade before by

Congress to help control organized lobby influence
on the lawmakers. What became clear by early 1982
was that the number of politically conservative
political action committees had strongly outnumbered
those from the liberal side; NCR leaders claimed
major responsibilty for that transformation.[7]

II

Easily the most important force uniting the many
conservative action programs was the enthusiasm they
all shared for having their man in the White House.
The religious Right believed they had every reason
to believe the President would press vigorously for
their legislative demands, dealing the first major
setback to the secular humanists in decades. Yet, as
became clearly evident in Reagan's first year, the
muscle and dynamics of the Presidency were to be
devoted largely to domestic economic and foreign policy issues; budget and tax issues received the highest
priorities.[8]

In at first a small but then in increasingly large
manner, New Right and NCR leaders started through press
conferences and comments to suggest the White House
was dragging its feet on the social agenda. The
executive Vice President of Moral Majority, Ron Godwin,
stated the members "have waited and waited for this
administration to demonstrate with actions the
verbal commitment to moral and social action that was
so evident during his campaign." Godwin expressed an
"underlying frustration over the lack of initiative
and action by this administration concerning moral
and social issues."[9]

At the same time, church leaders in both evangelical and fundamentalist circles had shown strong

enthusiasm for Reagan's general proposal that the
churches and synagogues of America should take over
federal welfare programs.   The President quoted
Billy Graham as stating that if those bodies adopted
an average of ten poor families apiece, "we could
eliminate all government welfare in this country.[10]
That proposal, apparently made in an informal, offhand
manner, helped to raise the hopes of the NCR leaders
that at last their man had taken a stand.   As it would
turn out over the next years before Campaign '84, the
President made no further reference in specific terms
to that suggestion.

From early 1982 through to the end of the Congressional session in the fall of that year, Congress and the
President battled primarily over the everyday stuff of
public policy making; taxes, budgets, foreign policy
and regulatory issues.   It became clear by mid-summer
that Reagan was not going to use the full or even much
of the partial clout he commanded to convince Congress
it should enact the social agenda.   As the focus from
the Oval Office stayed on economic issues, so too did
the criticism of Reagan from the Right.   The Conservative
Digest in July published an extended critique, with
direct quotations from conservative lawmakers calling
on the President to work more vigorously for the
social agenda.   Finally, in the late summer the Senate
did take up the school prayer and abortion issues (see
above, ch.4).

The New Christian Right proposals for those measures failed to receive the full, enthusiastic endorsement from the White House, which apparently was being
highly sensitive to counter pressures from mainline
churches.   The White House denied that it was stalling.
Press spokesman Larry Speakes stated, "We have gone all

out to get these issues passed in Congress. The President has expended a maximum effort"."[11] What became
recognized by all conservatives was that their social
agenda had not yet caught fire with the rank and
file grassroots constituency, with the one exception
of stopping the Equal Rights Amendment. And in Washington, those lawmakers not ideologically commited to
that agenda found no compelling reason in an election
year to vote for the New Christian Right.[12]

Despite this apparent stalemate, religious Right
forces entered directly into the elective battleground.
The Moral Majority, among other groups, turned its
mailing lists of potential donors to the Republican
National Committee. It sent out a plea for a $10 a
month contribution, which would entitle the contributors to see their name on a special "Honor Roll" to
be sent to the President which "will be kept forever
with your permanent papers." Using hand-stamped envelopes, the Committee included materials for how to
wage warfare against the Democrats. In other programs,
Christian Voice drew again on its highly publicized
"Moral Report Cards" and hit lists for targeted liberals
seeking re-election. However, the results fell considerably short of what Christian Voice had expected.
In Montana sharply worded attacks on incumbent Senator
John Melcher turned undecided voters against the Republicans. In Maryland, the New Right campaign against incumbent Senator Paul Sarbanes was halted weeks before
the election. Moral Majority itself, while zealously
attacking the nuclear freeze movement, found incoming
funds for planned campaigning falling far short of
projected totals. For all practical purposes, Moral
Majority failed to become a major elective force in
the 1982 campaign.[13]

Finally, Pat Robertson throughout the campaign kept
careful watch on the unfolding of the issues, speaking frequently for the social agenda and calling on
viewers to register and vote. He revealed his wife
had received a telephone call from the wife of a U.S.
Senatorial candidate, Paul Trible of Virginia, asking
for prayer because that race was so close. Robertson
told the audience of 700 Club that Trible was a righteous, God-loving Christian and had received Robertson's prayer to win. He added that God gave him a
"real peace and understanding" of the results, so he
knew Trible would be elected.[14]

Most of the attention from the general public over
the 1982 campaign regarding moral and religious issues
centered on the lobbying efforts of Moral Majority,
the Roundtable and the National Christian Action
Coalition. What became increasingly evident during
the campaign months was the rapidly escalating importance
of the Christian political action committees, interest
groups,attempting to persuade lawmakers to support their
proposals. The PACs were not really lobbies, but
had authorization to carry out their objectives by
working for the election of sympathetic legislators.
By late 1982 two major religious Right Political
Action Committees were in operation, Christian Voice
Moral Government Fund (CVMGF) and Christian Voter's
Victory Fund (CVVF). Two other related PACs, Moral
Majority and Christian Coalition for Legislation,
failed to attract enough funds to stay in operation.[15]

Christian Voice was the sponsor of the CVMGF,
controlling a mailing list including some 37,000 ministers and some 150,000 laity. Gary Jarmin, National
Director, organized the new PAC and served as its
treasurer. In 1980 it raised some $494,000 and spent

some $458,000 of that, centering on electing Reagan
as "the only Republican presidential candidate committed to Jesus Christ and Christian principles." It
also distributed some two million moral report cards.[16]
Two years later CVMGF had raised $432,069 and spent
some $425,565 for supporting pro-Christian Voice
legislators and gave energetic attention to distribut-
ing its updated moral report cards, especially in areas
where the elections were in doubt. The other PAC,
Christian Voter's Victory Fund, failed to attract
more than minimal funding.

The importance of these organizations revolved
around the report cards. These recorded the voting
records of all Senators and Representatives on issues
deemed "moral" by Christian Voice. They left the
unmistakeable impression that those who lawmakers voted
against their list were immoral. For instance in 1982
two ordained ministers, Representatives Robert Edgar
and William Gray in the House were given ratings of
zero.   These PACs were important in 1982 also because
they devoted considerable energy to using local
congregations as organizational precincts in voter education. The PACs also utilized local television, radio
and cooperating ministers to help register the citizenry.[17] They acknowledged they had learned how to use
the political expertise of the more secular New Right
specialists to get sympathetic voters involved and
to provide new outlets for the political energies
of the religious Right. The latter made its appeal
for support, not by pointing to bread and butter
issues as being determinative for voter motivation,
but calling on citizens to follow their religious
faith as their sole guide for political motivation.[18]

The question--in politics it is the only question--
is: Who won? What was the margin of victory for the
winners? As the results from the Congressional elections came to the political party experts for analysis,
it became clear that the New Christian Right had made
little if any difference in the many campaigns. In the
Senate the margin of Republican support, 54-56, remained
the same. In the House of Representatives the Democrats added 26 seats to their margin of control. Some
observers claimed the increase in House support came
from a shift in public opinion which led voters to
shun those candidates identified with the New Christian
Right and "made voters resistant to appeals couched in
religious or moral terms".[19]

Falwell made his assessment of Campaign '82. "We
are not in this battle simply to win a few elections
and then to brag about them. The fact is that, in
practically every campaign where our people were involved, the pro-moral candidates won, and your support
made this possible." "We are at least as strong as we
were before the elections--and perhaps a little stronger."[20] However, two analysts   from the conservative
think tank, The Free Congress Research Foundation
concluded the evangelical and fundamentalist vote as
such made little difference in 1982.[21]

But in good fundamentalist interpretation, such
results only meant it was time now to gird up one's
loins to do battle with the enemy again. That
would occur on the national level in Campaign '84.

Notes

1. Sidney Blumenthal, "The Righteous Empire", The
    New Republic, October 22, 1984, p.18.

2. Ibid., p. 23.

3. Shirley Rogers Radl, The Invisible Woman: Target
    of the Religious New Right (New York, Delta Books,
    1983), pp.156-57; editorial, Moral Majority
    Report, August, 1982, p.7; ibid., November, 1983,
    p.9; ibid., April, 1983, p.4,5,6; Minneapolis
    Star and Tribune, May 5, 1983, p.19A.

4. John S. Saloma, III., Ominous Politics: The New
    Conservative Labyrinth (New York, Hill and Wang,
    1984), pp.53-58.

5. Ibid., pp.58-59.

6. Group Research Report, June 26, 1981, 20, pp.21-22;
    ibid. February 20, 1982, pp.2-3; Stuart Rothenberg
    and Frank Newport, The Evangelical Voter: Religion
    and Politics in America (Washington, D.C., The
    Free Congress Research and Education Foundation,
    1984), pp.9-10.

7. News item, Christianity Today, June 18, 1982, p.68;
    also Group Research Report, May 28, 1982, pp.1-2;
    a sharp rivalry developed between Falwell and
    Robertson in this area; see Commonweal, October 22,
    1982,p.567.

8. Thomas E. Mann and Norman J. Ornstein, eds., The
    American Elections of 1982 (Washington, D.C.,
    American Enterprise Institute for Public Research,
    1983), p.2.

9. News story, Minneapolis Tribune, January 22, 1982,
    p.7A; ibid., January 7, 1982, pp.1A, 17A.

10. Editorial, Christian Century, January 27, 1982,
    p.75, endorsed in the evangelicalist journal
    Christianity Today, October 2, 1981, pp.1238-84.

11. Congressional Quarterly, September 25, 1982, p.
    2349; Time August 16, 1982, pp. 24-25; New York
    Times, September 25, 1982, p.9; column of Edwin
    M. Yoder, Minneapolis Star and Tribune, September
    29, 1982,p.15A; news story, ibid., October 4, 1982,

p.3A; <u>ibid</u>., September 9, 1982, p.3A; Mann and
Orstein, <u>1982</u>, pp.20,23; Richard V. Pierard,
"Religion and the New Right in the 1980s", James
E. Wood, Jr., ed., <u>Religion</u> and <u>the</u> <u>State</u>: <u>Essays</u>
<u>in</u> <u>Honor</u> <u>of</u> <u>Leo</u> <u>Pfeffer</u> (Waco, Baylor University
Press, 1985), pp.399-400.

12. See the excellent analysis by Bill Keller and
     Nadine Cohadas in <u>Congressional</u> <u>Quarterly</u>,
     October 16, 1982, pp.2675-78; and Alonzo L.
     Hamby, <u>Liberalism</u> and <u>Its</u> <u>Challengers</u>: <u>FDR</u> <u>to</u>
     <u>Reagan</u> (New York, Oxford University Press, 1985),
     pp.352-54. Perhaps the NCR judgment is well
     founded. For instance, shortly before the Novem-
     ber election, I received a letter from Ronald
     Reagan asking for my vote and contribution
     but not mentioning any social agenda items.

13. Letter from Ronald Reagan and Senator Bob Pack-
     wood, March 26, 1982, to "Jorstad:History"; the
     only group having that mailing address for me
     was Moral Majority; news letter, People for
     the American Way, September, 1982, p.4.

14. Dinesh D'Souza, <u>Falwell</u> <u>Before</u> <u>the</u> <u>Millennium</u>:
     <u>A</u> <u>Critical</u> <u>Biography</u> (Chicago, Gateway Regnery
     Books, 1984), p.22; 700 Club, November 1, 1982;
     <u>ibid</u>., November 2, 1982; <u>ibid</u>., November 3, 1982.

15. This section is based largely on the study by
     Margaret Ann Latus, "Mobilizing Christians for
     Political Action: Campaigning With God on Your
     Side", David G. Bromley and Anson Shupe, eds.,
     <u>New</u> <u>Christian</u> <u>Politics</u> (Macon, Mercer University
     Press, 1984),pp.251-68, here pp.251-52.

16. <u>Ibid</u>., p.253.

17. <u>Ibid</u>., pp.254-56; David Bollier, <u>Liberty</u> <u>and</u>
     <u>Justice</u> <u>for</u> <u>Some</u> (New York, Frederick Ungar
     Publishing Co., 1982; People for the American
     Way), pp.52-53.

18. Latus, "Mobilizing Christians", pp.257-58.

19. <u>Ibid</u>., p.266, see her documentation; Gillian
     Peele, <u>Revival</u> <u>and</u> <u>Reaction</u>: <u>The</u> <u>Right</u> <u>in</u>
     <u>Contemporary</u> <u>America</u> (Oxford, Clarendon Press,
     1984), p.115.

20. Falwell, fundraiser letter, November 17, 1982;
    Time, November 15, 1982, p.36; New York,
    November 22, 1982, p.13; Congressional
    Quarterly, September 22, 1984, p.2317.

21. Rothenberg and Newport, The Evangelical Voter,
    pp.85-91; Time, February 7, 1983, pp.21-22;
    ibid., February 28, 1983, p.15; Carol Flake,
    Redemptorama: Culture, Politics and the
    Evangelicalism (Garden City, Doubleday and
    Company, 1984), p.265; Morton Kondracke, "Hard
    Times for the Hard Right", The New Republic,
    December 20, 1982, pp.20-23; Peele, Revival
    and Reaction, p.123; an important case study
    is Stephen D. Johnson and Joseph B. Tamney,
    "Support for the Moral Majority: A Test of
    a Model", Journal for the Scientific Study
    of Religion, 1984; 23:2, pp.183-96.

1984: The New Agenda

The traditional blending of religion and politics
underwent a profound and rapid transformation in the
early 1980s during the lengthy campaign for the
Presidency. That event brought together the most
advanced tools of technology useful for politicking
such as computers, the 800 numbers and satellite television, witnessing their mastery by the highly energetic, well financed bloc of voters we call the New
Christian Right. That group should not be considered
the single key force which gave President Reagan his
landslide re-election margin of victory. But for the
first time in American history an incumbent President
"expressly and tirelessly courted" such a constituency
to a degree previously unknown.[1] And well he should
have, since the constituents were seen by political
strategists as a deliverable bloc of voters when
carefully organized, as a major source for increased
financial contributions, and as door to door campaigners. And for them the President seemed with his
often expressed endorsement of their social agenda
the ideal leader to continue the battle against secular humanists. Surely, they thought, it must be
providential that the nation's most effective leader
was in that office at this juncture in history. But,
that same identification with the White House led
millions of other Americans to insist with great
determination that the United States was a secular
state which required the equality of all religions
before the law. Thus was the role of the New
Christian Right to be defined in Campaign '84.[2]

One important qualification at this point is
necessary to make. The election was not a national
referendum on whether the New Christian Right agenda had been approved by the voters, even though some

NCR leaders claimed as much.[3] What it did contribute
was to greatly increase the religious, crusading kind
of tone to this campaign by both parties. The church
related ties of the major candidates including Gary
Hart, Jesse Jackson, and Walter Mondale received considerable attention. The Roman Catholic Church entered
directly into the fray with Archbishops jousting with
Geraldine Ferarro and Mario Cuomo. Congregations
served as voter registration centers. Mondale and
Reagan squared off on the "religion" issue early in
the formal campaign. Church-going people as such were
assiduously courted by the politicians. All of these
developments, when considered in tandem, suggest that
the religious issue in 1984 was more than that of the
social agenda. It was a pitched battle over religion
and politics, between the moderate mainline churches
and the fundamentalists and evangelicals. That war
had its origins far back in the 20th century, but
in this year the strategists of one side had the exclusive ear of the President. As one mainline leader
stated "'the President seems bent on establishing
a nondenominational religion with himself as its
defender'."[4]

National Presidential campaigns traditionally have
embraced a wide variety of appeals to special interest
groups. In this one, the social agenda of the religious Right became the major focus of attention.[5] The
so-called family issues were claimed by that group, a
move sharply contested by the Democrats. What the
debate, in a larger sense, involved was the extent
to which those favoring the social agenda were willing
to give the national government more influence in their
private lives to achieve its implementation.[6] Less
widely debated but equally at stake in the contest

over the family was the charge that the Republicans
were actually promoting anti-family values, opposing
"the struggle of women for full moral and political
agency." The NCR agenda, Elizabeth Bettenhausen
argued, was in fact a "whole set of issues that
directly affect the daily lives of millions of girls
and women: the ERA, day care, EEO and affirmative
action, sex education in the schools, AFDC, parental
control of education, access for teenage girls to
contraception that is safe and reliable, equal pay
for work of equal worth, civil rights for gay men
and lesbians, school lunch programs, '"no fault"'
divorce...."[7] Thus the polarization and the fuel
was furnished for continuing the warfare over the
American way.

By contrast to other Presidential campaigns in
which the candidates searched for a middle ground on
which to express their own religiosity, Reagan
linked himself directly to the New Christian Right.[8]
In 1983, for instance, he delivered addresses such
as to the National Religious Broadcasters convention
where he denounced legal abortion and called for tuition tax credits and school prayer. Later he offered
his "evil empire" speech regarding the Soviet Union
to the National Association of Evangelicals, and reaffirmed the social agenda. He accepted the honorary
chairmanship of the National Committee for "the Year
of the Bible"; he gave Billy Graham (who carefully
avoided the NCR) the Presidential Medal of Freedom;
he allowed his name to be placed on an anti-abortion
article in Human Life Review; he frequently denounced
the Supreme Court ruling on school prayer, and presented through videotape a greeting to a Campus
Crusade for Christ convention.[9]

The political dimension of this showed through when
Reagan proclaimed 1983 "The Year of the Bible" as
recognition of the place of that book in national
life; he proclaimed it to be in effect by his degree
"and that of the U.S. Congress". Critics of that
proclamation argued that to include the "U.S. Congress"
was to say it was attempting to use the Bible to con-
vert people to their groups. The Americans for Civil
Liberties Union sued the President for the proclamation.[10]

Critics also pointed out the anomaly of President
Reagan's decision to appoint an ambassador to the
Vatican, a proposal that had been overwhelmingly denounced by fundamentalists and mainliners alike in
earlier years. His decision, further, to break with
tradition by not attending Sunday church services
was interpreted favorably by Moral Majority; they
agreed he was correct in wanting to avoid disrupting
such services because of personal security considerations.[11]

Although no precise means for measuring the growth
of church member support for him existed, he apparently was not losing voters within those ranks. Many
could not help but appreciate his remarks speculating
on whether this generation was not that to witness
the end times—Armageddon. "I don't know if you've
noted any of these prophecies lately, but believe
me, they certainly describe the times we're going
through." That and related comments brought on considerable criticism. Before the November, 1984
elections he stated, "So I have never seriously
warned and said we must plan according to Armageddon."[12]

Such congenial but unmistakable identification
of the White House incumbent with one faction of

religionists created extended criticism from a variety
of others. Americans United, for instance, sharply
rebuked a White House liaison for religious affairs,
Carolyn Sundseth. She had stated that if former
counselor Edwin Meese became U.S. Attorney General,
"'saved Christians'" will no longer have anyone at
the top among President Reagan's closest advisers.
She added, "If you want to know how to pray for the
President, pray that anyone directly around him gets
saved or gets out". The AU leaders called this a
"blatant call for religious bigotry," and an "un-
American utterance."[13] Several critics found serious
fault with Reagan's statements on civil religion
which defended the themes of city on a hill, a
special place in God's providence, and needed in God's
plans for humankind. To Jim Wallis of Sojourners
the President's beliefs seemed idolatrous for their
lack of understanding of God's judgment on all
human institutions.[14] Finally, Reagan was criticized
for his policy of appearing only before those religious and church related groups favorable to his
position, and his refusal to meet with mainline
bodies.[15]

III

Another original feature of Campaign '84 was the
extensive attention given by both parties to voter registration. Republicans realized early in that year that
the Rev. Jesse Jackson was a serious candidate for the
Democrats and was potentially able to register millions
of Blacks in the South. But that region also embraced
large numbers of unregistered white evangelicals, perhaps enough to win it for the GOP. That group would
be "an auxiliary force, a division of Christian soldiers in the conservative Army."[16] Registration thus
became a prime concern for old and new campaigners.

By the summer months each of the major New
Christian Rights had started their own voter registration programs. Robertson's Freedom Council presented a separate, aggressive offensive to win
registrants through political education. Christian
Voice introduced what would turn out to be its decisive document among moral report cards, the forty-
page Presidential Biblical Scorecard rating Reagan/Bush
and Mondale/Ferarro by its definition of biblical standards. Ministers such as Rev. James Ahlemann of
Christian Fellowship Church in Vienna, Virginia,
utilized such material by conducting several voter
registration drives when he distributed the Scorecard.
Across the country, some 40,000 other evangelical
and fundamentalist ministers carried the message to
members to get registered and study the issues.[17]

Almost all of this potential energy and voting
power was channeled into a specific action program
by the New Christian Right with the founding of the
American Coalition for Traditional Values (ACTV) during
Campaign'84. To give its program legitimacy and
recognition, ACTV placed Tim LaHaye at the head of
its program aiming at registering some 2 million
voters and raising $1.5 million. Its Executive Committee
included Colonel V. Doner of Christian Voice, Ronald S.
Godwin of Moral Majority, and Jimmy Swaggart of
Jimmy Swaggart Ministries. The Executive Board included
Jim Bakker, Bill Bright, Kenneth Copeland, Jerry Falwell,
Rex Humbard, James Robison and other television luminaries. Robertson, among the top preachers, stayed
outside the group.

It caught potential voters' attention immediately
when it announced President Reagan had endorsed its
program. On the inside front cover of its descriptive

brochure, in a letter dated April 11, 1984, President
Reagan wrote, "your group of concerned religious leaders
has taken the important step of founding the non-partisan
American Coalition for Traditional Values (ACTV). ACTV
has the potential to speak to the millions of committed
Christians who, while they don't lack patriotism, have
for one reason or another never gotten involved in
"politics". In 1980, concerned Americans played a major
role in the victory of many candidates who stand for
traditional values. This nation needs this same level
of commitment even more in 1984 if our freedoms are to
remain secure. In 1984, America's promise can be renewed by millions of Americans dedicated to traditional
values. As your President, I thank you and your
colleagues for your faithful patriotism. Please continue
working to get eligible men and women in your area
registered to vote. And then do all you can to make
sure they go to the polls on election day."[18] In that document the President and the televangelists joined hands.

　　Excluding Robertson, the ACTV leadership aimed
its heaviest artillery at the full range of religious
Right targets; secular humanism, anti-family forces,
everything that would thwart their plan to "save
America."[19] During election months ACTV working with
related groups such as local National Association of
Evangelical organizations sponsored programs such
as a "Political Awareness Seminar". One such conference was held in Minneapolis in October with La-
Haye, advertised as "a non-partisan effort to encourage the involvement of Christian people. It will
give you the basis on how the Christian can truly be
the 'salt of the earth'."[20]

　　By contrast, the Democrats found few church-related
programs working for their voter registration drives.

The National Council of Churches launched a "Voter
Education/Registration Project" calling on members
to encourage potential voters to take full part in
the electoral process. Those church people found that
moderate evangelicals had started an "APJ Education
Fund" with the same basic goals. Democratic party
regulars worked especially hard with unregistered
Blacks and Hispanic-Americans in the Southwest and
South. However, none of these commanded the energy,
finances or ideological focus of the NCR.[21]

In politics, as in war, the final criterion for
evaluating any new program is its success. The religious Right claimed success for its efforts on the basis
that although twelve million more people were registered
in 1984 than in 1980, only four million more actually
voted, but of those the margin for Reagan was more
than two to one. "Every new registration group,
with the exception of Blacks, registered and voted
Republican" according to the specialists with the
Committee for the Study of the American Electorate.
LaHaye claimed some two million new "Christian" voters
had been registered by ACTV, but its national field
director, Gary Jarmin suggested that the total was
closer to 200,000. Buoyed by this claimed success of
numbers, ACTV after the November campaign moved its
headquarters to Washington, D.C.[22]

IV

Three other developments gave this campaign its
unique religious overtone; the candidacy of Jesse
Jackson, the Catholic Bishops' and Geraldine Ferarro's
imbroglio, and the Republican National Committee's
outreach for churchmembers' support. Regarding Jackson, the New Christian Right found itself criticizing its critics. The latter had during the early

1980s often sharply spoke out against the ministers
in Moral Majority or Christian Voice for improperly
mixing religion and politics or church and state
jurisdictions. Now an ordained minister was running
for the Democratic nomination, as total a "mixture"
as could occur. One Liberty University professor
commented, after discussing Jackson's liberal agenda,
"Can you imagine the protests of the media should
a Fundamentalist minister run for a major public
office?"[23] The religious Right showed no interest
in supporting Jackson's Rainbow Coalition.

A major uproar over religion and politics broke
out within Roman Catholic circles, centering on the
extent to which the Archbishops should make clear
to the faithful how they as Catholics could best use
their ballot. The specific issue was abortion; the
leading contestants were Archbishops John J. O'Connor
of New York and Bernard Law of Boston, versus Ferarro
and Governor Mario Cuomo. For whatever private reasons there might have prevailed, the leading New
Christian Right spokesmen avoided commenting on that
dispute, other than giving it perfunctory coverage
in their journals.[24]

Finally, the Republican Party made a very strong
effort to win and hold those church people they deemed
sympathetic to their cause. From the Reagan headquarters came a letter from Senator Paul Laxalt (R.--
Nev.), chairman of the Republican National Committee
to eighty thousand selected church leaders. Laxalt
asked them "to organize a voter registration drive
in your church" that "will surely help secure the
reelection of President Reagan and Vice President
Bush." He wrote that "President Reagan has been
faithful in his support of issues of concern to Chris-

tian citizens." Laxalt added, the President "has
made an unwavering commitment to the traditional
values which I know you share. In addition, he
has, on several occasions, articulated his own spiritual convictions. As leaders under God's authority,
we cannot afford to resign outselves to idle neutrality..."[25]

All of this was too much for columnist (and conservative) William Safire. He raised concern for the
strange "bedfellowship" of Christians now underway,
the bridge among them all being the President.[26]

That kind of discussion, accentuated by the newness of the debate over religion contributed directly
to considerable public unease over the issue. Throughout the late summer national pollsters such as Louis
Harris and CBS/New York Times showed that Americans
were uncomfortable and distressed over the discussion.
Some four voters in ten thought both parties had
improperly injected religion into the campaign and over
three quarters of those polled stated that members
of the clergy should not use religious arguments to
endorse candidates.[27]

The leading NCR preachers understood that, and also
had the opportunity to learn some other carefully documented, potentially bad news. Researchers Stuart
Rothenberg and Frank Newport had concluded earlier
that a voter's religious experience, even from those
claiming to be born again, would not determine the
way those people would vote. "The partisan identification of an evangelical is most determined by the
social background and current social standing of that
individual (in a sociological sense)". "There is no
necessary reason why a fundamentalist Christian in
this country is going to vote differently than his

or her neighbor with the same geographic and demographic characteristics."[28]

Such information meant for the newly energized
fundamentalists that their efforts for the cause must
be maintained at the highest possible level of activity at all times. Such zeal did, in fact, characterize
the work of the major bodies. Falwell, for instance,
carried out a unique Sunday service exercise. When
the regular service had ended he called on the congregation to stand. Then he asked the registered
voters to sit down, and went on to lecture those who
remained standing about their duty to get registered.
He promised to do the same every Sunday until election
day. This program was carried out in other fundamentalist churches as well, with some congregations setting
up registration facilities after services.[29] Falwell
also made several highly publicized speeches (see
below, ch.11) with Phyllis Schlafly at the Democratic
National Convention, intending to confront the gay
community with his critique. Just before Election
Day he called on Americans to observe a "National
Day of Fasting and Prayer" to help insure "that
religious men and women will be elected to public
office on Election Day."[30]

The PTL Club through its Director of World Missions
and International Programming published specific guides
for potential voters on how to register, study the
issues and vote. The booklet included a letter to
PTL and its director, Vernon K. McLellan, from President Reagan who endorsed the effort. From Jimmy
Swaggart came calls in his monthly, The Evangelist
magazine for studying the issues and the voting records of the candidates, to register and to vote.
Swaggart himself along with Falwell delivered his

opinions about specific issues to the Platform committee hearings of the Republican national convention.
Throughout the summer and fall Pat Robertson spoke
almost daily on the issues, chastising the secular
humanists and calling on voters: "We're asking
for Godly people to be in office. We're praying parti-
cularly in this election you want men of God in various
levels of life...men and women who love God, who believe in the Bible, who have a principle, who are
men and women of integrity and honesty and decency.
These are the kind of people we want in office."[31]

Unquestionably, the most aggressive of all NCR
forays was the publication by Christian Voice of a
40 page, full color magazine, Presidential Biblical
Scorecard. Claiming it distributed some ten million
copies, (some 200,000 free copies going to churches)
and it being "the nation's only Christian political
action committee" the editors had made a very large
expansion on their earlier moral report cards. Using
many photographs, compiling in tabular form the
voting records and specific statements on specific
issues by Reagan/Bush and Mondale/Ferarro, the CV
writers made clear their own stands on the agenda.
In each case the quotations used were favorable towards the incumbents and critical of the challengers.
On "Issues" the format was much the same. The latter
were portrayed as soft on pornography and on all
family issues as Christian Voice defined them. The
same use of quotations and voting records was utilized for contrasting the two tickets on secular humanism, religious freedom, euthanasia, capital punishment, balancing the national budget, ERA, marijuana,
parental and child rights, gay rights, voluntary
school prayer and national defense and disarmament.

The magazine also provided the updated 1984 edition
of moral report cards of all Senators and House members.

Obviously, no demonstrable means exist to determine how many votes such a publication changed. Of
real significance is the fact that its appearance
brought on a sharp repudiation   of it by Mondale.
The Christian Voice considered that attention as
proof its message was getting through.   In sum,
the full Christian Right by late, 1984 was a presidential campaign issue.[32]

All of this came to a very dramatic, brief
outburst of comment by both candidates in late August and early September. Reagan opened the war
of words when at an ecumenical prayer breakfast
in Dallas the day after his renomination he made
clear his convictions

Today there are those who are fighting to make
sure voluntary prayer is not returned to the
classrooms. And the frustrating thing for the
great majority of Americans who support and
understand the special importance of religion
in the national life, the frustrating thing
is that those who are attacking religion claim
they are doing it in the name of tolerance,
freedom and openmindedness. Question: Isn't
the real truth that they are intolerant of
religion?

Further in the speech he stated

There are, these days, many questions on which
religious leaders are obliged to offer their
moral and theological guidance. And such
guidance is a good and necessary thing.

To know how a church and its members feel on

a public issue expands the parameters of debate. It does not narrow the debate. It
expands it.
The truth is, politics and morality are in-
separable. And as morality's foundation is
religion, religion and politics are necessarily
related. We need religion as a guide. We need
it because we are imperfect. And our government needs the church because only those humble
enough to admit they're sinners can bring to
democracy the tolerance it requires in order
to survive.[33]

Those comments touched off a vigorous, highly
spirited debate among religionists, scholars, and
journalists. Opponents saw Reagan as dangerously
mixing church and state while supporters cheered his
linkage. In the context of the NCR impact on national
life, the President had directly accepted their
indictment of secular humanists as the enemies of
the Republic; once their influence could be eliminated,
the breakfast prayer speech suggested, America could
be well back on the road to righteousness.[34]

A few days later, candidate Mondale made his
rebuttal. He argued the President had called those who
disagreed with him to be "intolerant of religion" a
position which simply was wrong. Having known the
NCR criticism of his programs, Mondale addressed the
matter before the B'nai B'rith

I believe in an America where all the people
have the right to pursue their faith not just
freely, but also without insult or embarrass-
ment; where religious freedom is not a passive
tolerance, but an active celebration of our
pluralism. There is no more uplifting power

on earth than a religious faith which can not
be coerced and is tolerant of other beliefs.
To coerce it is to doubt the sturdiness of our
faith. To tell the state to enforce the religious life of our people is to betray a
telling cynicism about the American people.
Moreover, history teaches us that if force
is unleashed it will corrupt our faith, divide
our nation, and embitter our people. No
President should attempt to transform policy
debates into theological disputes. He must
not let it be thought that political dissent
from him is un-Christian. And he must not
cast opposition to his programs as opposition
to America.[38]

At that same program that day, President Reagan
also made a speech. But, one journalist concluded,
he "backed out of the fight he had picked; the clever
Republicans, solicitous of his September lead, would
risk nothing that might disturb it."[36] At that meeting Reagan reaffirmed his commitment to separation
of church and state, and religious pluralism. Although, as the press concluded, this exchange was
the first real fireworks between the two candidates,
they both moved on quickly to other issues, leaving
it for the interpreters to explain its importance.
Later, in their second face to face debates, the
two candidates repeated the stands they had already
taken on the social agenda issues.[37]

The religious Right attempted to carry on the
debate, using it to discredit the challengers. Moral
Majority writers pointed out that despite the fact
that Reagan often used terms such as "God", "faith",
"churches" and "religion" very often in his speeches,

it was the Rev. Jesse Jackson who "used more Bible
verses than Ronald Reagan and, perhaps, even the
entire Republican party know." Mondale was accused
of trying to "frighten the American people into believing that if reelected President Reagan will
determine the religious preference of every American."
Mondale, the writer pointed out, was attempting to
introduce humanistic religion "steeped in socialism"
into American life.[38]

From the critics on the other side came the point
that religious Right influence had led the President
and his party to be preaching, in this instance,
unassailable pieties. "To be for God means to be
for school prayer, anti-abortion legislation, government aid (or at least tuition rebates) for parents
sending their children to religious schools--in short
for a conscious re-insertion of what some call religion into public life. Those who oppose such things
are characterized as out-and-out secularists, as
people who are against God, or at least indifferent
to him."[39] Another critic suggested that the President in his "intolerance" statement was not presenting
a careful analysis of the issue, but "merely pressing
all available buttons, saying anything that would
please his immediate hearers and the rest of America's
righteous religionists, who may be in a majority.
In the process he was also adding to the confusion."[40]
Finally, another observer stated "Jerry Falwell tells
us that God has chosen Ronald Reagan and George
Bush as divine instruments for saving America. Who
knows? Falwell may be right."[41]

VI

As suggested above, the decisive question in political campaigning for special interest groups is:

Did they deliver? In this all too brief conclusion
(the writings on it are as of now voluminous and
show every sign of continuing to grow) we ask that
question. It should not be interpreted as being
in any way cynical or pragmatic. The New Christian
Right, armed with its absolutist theology and ideology, and its conspiracy thesis, entered knowingly
into the highly pragmatic, results-oriented battleground of elective politics. Their participation
should be evaluated on the basis of their successful
fulfillment of the criteria for success: Did they
deliver?

To answer that question directly at the outset
here: Given the information now available, the bloc
of New Christian Right votes as such had no measurable impact on the Presidential race. In one U.S.
Senate contest and in perhaps a half dozen House
battles, an arguable claim can be made for its being
able to deliver enough votes to win the battle away
from the Democratic condidates. Further, by contrast
to its (extremely debatable) claims of having
defeated five "liberal" Democratic Senators in the
1980 race, no NCR spokesmen made anywhere near comparable claims for Campaign '84. Apparently, its presence
did assist Senator Jesse Helms in a very close contest in North Carolina. Christian Voice claimed in
its post-mortem analyses it made the difference in
18 House and Senate races. ACTV claimed eight victories where its campaigning had been felt.[42] The
major news magazines, Time, Newsweek, and U.S. News
and World Report in their post-mortems scarcely
mentioned the religious Right, as was also true for
the analyses in the Washington Post, New York Times,
Congressional Quarterly and, later, several full
length book studies.

Yet the New Christian Right did make a significant contribution. As the statistics from regions, age
groups, races, occupations and the other demographics
reached the party and scholarly experts, they showed
some startling changes. The Democrats discovered
that the votes of 22 million Christian fundamentalists
and evangelicals had shifted form a pro-Democratic 56-43
percent margin in 1976 to an 81-19 Republican sweep
in 1984. Three political scientists through the New
York Times/CBS polls discovered that Reagan won more
than half of the vote among white Catholics and 7 out
of 10 white Protestants, actually 58 percent Catholic
and 73 percent Protestant. They also found "Reagan
was strongly supported by numerous fundamentalist
leaders...." "Reagan's appeal to fundamentalists
appears to have been translated into votes." He won
86 percent of the vote "among those who felt close to
evangelical groups." Among those whites claiming a
born again experience he received 81 percent, and
69 percent of the white Protestants who had not claimed
the born again experience."[44] This shift, according
to analyst Thomas B. Edsall was highly beneficial
to the Republicans because it brought in large amounts
of new contributions and "a source of sustained
moral commitment..."providing troops for day-to-day
combat. That alliance also sharply restricted the
capacity of the GOP to adapt flexibly on the issues
which were highly divisive; abortion, family, and
church/state issues. That decision apparently had
been a calculated risk in the Republican strategy.
Edward Rollins, a manager of the Reagan campaign,
stated the religious Right vote came to between 10
and 12 million, giving to the party a bloc comparable to what the Democrats had from Catholics in
the 1940s, 1950s and 1960s.[45]

Some discussion developed over whether the appearance of the NCR would in any significant manner influence the traditionally Democratic vote of Jewish
citizens. The issues were clouded because on the
one hand some Jews feared religious Right talk about
a Christian America and the return of religious exercises to the public schools. Polls showed most Jews
opposed much if not all of the social agenda. Yet
at the same time an increasing number of Jews responded
favorably to the NCR enthusiastic support for Israel
and Zionism. What seemed clear was that the religious
Right had made clear inroads into one of the most cohesive of all American voting blocs.[46]

Yet other scholars show, as do Thomas Ferguson
and Joel Rogers that when all the data from Campaign'84
are studied,"American attitudes betray no evidence
of a right turn. In general, religion, feminism,
civil liberties, abortion and race relations are the policies in which the public has shown the sharpest
increase in liberalism since the Second World War."
During Reagan's first term, in fact, "the public
became more liberal...." They called in increasing
numbers for the legalization of abortion, for opposing school prayers, for favoring an Equal Rights
Amendment, and in the number who thought negatively
of Jerry Falwell.[47]

The New Christian Right itself had no doubts
about its impact during the campaign. Rejecting
the critics' fear that the alliance with Reagan
threatened religious freedom in America, Tim LaHaye
said, "most Christians were ignorant about the
issues and their right to have an impact on those
issues" through the elective process. He added, "now
the liberal humanists are upset because they know the

silent Christian majority is no longer letting them
run the country. They know we have far more ground
troops than they do and they are terrified...."[48]
Robertson identified the fundamentalist and evangelical vote with the appeal of the Republican party,
agreeing with guest speakers on the 700 Club that
the Democrats had chosen to throw away their appeal
to religious people. Jimmy Swaggart's son, Donnie,
pointed out that three forces contributed to Reagan's
reelection; pocketbook issues, the new patriotism
and disgust over "liberal, humanistic ideology."[49]

In summation, the religion/politics debate over
the American way received extended if not always con-
structive public consideration during the campaign.
The presence of the New Christian Right intensified
that debate to a degree quite unknown in previous
campaigns. What that debate revealed sharply was
how increasingly bitterly divided Americans had become
over any issue that sounded as though it would involve
the religious commitment of any person of faith. In
harmony with the idea often expressed by analysts
such as Kevin Phillips that we were becoming "Balkanized"
or Martin E. Marty that we were becoming increasingly
tribalized and privatized, the 1984 campaign in the
realm of religion and politics underscored the
diagnoses of those two commentators.[50] The 1984
campaign gave the New Christian Right the opportunity
to place itself firmly on the political terra firma.
Its leaders utilized that opportunity to its advantage, becoming a household word. With direct access
now continuing into the Oval Office, those leaders
now had the opportunity in the next years to achieve
their agenda.

Notes

1. Editorial, James E. Wood, Jr., Journal of Church
   and State, Autumn, 1984, 26:3, p.402.

2. Ibid., p. 409.

3. News story, Christianity Today, October 5,
   1984, pp.54-58.

4. Quoted by Wood, see footnote 1 above, p.406; see
   again Sidney Blumenthal, "The Righteous Empire",
   The New Republic, October 22, 1984, pp.18-24;
   for Democrats see William Lee Miller, "The Semin-
   arian Strain", The New Republic, July 9, 1984,
   pp.18-21; Thomas B. Edsall, "Pulpit Power: Con-
   verting the GOP", The Washington Post National
   Weekly Edition, July 8, 1985, pp.9-10.

5. Well summarized in the brochure, "Ten Basic Causes"
   published in 1984 by the American Coalition for
   Traditional Values; a well written critique is Edd
   Doerr, "Will Religious Liberty Survive the 1980s"?,
   Americans for Religious Liberty, a 6 page pamph-
   let, n.d.; Time, September 2, 1985, pp.52,55,57.

6. "Insight" column, Beth Spring, Christianity Today,
   November 9, 1984, p.58; for more analysis see the
   articles on "Religion and the 1984 Election" in
   Review of Religious Research, December, 1985, 27:2,
   pp.98-188.

7. Elizabeth Bettenhausen, "Personal and political,
   private and public", Christianity and Crisis,
   October 29, 1984, pp.394-96.

8. Blumenthal, "The Righteous Empire", p. 18.

9. Richard V. Pierard, "Religion and the New Right",
   James E. Wood, Jr., ed., Religion and the State:
   Essays in Honor of Leo Pfeffer (Waco, Baylor
   University Press, 1985), p.411; see Richard V.
   Pierad, "Reagan and the Evangelicals: The Making
   of a Love Affair", Christian Century, December
   21-28, 1983, pp.1182-85; "Insight" in Christianity
   Today, October 7, 1983, pp.44-50; see Ronald
   Reagan, In God I Trust, David R. Shepherd, comp.
   (Wheaton, Tyndale House Publishers, 1984); and
   Bob Slosser, Reagan Inside Out (Waco, Word
   Books,1984).

10. See Marty in Christian Century, January 25, 1984,
     p.71; news item, The Fundamentalist Journal,
     September, 1983, p.64.

11. Moral Majority Report, February, 1985, p.5; news
     item, Christianity Today, December 16, 1983, pp.
     36-37; Charles Krauthammer, "America's Holy War",
     The New Republic, April 9, 1984, pp.15-19.

12. News item, Sojourners, January, 1984, p.7; Time,
     November 5, 1984, p.73; Newsweek, November 5, 1984,
     pp.84-91; Minneapolis Star and Tribune, October 24,
     1984, p.19A; news item, America, November 10, 1984,
     p.286; Christianity Today, December 14, 1984, pp.
     48-51.

13. News item, Christian Century, March 7,1984, p.241;
     news item, Religious News Service, February 17,
     1984; see the debate with Norman Lear in "Readings",
     Harper's, October, 1984, pp.15-20.

14. Jim Wallis, Sojourners, September, 1984, pp.18-21;
     editorial in Christian Century, September 21,
     1984, pp.483-85; see Steven M. Tipton, "Religion
     and the Moral Rhetoric of Presidential Politics",
     Christian Century, October 31, 1984, pp.1010-13.

15. Editorial, Christian Century, March 23-30, p.259,
     and ibid., February 15, 1984, p.155; Lutheran Council
     in the U.S.A., Focus on Governmental Affairs,
     August, 1984, 18:8,p.3; news item, Los Angeles
     Times, November 3, 1984. These, plus several
     other references are reprints of stories in these
     newspapers which have been collected and distri-
     buted by People for the American Way, available
     from that office, 1015 18th St., NW, Suite 300,
     Washington, D.C. 20036. Unfortunately, PAW
     did not include the page references; see also
     the analysis by John H. Simpson, "Socio-Moral
     Issues and Recent Presidential Elections,"
     Review of Religious Research, December, 1985,
     27:2, p.116-26; Sidney Blumenthal, "The GOP
     'ME' Decade;", The New Republic, September 17-24,
     1984, pp.12-15; see also "Doonesbury" for November
     4, 1984; and "M.E.M.O", Christian Century, October
     17, 1984, p.967.

16. Blumenthal, "The Righteous Empire", p.18; Stuart
     Rothenberg and Frank Newport, The Evangelical
     Voter: Religion and Politics in America (Washing-
     ton,D.C., The Free Congress Research and Educa-
     tion Foundation,1984),pp.116-20.

17. <u>Newsweek</u>, July 9, 1984, p.52; <u>New York Times</u>,
     August 17, 1984, p.10; <u>Congressional Quarterly</u>,
     September 22, 1984, p.2318.

18. ACTV, "National Voter Registration Leadership
     Manual", 1984, inside cover; and flyer, "The
     Second Most Important Day in Your Life", ACTV,
     1984, n.p.

19. Editorial, <u>Christian Century</u>, June 20-27, 1984,
     p.619; <u>New York Times</u>, August 17, 1984, p.10;
     Jack Germond and Jules Witcover in "Commentary",
     <u>Minneapolis Star and Tribune</u>, June 23, 1984,p.17A.

20. General mailing letter, Greater Minneapolis
     National Association of E7angelicals, October
     1984, signed by Quinton Alfors; <u>Moral Majority
     Report</u>, October, 1984, p.6; <u>The Freedom Report</u>,
     August/September, 1984, 2:7, passim; see voter
     registration instructions from the PTL in Vernon
     K. McLellen, <u>The Great American Arena!</u> Positive
     <u>Strategies for 20th Century Patriots</u> (Charlotte,
     Associates Press, 1984), chs.11,12; article by
     Donnie Swaggart in <u>The Evangelist</u>, July, 1984,
     pp.40-42 using Christian Voice materials; <u>Moral
     Majority Report</u>, April, 1984, pp.1,15; Old-Time
     Gospel Hour, June 17, 1984; Bill Bright of
     Campus Crusade also used Christian Voice materials
     in his 1984 brochure, "Your Five Duties as a
     Christian Citizen".

21. News story, <u>Christian Science Monitor</u>, November
     6, 1984, pp.1,40; news story, <u>Minneapolis Star
     and Tribune</u>, September 9, 1985, p.1A; packet
     and letter to me from Debra Livingstone of the
     NCC, August 10, 1984; the "Nighttime" show on
     ABC-TV of September 6, 1984, explored the regis-
     tration issues; <u>Newsweek</u>, September 17, 1984,
     p.39; <u>Time</u>, September 2, 1985, p.51.

22. Pierard, "Religion and the 1984 Election",
     pp.102-03; David Osborne,"Registration Boomerang",
     <u>The New Republic</u>, February 25, 1985, p.15; news
     story, <u>Christianity Today</u>, November 9, 1984,
     p.46; news story, <u>Congressional Quarterly</u>,
     September 22, 1984, p.2316; news item,
     <u>Christianity Today</u>, December 14, 1984, p.57.

23. <u>The Fundamentalist Journal</u>, April, 1984, p.28;
     <u>National Catholic Reporter</u>, September 14, 1984,
     p.8; news item, <u>Journal of Church and State</u>,

1985, 26:3, p.584; editorial, Conservative Digest,
July, 1984, p.35; see also Adolph L. Reed, Jr.,
The Jesse Jackson Phenomenon (New Haven, Yale
University Press, 1986).

24. Richard Brookhiser, The Outside Story(Garden
     City, Doubleday and Company, 1986), pp.236-41.

25. Pierard, "Religion and the 1984 Election", p.103;
     Congressional Quarterly, September 15, 1984,
     p.2267; Wood, "Religion and Politics", Journal
     of Church and State, Autumn, 1984, 26:3, p.407.

26. Column of August 29, 1984, in the Minneapolis
     Star and Tribune, p.17A.

27. New York Times, September 9, 1984, p.13.

28. Ibid; and Rothenberg and Newport, The Evangelical
     Voter, pp.111-12, 130, 148; news item, Christianity
     Today, December 14, 1984, pp.61-62; further support-
     ing data are in "Appendix E", Lance Tarrance and
     Frank Newport, "Evangelicals, Fundamentalists, and
     Political Issues in the 1984 Election", a 104 page
     booklet issued by The Institute of Politics and
     Harvard Divinity School, Cambridge, 1984,pp.101-04.

29. A. James Reichley, Religion in American Public
     Life (Washington, D.C., The Brookings Institu-
     tion, 1985), p.321.

30. Minneapolis Star and Tribune, July 13, 1984, p.13A;
     Bangor(Me.) Daily News, October 11, 1984, pp.1;3;
     brochure on "Fasting and Prayer", Old-Time Gospel
     Hour, October 7, 1984; and November 4, 1984;
     Moral Majority Report, August, 1984, p.1.

31. McLennen, The Great American Arena!, p.113, see
     pp.112-20; The Evangelist, June, 1984, p.36, and
     ibid., October, 1984, p.38, and December, 1984,
     p.20; 700 Club, October 3, 1984 through October 10,
     1984; the quote is from October 14, 1984; The
     Freedom Report, October, 1984, 2:8, pp.5-8;
     William Greider, "Attack of the Christian
     Soldiers", Rolling Stone, May 9, 1985, pp.64,
     85; news item, Chicago Sun-Times, October 1,
     1984, p.1.

32. News story, Christian Herald, September, 1984,
     p.4; see also the CV publication "Revive America",
     1985, 2:1, pp.1-6; New York Times, August 17,

1984, p.10, and ibid., September 7, 1984,p.1;
Congressional Quarterly, September 22, 1984,
pp.2315-19, and see the issues of Christian
Inquirer for these months.

33. New York Times, August 24, 1984, p.11.

34. Brookhiser, The Outside Story, pp.242-43.

35. New York Times, September 9, 1984, pp.1,12.

36. Brookhiser, The Outside Story, pp.243-44; New
    York Times, September 7, 1984, pp.1,12.

37. New York Times, October 9, 1984, p.15; news
    item, Christianity Today, October 19, 1984,
    pp.32-36.

38. Moral Majority Report, October, 1984, pp.1,26.

39. John Garvey, "Politics and Religion", Commonweal,
    November 2-16,1984, p.584.

40. Robert G. Hoyt, "Politics, Religion, Confusion",
    Christianity and Crisis, September 17, 1984,
    pp.316-17.

41. William Greider, "Will God Vote Republican?",
    Rolling Stone, October 25, 1984, pp.11-13.

42. Christian Voice, "1984 Election Report", in
    "Memorandum", March 8, 1985; news item, Christian
    Herald, January, 1985, p.7; Cox News Service,
    "Analysis", in Minneapolis Star and Tribune,
    November 15, 1984, pp.25A, 26A; Pierard, "Reli-
    gion and the 1984 Campaign", pp.111-13.

43. Thomas B. Edsall review in The New Republic,
    March 3, 1986, p.32; see the statistical analyses
    in Public Opinion, December/January, 1984/1985,
    7:6, p.2 ff; and a flyer, "Christian Voice
    Attack Facts", September 30, 1985, 3 pages.

44. News story, New York Times, March 7, 1986, p.12;
    ibid., November 25, 1984, p. E2; Paul Abrahamson,
    John H. Aldrich, David H. Rohde, Change and
    Continuity in the 1984 Elections(Washington, D.C.,
    Congressional Quarterly Press, 1986), pp.141-42;
    news story, U.S.News and World Report, November
    4, 1985, p.70.

45. Edsall, The New Republic, p.32; U.S.News and World
     Report, November 4, 1985, p.10.

46. Martin E. Marty, "Transpositions: American Reli-
     gion in the 1980s", Wade Clark Roof, ed., Religion
     in America, The Annals of The American Academy
     of Political and Social Science (Beverley Hills,
     Sage Publications, 1985), pp.15-16; Pierard,
     "Religion and the 1984 Campaign", pp.106-08;
     see the symposium, "Jews and American Politics--
     1984...and After", This World, Winter,1985, no.10,
     pp.28 ff; also Commentary, May, 1985, has dis-
     cussion, and Milton Himmelfarb, "Another Look at
     the Jewish Vote", in ibid., December, 1985,pp.
     39-44.

47. Thomas Ferguson and Joel Rogers, "The Myth of
     America's Turn to the Right", The Atlantic
     Monthly, May, 1986, pp.45-46; Barry Sussman's
     evaluation in The Washington Post National
     Weekly Edition, July 21, 1986, p.37.

48. Moral Majority Report, November, 1984, p.15.

49. 700 Club, November 7, 1984; Old-Time Gospel
     Hour, November 11, 1984,; editorial, The
     Evangelist, February, 1985, pp.24-25.

50. See the stimulating interpretation by Rodney
     Clapp, "The God and Politics Debate", Christianity
     Today, December 14, 1984, pp.26-29.

PART TWO. 1985-1986
The Televangelists

It may seem to readers presumptuous for a historian
to be writing a history of a movement as it still re-
mains in transition. However, thus far we have already
identified those elements which continue to be steadfast in that movement; the theology, the political ideology, the conspiracy thesis, and the strong cooperation
with the office of the President. Continuity also
exists from the early 1980s into their later years
with the continued expansion of televangelist preaching,
the common pursuit of the social agenda, the addition
of new, and to many religious Rightists attractive
causes (such as the "Hatch Amendment", see ch.11),
and finally, the irresistibly attractive need to get
involved in choosing a successor to President Reagan.
Those parameters serve as the sources of continuity
into the immediate future of the late 1980s.

Since the New Christian Right came into national
prominence largely through television, its continued
growth after Campaign '84 continued to depend on its
ongoing financial expansion. Such enlargement did
occur, due largely to its leaders' understanding of
what the viewers wanted to see and their ability to
translate that into target programming. By early
1986 Pat Robertson's daily program reached 16.3 million
households per month, Jimmy Swaggart's weekly some
9.3 million, Jim Bakker's daily show some 5.8 million
and Jerry Falwell's weekly service some 5.6 million.[1]

Such impressive strength suggested their numbers
were growing, and with that strength so too might
their influence on national public policy. The NCR
leaders knew they furnished an indispensable source
of votes for the new Reagan coalition; white Protestant

evangelicals favoring the social agenda, Northern blue-
collar Roman Catholics supporting pro life and tax
vouchers, and neo-conservative intellectuals promoting increased support for Israel.[2] They knew also
the President would work for the promulgation of
the social agenda, understanding this was something
of a risk because in "every preceding period of broad
cultural change in American history, the forces supporting tradition have ultimately lost."[3]

That issue would become the crucial test for the
political muscle of the New Christian Right. As did
other long range analysts, they would have to face
the question of whether a genuine shift had been made
rightward during the 1980s. Was it not possible that
with all their bombast and headline getting rhetoric,
the religious Right leaders really were not all that
powerful a political force? Polls such as that of the
New York Times/CBS in January, 1986, showed little
support for any move to the right. In 1981, some 37
percent of those polled considered themselves "conservative"; in January, 1986 the total was 36 percent.
Some 24 percent thought in 1986 their views were more
conservative than before and some 39 percent thought
the country's political thinking was more conservative.
Kevin Phillips suggested that the 1984 election was
perhaps the peak of conservative energy; that shortly
citizens would want an increase in government activism
in their economic and social lives. He, as well as
another Reagan supporter, David R. Gergan, concluded
that "social conservativism isn't catching fire", the
social agenda lacked appeal.[4]

                              II

Whatever strength those arguments contained, the
Administration in 1985-86 started several programs and

new appointments which received strong support from
the religious Right. They backed Reagan on supporting the contras in Nicaragua, on the Strategic Defense
Initiative programs, on the Administration's decision
to appoint to Federal judgeships only justices friendly
to its philosophy, on the White House decision to
press again for tuition tax vouchers, and for the Department of Education investigation of evaluating public
school textbooks for "untruths" and "inadequacies."
In 1985 the Oval Office reaffirmed its commitment to
press for the abolition of legal abortion and for the
passage of a school prayer amendment. By the Spring
of the next year, however, when opposition to both
became evident, the two measures were postponed.[5]

In an appointment attracting little media attention,
but taken very serously by the religious Right, Reagan
named Herbert Ellingwood to head the Justice Department's Office of Legal Policy. That office screened
candidates for federal judgeship appointments. Ellingwood had already taken a firm stand in favor of the
social agenda. Then the executive director of ACTV,
Curtis Maynard, stated that when Ellingwood learned
of civil service job appointments, the latter "submits
them to us." Critics demanded Ellingwood's promotion
be rejected because of that link. Ellingwood replied
that ACTV had an "advisory service" to help people
seeking civil service jobs, but denied complicity
with ACTV. However, Gary Jarmin of Christian Voice
stated that the talent bank idea had been Ellingwood's
"brainchild" but that no wrong had been done. Under
strong pressure from groups such as People For and
civil liberties associations, Ellingwood's name was
withdrawn by the Administration.[6]

Yet the religious Right continued to support the
President, not the least because of two statements
from him regarding theology and polity. In a speech
in February, 1986, before the National Religious
Broadcasters Conference, he quoted Luke 14:31 as
justification for increasing defense spending. The
statements are worth quoting at length

> ...in which Jesus is talking to the disciples
> spoke about a king who might be contemplating
> going to war against another king with his
> 10,000 men, but he sits down and counsels
> how good he's going to do against the other
> fellow's 20,000 and then says he may have to
> send a delegation to talk peace terms. I
> don't think the Lord that blessed this country
> as no other country has ever been blessed in-
> tends for us to someday negotiate because
> of our weakness.[7]

After extensive criticism of his exegesis had been
made, Reagan replied, "I checked with a few theolo-
gians, if it was appropriate. And they seemed to
think that it was perfectly fitting. It was a cau-
tion to those people in our country who would, if
given the opportunity, unilaterally disarm us."[8]

In the June, 1986, battle among the Southern
Baptist Convention delegates (or "messengers") over
nominating a new President, Reagan telephoned
congratulations to the winner, known as a "fundamentalist" in scriptural interpretation. The message
was read to the convention; it declared that "liberalism" which had seemed triumphant so long, "had been
thrown on the defensive."[9]

As criticism continued to be made, President
Reagan stated, "I don't think I've ever used the Bible

to further political ends. But I've found that the
Bible contains an answer to just about everything
and every problem that confronts us, and I wonder
why sometimes we won't recognize that one Book could
solve a lot of problems for us."[10] Colman McCarthy
of the Washington Post responded, "Religion is honored
when it is separated from party platforms and valued
for the moral force of faith and hope. It is dis-
honored when it is Americanized and militarized. Earlier
presidents have done one or the other. Reagan is
the first to do both."[11]

                            III

    With the informal alliance of White House and NCR
public policies made clear by both sides, religious
Right leaders moved quickly to expand the full range
of their programs. The frontrunner, Jerry Falwell,
enlarged the scope of outreach. In "Operation Uplift"
considerable support was sent to the famine areas
of the Sudan. At home the enrollment of Liberty College
(changed to a university) grew to some 6,000. The
facilities for unwed pregnant women were likewise
expanded. All in all, by mid-1985 Falwell's domain
was bringing in some $200 million annually.[12]

    In politics, however, the fortunes took a different
turn. Aware that many critics believed that "in many
ways Ronald Reagan made Jerry Falwell possible", the
latter continued his staunch advocacy of the White
House agenda for domestic and foreign issues. He
opposed the nuclear freeze movement, endorsed Reagan's
proposals for "meaningful and verifiable arms reduction"
and staunchly opposed all threats of "Communist expansion in Central America. Nicaragua is gone and
El Salvador is tottering". At home, in May, 1985, he
stated "As for me, I have no intentions of allowing

Tip O'Neill and Jim Wright [Democratic party leaders
in the House of Representatives] to place my children
and grandchildren in Communist slavery or worse."[13]

Falwell also involved himself aggressively in
the social agenda issue of gay rights. He started
working for national legislation to stop the spread
of Acquired Immune Deficiency Syndrome, AIDS. The
proposal would allow civil lawsuits to be brought against
AIDS carriers, allocate federal funds for public education about AIDS, require "mandatory testing of blood
for AIDS during all routine physical examinations---
with documentation on individuals who are diagnosed
as having AIDS filed with the State Board of Health",
authorization by state health departments "to quaran-
tine or isolate individuals with AIDS..." and an im-
position of mandatory prison sentences for persistent
offenders".[14]

The gay community, through its local chapters,
nationally suggested that members call Falwell's
800 number to order his offer of a free Bible, or
simply to run up the costs by Ma Bell. Eventually
those costs came in Falwell's estimate to over $2
million; the 800 number was removed.[15]

In another domain, Falwell in 1985 went on record
before the Rabbinical Assembly of Conservative Rabbis
with the statement it was "wrong" for conservative
Christians to assert that the United States is a
Christian nation. He explained his support for the
State of Israel was not based on a belief that the
country's existence is necessary for the second
coming of Christ. Apparently, he made the statement
in light of increased criticism in the Jewish
community over the statements by some NCR leaders
about the necessity to "Christianize" America.

Responding to Falwell, Rabbi Marc Tannenbaum, director
of international relations for the American Jewish
Committee, stated that Falwell's remarks represented
"a new hermeneutic on classic premillenarian doctrine".
Tannenbaum added that Falwell "had assured him" that
he is opposed to the conception of America as a 'Christian
republic' and remained opposed to any religious test
for office seekers."[16]

The statements and proposals on domestic issues
might not in themselves have contributed to his down-
ward plunge in public esteem in these years. But, by
his own admission, Falwell's interpretation of two
areas of foreign policy debate, that of the Philippines
and of South Africa, proved to be near disastrous. They
are thus important to explore at some length.

After a two-day tour of the Philippine Islands
late in 1985, Falwell told the press he was tired of
those American policy makers for "bellyaching" about
that nation. He claimed its citizens enjoyed freedom thanks to President Ferdinand E. Marcos. "I don't
think any fair person can deny the fact that had it
not been for the Marcos family the chances are that
the freedoms you enjoy now would not be here." "This
is a great land and a free country and we need the
Republic of the Philippines as our friend."[17]

That statement in itself might have found its
way into oblivion. But it became coupled in the news
media and public mind with his statements on the conclusions he reached after touring with nine other
American ministers for five and a half days in the
Republic of South Africa. As the tour ended, on
August 19, Falwell announced his steadfast support
for President B. W. Botha's limited racial reform
program and his total opposition to economic sanctions

by the United States. Falwell stated he would urge
"millions of Christians to buy Krugerrands", the
South African gold coin. He would call on those
American firms which had withdrawn investments to
return those into the republic. He added that he had
not found "one person--black, colored, white or Indian--
who wants divestment." He pledged that Moral Majority
would do everything it could to overturn the move in
Congress to impose sanctions on the nation. He concluded the conference by stating the Blacks in South
Africa did not consider Bishop Desmond M. Tutu as
their spokesman.[18]

Back in Washington, Falwell amplified his re-
markings, stating that if Bishop Tutu maintained that
he spoke for the Black people of South Africa, then
he was a phony. "I think he's a phony, period, as
far as representing the black people of South Africa.
And if anyone here doubts that, go out to the black
public in South Africa and ask them. We did. We have
it on videotape." That interpretation, especially
the use of the word "phony" made the lead stories of
world and national television, of radio and the press
coming as it did after Tutu had been a Nobel Peace
Prize winner and celebrated critic of racial oppression in his homeland. The protest from all areas
of the country and all points of the religious spectrum
was virtually instant and sustained. Falwell, for
so long an adroit user of the media, found himself
the object of scorn and ridicule. He struck back,
however, claiming he had been mistreated. Admitting
to the use of "phony", he added: Well, I said more
than that. I said if he represents himself as speaking for the black people of South Africa, that he
is a phony. And he no more speaks for the black people

of South Africa than I speak for the whites or the
blacks or both of America. No one does that."[19]

But the damage had been done. Media criticism
continued on for several days, with denunciations
of Falwell by Black clergy and Black Congressmen
such as the Rev. Joseph E. Lowrey and Representative William Gray(D.--Pa.). Falwell made a conditional
apology, explaining such was in order if Bishop
Tutu took it to mean that Falwell was impugning him
"as a person or minister." He told reporters, "I'm
saying that if the word 'phony' to you, as communicated
to you, meant that I was impugning you as a person
or minister, I apologize. I was impugning the fact
that you, sir do not speak for the South Africans
any more than I speak for all Americans." "It was
an unfortunate choice of words. The word 'phony'
I should not have used. I should have used the
word that he was incorrect or wrong, and I have
since apologized."[20]

As further evidence that he had lost his once
firm mastery over the media, Falwell turned to insult-
trading. This reached the front pages with an exchange with Rev. Lowrey who had claimed Falwell was
"throwing some jazz at reporters." Falwell replied
that Lowrey was on the payroll of the Unification
Church and "will speak on any position he's paid
for it."[21]

Within days, Falwell found himself being criticized sharply from a wide variety of sources,
conservative as well as liberal, adding up to (in
his estimate) the loss of a million dollars in
gifts. Critics rejected his position on three
counts; that unless Botha was in power, the communists would take over; that Falwell had defamed a

fellow Christian minister, and that he was in "over
his head in international affairs, out of bounds
when he presumes to speak for evangelicals, and
far from the pulpit which he claims to be his
primary calling."[22]

Recognizing the damage done, Falwell spoke
frequently through a variety of media opportunities.
He appeared often on late night talk shows; he
wrote letters to national newspapers such as U.S.A.
Today; he defended himself frequently on his Sunday
television service, and wrote extensively for the
publications coming out of his empire in Lynchburg.
In early 1986 he concluded, "The South African
debate is probably the most volatile one we have
been involved in because there are really good
people on both sides of the issue."[23]

That volatility surfaced in early, January,
1986. Falwell announced the creation of a new political organization aimed at winning wider support than
the original Moral Majority, Inc. The latter would
remain, centered on "strictly moral" issues such
as the social agenda. The new group, "Liberty
Federation", would be free to concentrate on matters
such as a balanced federal budget, the Star Wars
issues, and Communist offensives in Central America,
Taiwan, South Korea, the Philippines, South Africa
and elsewhere. The new organization would be "no
more or less religious than Moral Majority". Falwell also announced the new group already had the
approval of the Administration; for its first national
meeting, a gala banquet scheduled for late January,
Vice President Bush had accepted the offer to be
the speaker. Falwell also announced he was supporting the candidacy of Bush for the Presidency in
Campaign '88.[24]

When pressed by reporters, Falwell acknowledged
that Moral Majority had slipped considerably in
approval throughout the general public. Conservative Paul Weyrich suggested "I'm not sure that...
[a name change] will do them a lot of good." The
chair of the Democratic National Committee, Paul
G. Kirk suggested that "Liberty Federation won't stand
for true liberty any more than the Moral Majority
represents the moral values of most Americans."[25]

IV

The fortunes of the other major televangelist,
Pat Robertson, after Campaign '84 moved in a different
direction. From the outset of his ministry he chose
to work through television, rather than a congregation in which Falwell first received national attention. In Virginia Beach Robertson was able to build
a mammoth, heavily endowed empire by skillful use of
making his agenda palatable to a growing number of
American and overseas viewers. In this section we
explore that growth; in chapter 14 we look at his
candidacy for the Presidency.

As did Falwell, Robertson expanded the full
range of his programs in line with the increase in
financial support. Early in 1986 he accepted the
transfer of the Oral Roberts School of Law, Tulsa,
Oklahoma, to CBN University. Through "Operation
Blessing" resources for the famine-struck areas
of the Sudan and Ethiopia were provided. Some $20
million also in supplies was sent to refugee organizations in El Salvador, Guatemala, and Honduras.
In June, 1985, Robertson accomplished the delivery
of some $1 million in medical supplies to Guatema-
la's government.[26]

Throughout 1985 and until the next year when he became heavily involved in day to day politicking, Robertson presented the well established NCR case for the social agenda; he also spoke often on foreign policy. He warned against "Marxian communists" in South Africa who would make life for the Blacks there far worse than what they now experienced. On Nicaragua Robertson encountered something close to Falwell's South Africa debacle. Reporters and some evangelicals claimed he had pledged some 3 million new dollars to a contra group, the Nicaraguan Patriotic Association, and $2 million to former Brigadier General Hienie Aderholt for distribution to appropriate military sources. Sojourners in Washington, D.C. found CBN funds being used to sustain the contras and perpetuating their terrors. The CBN officals replied to the charges by stating the implications of Sojourners as being "false and perhaps border on being libelous." The charges could well have led to a discrediting of Robertson as the "phony" statement of Falwell. But the issue failed to attract national media attention largely because investigators could not discover with any degree of accuracy what actually was taking place.[27]

Speaking on domestic issues, Robertson continued his searching criticism of secular humanism, the legal abortion choice for women, and the full social agenda. He found the public schools tottering on the brink of atheism because of curriculum innovations by liberals and the humanist conspirators. Robertson presented video tapes of an interview with President Reagan who explained his position on the budget deficit, tax reform, and trade protectionism. Robertson concluded, "We appreciate a President who knows

the greatness of this people and the greatness that
God will give us a nation under God." On AIDS, he
pointed out that the disease was God's punishment
for breaking His laws, for starting "this sexual
adventure", homosexuality.[28]

By contrast to Falwell's fortunes, Robertson
continued to maintain a growing rate of acceptance
by the viewers of religious television. His loyalty
to the religious Right was as pointed and as militant as that of Falwell. But he avoided making the
kind of shoot-from-the-hip commentaries which by
his own admission Falwell could not avoid. Robertson (in this writer's estimate) had become to his
viewers a sort of fundamentalist Walter Cronkite:
authoritative, calm, in command, perfectly attuned
to the demands of the pressures of the wizardry of
television. He seemed to be the person they could
trust to explain what were obviously some exceedingly complicated, often frightening implications
of survival in an increasingly violent world.

V

During the years immediately after Campaign
1984 the third of the major television preachers,
Jimmy Swaggart, significantly enlarged both the
scope and the energy of his ministry. Conscious
always of the need to maintain his own identity
("product differentiation") Swaggart used his increasingly sophisticated command of televangelism
and market skills to help enlarge his vigorous
credibility as a religious Right commentator on
public issues. That is to say, by contrast to
earlier years, he clearly in the mid 1980s joined
hands with Falwell and Robertson to present his
version of the blend of theology, political ideology, and the secular humanistic conspiracy.

But by contrast to the other two, Swaggart was
far more the entrepreneur presenting to supporters
a wide variety of items for sale; tapes, cassettes,
sermons, tracts, booklets, books, and related
materials identified with Swaggart himself. Much
material centered on his charismatic, "neo-Pentecostal"
ministry of the spiritual gifts, of devotional aids
and inspirational items all identified with Swaggart's
personality. The catalogs also included the books
available to viewers which clearly identified his
ministry with that of the political New Christian
Right. Included were books by Francis and Franky
Schaeffer and John Whitehead, all classic interpretations of NCR themes.[29]

With increasing revenues, Swaggart enlarged the
scope of his expression of evangelism. By 1986,
through satellite electronics, "The Jimmy Swaggart
Telecast" was being broadcast in 125 countries.
The "Child Care International" outreach program
offered supplies and leaders to schools, orphanages,
and famine struck nations in most third-world locales.
At national headquarters in Baton Rouge, Louisiana,
the Jimmy Swaggart Bible College has been established
with some 700 students. Swaggart preached in South
America and Africa, following through on his television appearances. Throughout the United States,
Swaggart appeared in one to three day preaching
missions.[30]

Swaggart in post-Campaign '84 America accepted
the religious Right social agenda, adding at times
a unique personal interpretation. Regarding abortion, "The Supreme Court of the United States of
America because of this one thing has been damned
as an institution by God Almighty. The Congress of

the United States because of this one thing has been
damned by God Almighty." Swaggart took equally
strong stands against homosexual behavior, against
feminists "that disregard the God of the Bible and
laud that which is perverted", against the teaching
of evolution, "the garbage my children are being
taught in the public schools, that we came from
monkeys and disregarding God."[31]

Swaggart found the secular humanist conspiracy
at work in the Supreme Court and in television; "this
carefully guarded élite is not a force for righteousness, brother, but rather an insidious cabal blatant-
ly working against God's behalf", a condition he
traced to secular humanists dominating the faculties
of the schools of journalism. "For those who criticize the believers in the conspiracy," Swaggart concluded, "you sir have not set yourself against
the so-called right-wing, moral McCarthyites. You
have not set yourself against the hick fundamentalists. You have set yourself against God."[32]

In sum, Swaggart more than the other major preachers, chose to make himself and his specific Pentecostal
tradition the centerpiece of his ministry. The excitement of a Jimmy Swaggart program depended on
his being in front of the camera. During the mid
1980s an increasing number of television viewers
found Swaggart and discovered the right blend of
religion and politics.

VI

Finally, one of the true founders of televangelism,
Jim Bakker of the PTL Club, also found the opportunity
in the mid 1980s to move that ministry into new areas.
By choice, he and Tammy Faye Bakker had avoided the
more polemical and divisive tones of the other leaders,

with the exception of the question of abortion. Much
of their time before and after Campaign '84 was spent
responding to criticism by the newspapers of their
financial arrangements. Investigative reporters
raised questions about the fundraising connected
with the development of "Heritage,U.S.A.", a resort
complex of some 2,500 acres in Charlotte, North
Carolina with luxury hotel facilities, campgrounds
and rental condominiums along with the broadcast
auditorium for their daily television programs.
At times the cash flow dwindled down to a trickle,
prompting the Bakkers to use aggressive fundraising
techniques over the air. Bakker justified this:
"Well, if the Bible says we are to be fishers of
men, then a water park [a new part of the complex]
is just the bait. And I don't see anything wrong in
using some pretty fancy bait." That approach, by
contrast to the other NCR leaders, was a part of
Bakker's evolving understanding of the essence of
religious faith as being the promise to believers
that God would provide for their material lives
as well as their spiritual ones.[33]

Pursuing that theme carefully, the PTL program
in the Spring of 1986 announced plans to shift its
emphasis. In accenting the new priorities of
health, wealth, happiness and family, the daily
program was retitled, "The Jim and Tammy Program".
The new emphasis would include more guests, more vocal contributions and less talk about the internal
conspiracy and related divisive issues.[34] And as
events unfolded, the new agenda proved to be popular
with viewers and visitors. Some 4,000 supporters
were on the waiting list in mid-1986 to rent vaca-
tion homes at Heritage, U.S.A. They also filled

the auditorium each day for the television broadcasts
which on occasion offered the "passion play with a
cast of 100 and three camels."[35]

The highlight, however, revolves around the PTL
extravaganza each year between Thanksgiving and New
Year's, focusing on a visual celebration of Christmas.
Thousands of visitors take a two hour tour of Heritage, USA, where they find a million lights, illumin-
ating thousands of Christmas trees, candy canes, ani-
mated scenes from Christmas cards, and angels, the
latter being 50 in number and measuring eight feet
in height. The most popular crowd pleaser is Candy
Cane Lane, with five foot high striped candy canes
lit with red and white lights; in between are brightly
colored gingerbread men and lollipops. The center
of the display is a large Christmas tree atop being
a star of David. Local citizens tell visiters that
"children are always brought to Christmas City--this
may be the very way they first learn about the
Lord."[36]

Ch. X: Notes

1.   Time, February 17, 1986, p.67; see also a CBN sur-
     vey reported in the Minneapolis Star and Tribune,
     October 26, 1985,p.14A.

2.   "Opinion", Joseph C. Harsch, Christian Science
     Monitor, January 16, 1986, p.15.

3.   Richard F. Schier, "Politics After Ronald Reagan",
     U.S.A. Today, March,1985, p.17 (this is the maga-
     zine, not the daily newspaper).

4.   Kevin Phillips, "Hubris on the Right", New York
     Times Magazine, May 12, 1985, p.48 ff.; David R.
     Gergen, "Following the Leaders", Public Opinion,
     June/July,1985, p.57; also Danny Collum, "The
     Big Picture", Sojourners, May, 1986, pp.15-20.

5.   News item, Baptist Joint Committee for Public
     Affairs, Report from the Capital, April, 1986,
     p.6; ibid., March 1985, p.5; Dwight R. Lee,
     "The Uncertain Prospects for Educational Vouch-
     ers", The Inter-Collegiate Review, Spring, 1986,
     pp.29-38; news story, The Chronicle of Higher
     Education, April 16, 1986, pp.13,24; the ongoing
     influence of conservatism on the President is
     documented in Sally Weymouth, "The Great Right
     Hope: Pat Buchanan on the Inside", New York,
     June 10, 1985, pp.48-54; Christian Inquirer,
     March, 1985, p.26.

6.   Newsweek, June 3, 1985, p.19; Christian Century,
     May 22, 1985, p.527; Madison(Wis.) Capital-Times,
     April 5, 1985; Swaggart, Falwell, and Robertson
     endorsed Ellingwood's appointment.

7.   Quoted in Minneapolis Star and Tribune, February
     12, 1985, p.14A.

8.   New York Times, February 22, 1985, p.11; see
     the searching critique by Alan M. Olson of
     the Religion Department, Boston University,
     in Minneapolis Star and Tribune, April 12,
     1985, p.17A.

9.   Ibid.

10. New York Times, February 22, 1985, p.11.

11. McCarthy in Minneapolis Star and Tribune, February
    12, 1985, p.14A.

12. Ibid., June 17, 1985, p.2A; Time, February 17,
    1986, p.62; The Fundamentalist Journal, April,
    1985, p.57; Washington Post Weekly National
    Edition, May 27, 1985, p.7; Time, September 2,
    1985, pp.57-61.

13. Time, September 2, 1985, p.59; Falwell, "The
    Issues of '85" in The Fundamentalist Journal,
    April, 1985,p.10; Old-Time Gospel Hour,
    September 8, 1985.

14. See Liberty Report, April, 1986, p.7; Falwell
    fundraising letter of May 3, 1985; April, 1986;
    letter from Moral Majority; May 31, 1985; ibid;
    Newsweek, January 6, 1986, p.23.

15. News item, Christian Life, July, 1986, p.14.

16. News story, Christian Century, April 17, 1985,
    p.376.

17. New York Times, November 13, 1985, p.5.

18. Ibid., August 20, 1985, p.6.

19. Ibid., August 21, 1985, p.3; Falwell on McNeil/
    Lehrer News Hour, August 20, 1985, Transcript
    number 2582, p.4; Associated Press news story
    in Minneapolis Star and Tribune, August 21,
    1985,p.1A,7A.

20. New York Times, August 24, 1985, p.4.

21. Ibid.; Stephen D. Johnson and Joseph B. Tammey,
    "The Christian Right and the 1984 Presidential
    Election", Review of Religious Research, Decem-
    ber, 1985, 27:2, p.131.

22. U.S.News and World Report, September 2, 1985,
    p.11; Washington Post, Weekly National Edition,
    September 2, 1985, p.26; "Doonesbury", Septem-
    ber 9,10,1985; Meg Greenfield in Newsweek,
    September 9,1985, p.100; Newsweek, September
    2, 1985, p.30-32; Time, September 2, 1985, p.
    5; editorial, The Reformed Journal, October,

1985, pp.5-7; news story, Christianity Today,
October 4, 1985, pp.52-56; Joseph Bayly in
Eternity, November, 1985, p.96.

23. See "Special Report", The Fundamentalist
    Journal, October,1985,pp.1-16; USA Today
    (newspaper), January 7, 1986, p.1A; Old-Time
    Gospel Hour, October 6, 1985; interview in
    Christianity Today, February 21,1986, p.41.

24. Fundraiser letter from Falwell of Moral Majority,
    January 6, 1986; New York Times, January 4, 1986,
    p.6; news story, Journal of Church and State,
    1986, 28:2, pp.365-66.

25. Editorial, Christian Century, January 22, 1986,
    pp.59-60; Time, January 13, 1986, p.25; news
    item, Christianity Today, February 7, 1986,
    p.60; see the extensive comments in Liberty
    Journal, January through June, 1986; The
    Fundamentalist Journal, June 1986, p.11.

26. News story, Christianity Today, February 7,
    1986, p.48; news story, Mother Jones, January,
    1986, p.9; news story, Conservative Digest,
    August, 1985, p.4.

27. 700 Club, September 9, 1985; ibid., February
    28, 1986; Vicki Kemper, "In the Name of Relief",
    Sojourners, October, 1985, pp.12-20; Arizona
    Star, July 7, 1986; news story, Lutheran
    Standard, March 7, 1986, p.49; news story,
    Christian Century, March 5, 1986, p.232;
    news story, Sojourners, April, 1986, pp.10-11.

28. 700 Club, September 17,19,20,23,1985; ibid.,
    March 2-5, 1986.

29. The Christian's Catalog, November, 1984, 16:11,
    n.p.; Swaggart also printed speeches of con-
    servatives such as Representative Newt Gingrich
    (R.--Ga.), in The Evangelist, March, 1985,
    pp.31-35.

30. The Evangelist, July, 1986, p.28; Steve Chapple,
    "Whole Lotta Savin' Going' On", Mother Jones,
    July/August, 1986, pp.36-45, 86.

31. The Jimmy Swaggart Television Program, February
    3, and October 6, 1985.

32. Ibid., January 5, 1986.

33. PTL programs, March 14, March 23, 1986: New
    York Times, December 24, 1985, p.7.

34. Christian Life, April, 1986, p.16.

35. New York Times, December 24, 1985, p.7; Context,
    December 1, 1985, p.3.

36. Kathryn Dantzler, "Christmas City", Christian
    Life, December, 1985, pp. 20-21.

Public Education Under Siege

Nowhere was the new clout and aggressiveness of the New Christian Right after Campaign '84 more strongly felt than in its expanded offensive to purge secular humanism and restore traditional religious expression within the public schools. The leadership here emerged not directly from the celebrity preachers as from another familiar face on the far right, Phyllis Schlafly with her Eagle Forum of Alton, Illinois. Fresh from her victory in stopping the ratification of the Equal Rights Amendment, in 1984 she organized her considerable skills and resources again for uniting the New Christian Right for this new crusade. Her offensive attracted the full support of the religious Right, hence it here receives an extended discussion. And the war continues unabated into the late 1980s.

For a variety of reasons, some more clear than others, public education in the United States since the early 1960s had been deemed by a growing number of citizens and observers as continually sinking into one desperate crisis after another.[1] Teachers allegedly were failing to instill the basic educational skills; classroom discipline had long since disappeared; drugs were abundantly available. The New Christian Right discovered the internal conspiracy at work in textbooks which eliminated or downplayed the role of religion in American society, or advocated promiscuous sexual activity, or denigrated traditional authority. Evolutionism had in many texts triumphed over any kind of creationism in biology texts, and "values clarification" had supplanted any attention given to morals education.

The televangelists found this indictment highly
congenial. Pat Robertson told the National Press
Club that the schools had become the centers of
serious crime making the public school "the most
dangerous place to be...outside the mother's womb."
Its values were "totally contrary to the Judeo-
Christian tradition." He indicted the secular humanists
as the culprits. Jimmy Swaggart and Jerry Falwell
stepped up their criticisms also, finding the conspiracy thesis to be satanic. Swaggart added "evolu-
tionists in our schools try to tell us that we came
from monkeys. Go to Africa and teach the monkeys.
Don't insult the monkeys."[2]

In post Campaign '84 America, the issue came to
focus on a specific piece of Congressional legislation, the so-called "Hatch Amendment", actually two
amendments by the same Senator(1978,1984). So explo-
sive and controversial did the Amendment become in
public educational circles as to create for everyone
concerned a new, no-holds-barred battleground from
which no contestant would retreat. The NCR attack,
chronicled in this chapter, came to challenge the very
existence and credibility of the professional community
of educators as well as civil libertarian groups.
They in turn responded by turning their full research
and public relations resources against letting the
NCR win even a preliminary skirmish.

The story is exceedingly complex, often freighted
with professional jargon, requiring more than a little
background information. As early as 1962 some parents
began expressing concern over what they believed were
non-academic, psycho-social programs conducted in the
public schools which they believed were invading the
privacy of the family. Congressman John Ashbrook(R.--

Ohio) proposed a bill requiring parental knowledge of
and consent for their childrens' involvement "in any
federally funded programs, examinations, relationships,
sexual behaviors and religious beliefs."[3] The bill
failed in the House.

Another conservative legislator, Senator James
Buckley(R.--N.Y.) in 1974 produced something of an
alternative, a measure to protect the privacy and
rights of parents and students by giving them access to
students' school records. Parents and students, under
its terms, could examine and, if necessary, correct
those records. Buckley pressed for more, proposing a
measure which would require parental consent by school
officials before children were required to take certain forms of testing or be involved in certain experimental or attitude-affecting programs. That
measure was defeated.[4]

Congressional interest was kept alive in that year
by the General Education Provisions Act (GEPA) introduced by Representative Jack Kemp (R.--N.Y.). His
amendment to it, which was approved, required education
grant recipients or contracts working through the
programs administered by the Department of Education
to obey the following provision

All instructional material, including teachers'
manuals, films, tapes, or other supplementary
instructional material which will be used in
connection with any research or experimentation
program or project shall be available for inspection by the parents or guardians of the
children engaged in such program or project.
For the purpose of this section "research or
experimentation program or project" means any
program or project in any applicable program

or project in any applicable program designed
to explore or develop new or unproven teaching
methods or techniques.[5]

Kemp proposed another amendment, which was approved,
requiring that "no child shall participate or be used
in any research or experimentation program or project, or in any pilot project if the parents of such
child object to such participation in writing." Kemp
explained he intended by that amendment to ensure that
parents be given the right of consent to any proposed
but untried teaching method or program which could
be detrimental to their child.[6]

II

Little came of the Kemp amendments because schools
had no policies which ran counter to the new provisos.
The matter remained quiet until 1978 when Senator
Orrin Hatch(R.--Utah) proposed an amendment. As it
would unfold, even contrary to what Hatch had intended
in 1978, that the proposal would turn out to be something of a trojan horse, one giving the New Christian
Right access into combat to eliminate the humanists
from public education.

Three major goals were attempted by the Hatch Amendment of 1978; it would remove the parental consent
proviso from the Kemp proposal; it would require local
school districts to make available for parental inspection any materials associated with federally funded
experimental programs, and, finally, it would provide
that students could not be examined, tested, or
treated psychiatrically or psychologically without
prior parental consent.

In concrete detail, the Hatch Amendment established
barriers against research programs in the public schools
which would require the students to reveal information

on one or more of these: (1), political affiliation;
(2) mental and psychological problems potentially embarrassing to the student or her family; (3) sex
behavior and attitudes; (4) illegal anti-social, self-
incriminating and demeaning behavior; (5) critical
appraisals of other individuals with whom respondents
had close family relationships; (6) legally recognized
privileged and analogous relationships such as lawyers,
physicians, and ministers; (7) income (other than that
required by law to determine eligibility for participation in a program or for receiving financial aid
under such a program) without the consent of the student
(if the student is an adult or an emancipated minor)
or in the case of an unemancipated minor without prior
written consent of the parent.[7]

As two close observers of the amendment note, "from
the day the Hatch Amendment was passed, the written consent requirement lay dormant, that is, until 1984" because "such permission is routine procedure in most
school systems..." thus defusing the need for new rules,
such as Hatch's. The Senator himself commented, "our
amendment does not add to or subtract from any monies.
It does not presume to redirect any of the programs
involved...." Later, Phyllis Schlafly interpreted
this period of dormancy to be the result of lawmakers
refusing to think that anyone could object to providing school children "with this mantle of protection
against such classroom abuse of their personal rights
or family privacy."[8] She found them to be wrong.

Yet this period of dormancy proved to be the time
period in which the trojan horse came into the battle.
The Hatch Amendment of 1978 would become the energiz-
ing, rallying force for theological and political right
wing groups convinced that the secular humanist

conspiracy had now threatened to envelope even school children. However, the original leadership for this rightist crusade came not from the NCR preachers nor Schlafly, but from a sometime policy maker in the educational bureaucracy in Washington, D.C., Charlotte Iserbyt, at one time executive assistant to Donald Sense, Associate Secretary for the Office of Educational Research and Improvement and later head of G.E.M.-- Guardians of Education for Maine. After the Reagan administration in 1981 placed its people in the various offices, including Education, Iserbyt sent a memo outlining her plans for implementing the Hatch Amendment to serve conservative ideological goals to the director of the Office of the General Counsel of the Department of Education. Apparently, some such regulations were drafted but failed to receive approval of the Secretary of Education, Terrell Bell.[9]

But from that point on, the matter became exceedingly complex for two reasons; the Kemp and Hatch amendments themselves were vaguely worded, leaving specific implementation very much in doubt; and, second, the call for the promulgation of the provisions of enforcement would emerge from "very strong political pressures from well organized conservative groups".[10]

Although the records for documenting the story from this point on are hazy, apparently Schlafly learned of the potential for using the Hatch Amendment to further her goal of eliminating the humanists from the schools. In her October, 1981, "The Phyllis Schlafly Report" she called on supporters to "reassert their authority find out what is being taught in the name of 'education', and stop any assault on traditional and family values."[11] That phrase constituted, of course, the legitimizing claims to

political involvement of the religious Right. In 1982
Iserbyt moved to take control of the situation. She
resigned from the Department of Education, and headed
up the Guardians of Education for Maine. She called
on supporters to demand that Secretary Bell issue regulations which would implement, in concrete form, the
mandate of the Hatch Amendment. In the years when the
NCR was growing quickly, Iserbyt asked supporters "to
put intense pressure on Secretary Bell to approve draft
regulations for the Hatch Amendment, which have been
written by a Reaganite political appointee in the Department of Education's Office of the General Counsel". She added, "without regs, the hard-fought-
for-amendment is nothing but a worthless scrap of
paper."[12]

     With the Reagan administration endorsement of the
social agenda, the momentum for implementing Hatch
Amendment regulations shortly got under way. The
specific details of informal politicking are missing,
but it is clear that Iserbyt, using her personal
knowledge of Department of Education dynamics, knew
where to apply the pressure. As she wrote her supporters in early 1982 she knew the horse was being
groomed for battle. Iserbyt argued that her supporters must demand from their Congressmen the passage
of regulations for the Hatch Amendment; "This is
our only chance to gum up the works, and the effort
is crucial." "If all of us would stop what we are
doing and put all our energy and talents into
efforts to get very strong regulations, we could...
stop the socialist change agents dead in their
tracks."[13] She wrote that Secretary Bell opposed
implementing the Amendment because he "does not
want to offend his educationist friends by signing

off on regulations that will disturb their modus
operandi, their persistent efforts to change the
values, attitudes and beliefs of students to conform
with those necessary to bring about a socialist/
humanist one world government".[14]   She argued that
by the use of regulations, the conspirators could at
least be checked until all the resources of the
Hatch Amendment regulations could be brought to
bear in the schools.

Iserbyt also knew as she wrote a second memo of
January 10, 1982, that the Department of Education
had decided already, in a reversal of its position
in the President Carter years, to hold hearings "to
determine the content of regulations for the Hatch
amendment". To supporters Iserbyt enclosed draft
copy regulations written "by conservatives in the
Department" and the types they proposed to be taken
for carrying out the attack against the humanists.
The Department of Education, she had learned, would
be holding hearings in selected locations around
the country to take testimony on how best the Hatch
Amendment could be utilized to preserve the rights
of the students and their parents. She made a request of her supporters; "It is important that you
advise me of confirmation of your testifying, or
if you have had problems getting on the list." That
last phrase referred to her admonition to supporters
to be sure to get on the list of those testifying
for the Hatch Amendment.

By way of convincing her readers that they should
act immediately, Iserbyt added(her emphasis); "the
intent of Congress was to cover all the mindbending
techniques and materials used in our children's classrooms, in special ed and in guidance, not just the

narrow and difficult to define areas of psychological
and psychiatric testing or treatment." To those she
had encouraged to get on the list, Iserbyt offered
advice, "You can expect to be up against lobbyists
from all the special interest groups and educational
associations (there are over 900 of them in the
country). They and Bell detest the Hatch Amendment
and are responsible for us never getting regulations."[15]

After more negotiations the Department of Education in January, 1984, announced it would sponsor
hearings on Hatch Amendment regulations in seven
cities across the country: Seattle, Pittsburgh,
Kansas City, Concord, N.H., Orlando, and Washington.
Iserbyt now gave detailed instructions to supporters
on how they should testify. When looking at public
school course descriptions they should search for
"key words" to see if such were controversial, to
search for names and addresses of persons involved in
such programs, and to collect information on "decision making, role playing, values, attitudes...creative
thinking, etc." She added, "When you testify at the
hearings, don't wear conservative buttons. Identify
yourself as a housewife, schoolboard member, teacher,
businessman, whatever, but do not identify yourself
as a member of a conservative political action
group...."[16]

The longsought implementation of Rightist planning
came to fruition when on February 22, 1984, the
Federal Register published information on the regional
hearings. At this point Schlafly made an important
decision. Knowing that supporters of her cause would
be those who would do the greatest share of the
testifying in the 7 hearings, she realized that such
testimony would be the documentation she and her

supporters needed to prove their case against the
humanists. As the matter would unfold, Schlafly
reviewed the testimony of "hundreds of parents,
teachers, and concerned citizens" using it as her
documentation for her case. Of fundamental importance
in her stated objectives for getting involved was
her determination to see that the Hatch regulations
would require that "all instructional items, including teacher's manuals, films, and tapes, would have
to be made available for parental inspection."[17]

Iserbyt's plans now materialized according to
schedule. As the hearings took place in the seven
cities, some 163 citizens from 29 states testified.
All but two urged passage of regulations congenial
to the Rightist agenda. According to careful observers at the hearings, the witnesses exhibited
"anger, distrust, and loathing...about what they
believed was the nature of education in the nation's
public schools." Three specific charges emerged out
of their testimony: (1) resentment over a perceived
invasion by educators of students' privacy and teachers' attempts at brainwashing; (2) deprivation of
instruction in the basic academic skills, the 3 R's;
(3), a demand to return school administration and
curriculum to local control. In her reports to
the news media about this, Schlafly talked of "the
thunderous voice of hundreds of parents who are
angry at how their children have been emotionally
and mentally abused...during classroom hours..."[18]
The troops had climbed out of the trojan horse and
were testifying before sympathetic officials of
the Department of Education. The battle was joined.

After the testimony sessions closed in May, DoE
officials started to process the evidence. At

that point, in a move apparently not directly related
to the first amendment, Senator Hatch offered another
regulation. In a bill to help "magnet schools",
those undertaking major desegregation plans, he
offered Sec.509

> Grants under this title may not be used for con-
> sultants, for transportation, or for any acti-
> vity which does not augment academic improve-
> ment, or for courses of instruction the sub-
> ject of which is secular humanism(emphasis mine).

In floor remarks he stated, "I'm tired of seeing the
dumbing down of textbooks and schools to ignore all
reference to religion and patriotic values."[19]
Some months later Hatch would come to change his
mind about that proposal, but coming now as it did in
1984 in the din of election-year politicking, his amendment as approved by the Congress of the United States
meant that the phrase "secular humanism" was on the
books of both the Congress and the Supreme Court. For
its opponents, that was of the utmost importance.

III

The several professional associations of public
school teachers understood the implications of Hatch's
phrase. Long a target of NCR artillery, the National
Education Association (hereafter, NEA) called on its
members to demand that the "509" phrase be deleted.
It reasoned that no official definition of "secular
humanism" had been included in the terms of the measure, nor was the Secretary of the DoE authorized
by the terms of the bill to make such a definition.
Thus it should be expunged.[20]

Meanwhile, Schlafly had utilized the voluminous
testimony as documentation to prove the need for implementing the Hatch Amendment. In August, 1984, her

publication, <u>Child</u> <u>Abuse</u> <u>in</u> <u>the</u> <u>Classroom</u> appeared
for sale to the general public. Three weeks later,
President Reagan announced to the annual conference
of the Eagle Forum, "I'm happy to tell you today
that new regulations to enforce the Protection of
Pupil Rights Act, sometimes called the Hatch Amendment, have been completed by the Department of
Education...Like you, I believe that parents'
rights in education must be respected."[21]

At the same time, the NEA and a newly formed
coalition of thirty professional education associations announced their opposition to the promulgation
of the forthcoming regulations. Known as "The
Hatch Amendment Coalition", it along with the NEA
negotiated extensively with DoE officials during
the last months of 1984 for withdrawal or at least
modification of the proposed regulations. But no
such changes were made. On November 12, 1984, a
week after the national elections, the newly drafted
Hatch regulations went into effect. Unpalatable as
they were to the educationists, the "regs" also
proved to be unacceptable to the Rightists. Within
two weeks, activists such as Schlafly and the Maryland Coalition of Concerned Parents met with DoE
officials. As the meeting ended the spokespersons
for the latter group stated that the regulations "are
much too weak and limited in several respects. [We
reserve] the right to seek a strengthening of the
regulations after the new Secretary [of Education]
takes office." Secretary Terrell Bell had recently
announced his resignation.[22]

In effect, the new regulations amplified the
1978 Amendment. They required prior parental consent before a school could ask students for information about political affiliations, mental or psycho-

logical problems that could embarrass a student or her/
his family, sexual behavior and attitudes, illegal
or anti-social, or self-incriminating or demeaning
behavior; critical appraisals of members of a student's family, privileged relationships such as those
with lawyers, physicians, or clergy, and income,
except where required for eligibility for a government
program.[23] Schlafly reported that Eagle Forum had
sent a letter to some 250,000 parents calling on them
to use the Hatch regulations to bar the schools from
"manipulating" children's "values and moral standards"
through "curricula, textbooks, audiovisual materials,
or supplementary assignments". The letter also asked
school officials to seek written parental consent
before taking up in the classroom setting a lengthy
list of topics far removed from Senator Hatch's concern with psychological and psychiatric testing.
Schlafly asked parents to give consent before subjects such as the following could be brought up in
the classroom: nuclear war, global curricula,
every aspect of human sexuality, autobiographical
assignments, evolution, alcohol and drug abuse, non-
Western religions, abortion, suicide and drug abuse,
all linked in Rightist thought to secular humanism.[24]

    Throughout the winter months the conservatives,
the education lobbies and the DoE attempted to keep
one another from dominating the enforcement of the
regulations. The new Secretary, William Bennett,
announced his endorsement of them; "I would take
a very close look at what my son was being asked to
study, because there are a lot of things in schools...
that don't belong there".[25] NCR leaders such as
LaHaye, Mel and Norma Gabler and Dr. James Kennedy
spoke out in support of the Schlafly interpretation

of the regulations. In turn, activists from civil
liberties groups and People for the American Way
insisted that if enacted, the regulations would
remove the school classroom from being a place where
students would learn to think for themselves.
Barbara Parker of PAW argued that the Schlafly forces
hoped to turn the classroom into "a sterile place in
which students memorize officially sanctioned facts"
and indeed the Right "would like to do away with
the public schools as they exist today." "Requiring
parental consent would mean most of what is taught
in social studies and other classes would be out-
of-bounds."[26]

During the battles, Senator Hatch in February
attempted to clarify his original intentions. He
started by showing that everyone concerned--the conservatives, the education lobbies, and the DoE had made
the worst possible interpretations of his intentions.
He criticized the activists when he stated that some
"parent groups" apparently wanted to extend Hatch to
apply to all curriculum materials, library books, and
teacher's guides, as well as to all tests used by
teachers in courses in physical education, health,
sociology, etc., reviewed by parents before they
could be administered by them. Hatch stated, "Because there are no Federal funds in such courses, the
Hatch Amendment is not applicable to them." "All
that the amendment did apply to were those federally
funded programs, the primary purpose of which is
to elicit the type of information prescribed by the
Hatch Amendment."[27] In short, the author stated,
the federal government was not the agency which
concerned parents should use to implement their
goals.

That did not slow down the agitation. As the vague-
ness of the wording and the difficulty of defining
criteria continued to upset any smooth enforcement
of the regulations, the DoE stated "Hatch violations
that make it to the Department level will be judged
on a case-by-case basis". It was added the DoE had
"no criteria" against which alleged violations would
be assessed. The Department gave up trying to define
key terms such as "non-academic" in the phrase of the
1978 Amendment centered on "psychological and psychiatric examinations or tests"... "of a non-academic
nature." Since it could not define "non-academic",
it would be forced to review each case individually.[28]

Schlafly, meanwhile, proposed a new series of
maneuvers. She called on supporters to promote state-
level parent right groups (now that Hatch had shown
federal endorsement was not possible) to sponsor
legislation on the state level. By May 29 some 10
states were in varying stages of readiness considering bills endorsed by, among others, the Eagle Forum
people. Parent vigilante groups throughout the nation
started demanding prior inspection and approval of
a variety of classroom and testing procedures, citing
the Hatch amendment as their justification.[29] The high-
water point came when in May, 1985, the Arizona Senate
and House passed a state level Pupil Rights Protection
bill, modeled after the Schlafly proposal. The
Governor, Bruce E. Babbitt, vetoed the measure stating the legislation was an attempt to usurp control
of local school districts. No other similar legislation reached that level of approval, failing in either
one or both of the several state houses.[30]

The same general momentum against parent groups
continued to influence the United States Senate. In

October, by a voice vote, the Senators deleted from
the magnet bill of 1984 the wording "for courses of
instruction the substance of which is secular humanism." That phrase was struck by the leadership of
Senator Hatch and senators from both parties. Its
repeal also nullified a potentially embarrassing
lawsuit against the DoE being proposed by certain
intellectual leaders (such as Isaac Asimov and B.F.
Skinner) asking that the law be removed.[31]

Meanwhile parental groups maintained pressure on
school districts for increasing their own control over
curriculum and extra curricular activities. Both
old and new lobbies such as Save Our Schools, Christian
Inquirer, the National Association of Christian Educators and Robertson and Falwell kept calling on
supporters to renew their fights against the conspiracy.
Jimmy Swaggart called the public schools "the greatest
enemy of our children today...whether you know it
or not...." He called on supporters to send their
children to private religious schools.[32]

Clearly the issue, in its broadest implications,
reflected the head-on collision of the NCR with its
social agenda against those citizens, in this case
the educators, who rejected that agenda. The NEA,
in fact, chose openly to repudiate the religious Right
bill of fare. It, for instance, opposed voluntary
school prayer in schools which were mandatory, state
sponsored and organized. It opposed the equal access
of school facilities for voluntary religious meetings;
it opposed the tuition tax voucher proposals; it
endorsed the nuclear freeze proposals; it favored sex
education being taught without parental choice or
review; it endorsed the Equal Rights Amendment and
forced busing of school children to achieve racial
balance.[33]

Schlafly found new ways to keep up the offensive.
In the Spring of 1986 she distributed "A Student's
Bill of Rights" in response to what she said were
some 500 complaints by parents who thought their
childrens' beliefs were under attack in the public
schools. Among the ten rights were "the right to
my religious faith and beliefs", and "the right to have
and to hold my moral values and standards, my political opinions, and my cultural attitudes". "Schoolpersons
may not force me to do assignments or engage in classroom activities which criticize or downgrade my religion."
The NEA commented: "there can be little argument
with this list of student rights. Simply by enumerat-
ing all these forms of abuse, however, Schlafly seems
to imply that 'schoolpersons' commonly commit such
abuses. Her insinuations here, as in all the other
listed rights, are obviously an attempt to exploit
parents' concerns for the safety of their children,
and to undermine their trust in public schools and
educators."34

                               IV
Closely allied to the parent activities has been
"the schoolbook protest movement" of the 1980s. It is
defined by its closest student, Professor Edward B.
Jenkinson, as the attempt to remove books from school
classrooms and school libraries; and(2) the work of
school critics attempting to remove or keep books
from being adopted on a state and national scale. Re-
fraining from calling the movement "censorship", Jenkinson finds that where the activists have enforced their
restrictions, schoolchildren are denied the right
to learn, the atmosphere for respect for learning
is weakened, banned books are turned into best sellers,
and educators are pitted against action groups ostensibly

acting for parents but in reality pursuing their own
social agenda. The statistics show that attempts by
citizen groups to influence text choice and library
book choice has increased steadily in the 1980s.[35]
    Obviously proponents of the movement see it in a
much different light. Worried over the influence
of the secular humanists and professional educators,
they are attempting to "return education and textbook adoptions to the parents and the community of
which the educational system is a part...."[36] Starting informally after World War II, the schoolbook
protest movement became institutionalized and often
highly effective under the leadership of Mel and Norma
Gabler of the Educational Research Analysts program
of Longview, Texas. Since 1961 they have conducted
formal reviews of public school textbooks, offering
their evaluations to school boards, citizen groups,
and state boards of education. They start from the
premise that "textbooks mold nations because textbooks largely determine how a nation votes, what it
becomes and where it goes".[37] In Texas especially
where one committee chooses the texts for all of the
state public schools, the Gablers became a powerful force for implementing texts endorsing the social
agenda of the religious Right. They have become
television celebrities speaking frequently on talk
and interview shows about the impact of their work,
as they state, in the 50 states and 25 foreign nations.
    The targets of the Gablers and similar textbook
protesters include an extremely wide variety of topics,
only some of which can be summarized here. They look
for writing which suggests values or endorsements
with which they take exceptions such as sex and drug
education, values clarification, Soviet propaganda,

evolution, stories portraying conflict between parents
and children or other authority figures or women in non-
traditional roles, stories of pagan cultures, violence,
sexual behavior, sensitivity training, death education,
and others closely related to those subjects the Schlafly proponents also want to remove from the public
schools.[38]

The work of the Gablers receives the full and enthusiastic approval of the New Christian Right leaders.
In 1983-84, for instance, among the instances of local
activist groups protesting the use of certain books,
some 20 percent had received support from groups such
as Eagle Forum, Moral Majority and Bev LaHaye's Concerned Women for America (see below, ch.12). Works
under criticism included Arthur Miller, The Crucible,
Harper Lee, To Kill a Mockingbird, William Golding,
Lord of the Flies, Studs Terkel, Working, and Alice
Walker, The Color Purple. Falwell in 1985 interviewed
Mel Gabler offering the latter his congratulations
for the program. "You can tell somebody by their
enemies. And you have all the right enemies." Gabler,
in the same program, acknowledged support from Pat
Robertson in their common battle against the enemy;
fighting secular humanism was "a spiritual battle. It's
Christ against humanism."[39]

In their advice to parent and other activist groups,
the Gablers recommend less confrontational strategy.
They propose more low key methods in talking with
school officials, careful planning and development of
specific facts before questioning the choice of texts,
keeping the focus on a specified number of targets
rather than taking on all their adversaries at one
time. But the Gablers also admonished supporters
to keep careful watch on how texts treat patriotism

and free enterprise, attitudes on the family and any
tendencies in texts "to deal with inward thoughts
and emotions rather than 'academics'."[40]

In the late 1980s the battles continue. The NCR
has chosen some law suits to support where parents
contest schoolboards over textbook selection. They
are countered by People for the American Way who
offer counsel for the anti-schoolbook textbook leaders.
In cases in Tennessee and Alabama the battle is
clearly joined between Robertson's Freedom Council
and People For. The former drew from the Gablers'
evaluations which pointed out that secular humanism
is a religion; its religion is manifest in the
texts to which the Council objects and the school
must remain neutral on all religious issues. Thus
the texts in question must be rejected. The defendants
reply that if the courts rule that secular humanism
is a religion whose evidence must be purged from
school materials, "every school board in the country
is going to be confronted with it. And it will wreak
havoc and confusion until it is reversed."[41]

XI. Notes

1.   See the background and documentation in Erling
     Jorstad, Being Religious in America: The
     Deepening Crisis over Public Faith (Minneapolis,
     Augsburg Publishing House, 1986),ch.6; On "The
     CBS Evening News", May 14, 1986, much the same
     picture was given. Editorial, James E. Wood,
     Jr., "The Battle Over the Public Schools",
     Journal of Church and State, Winter, 1986,
     28:1, pp.7,8.

2.   Swaggart, television program, December 12, 1984;
     Old-Time Gospel Hour, August 26, 1984; see also
     the NEA study published by its "Human and Civil
     Rights" agency, Understanding the Smear Tactics
     of the Far Right(February, 1984).

3.   Documented with appropriate references to The
     Congressional Record in the Hatch Coalition
     and American Educational Research Association,
     The Hatch Amendment Regulations(Washington, D.C.,
     A.E.R.A., 1985), pp.4-11, hereafter cited as
     Coalition, Hatch.

4.   Ibid., p.4.

5.   The General Education Provisions Act, 20 U.S.
     Congress 1232h,Sec.439; Bert I. Greene and
     Marvin Pasch, "Observing the Birth of the Hatch
     Amendment Regulations: Lessons for the Educator
     Profession", Educational Leadership, December,
     1985, January, 1986, p.43.

6.   Kemp's remarks in the U.S. House Congressional
     Record, vol.120, March 20, 1974, p.8505; Coali-
     tion, Hatch, pp.4-5.

7.   Greene, "Observing", p.43; Willard Hogeboom, "The
     New Right, the Hatch Amendment, and Public Educa-
     tion", U.S.A.Today, May,1986,p.78.

8.   Greene, "Observing", p.44; New York Times, April
     16, 1985; Coalition, Hatch, pp.15,25, see documen-
     tation' Hatch remarks, Congressional Record,
     August 23, 1978, p.27423; Phyllis Schlafly, ed.,
     Child Abuse in the Classroom(Alton, Pere Marquette
     Press, 1984), p.16.

9.   Coalition, Hatch, pp.15,25,26.

10. Ibid., p.26.

11. Ibid., p.16.

12. Ibid., p.15.

13. Ibid.; Greene, "Observing", p.44 also quotes from this memo.

14. Greene, "Observing", p.44; see the documentation, p.48.

15. Coalition, Hatch, pp.15-16; Greene, "Observing", pp.44-45; see the documentation there.

16. Coalition, Hatch, p.16.

17. Schlafly, Child Abuse, p.16.

18. Greene, "Observing", pp.45-46.

19. News story, New York Times, February 22, 1985; Jorstad, Being Religious, ch. 6.

20. See Congressional Record, July 25, 1984, p.H7742; see NEA Memo to Department of Education, January 3, 1985, p.3.

21. Schlafly, Child Abuse, p.20; the regulations are printed in toto here, pp.9-10.

22. Coalition, Hatch, p.17.

23. Hogeboom, "The New Right", 78; NEA Human and Civil Rights News, February, 1985, p.3.

24. New York Times, August 20, 1985, p.22; see the Maryland Coalition letter which has many more topics in Coalition, Hatch, "Appendix", n.p.

25. Coalition, Hatch, p.17.

26. Ibid.; quotation from The Social Studies Professional, May/June, 1985, p.4; editorial, Christian Century, April 24, 1985, p.403; NEA, Human and Civil Rights, February, 1985, pp.1-2, 6; news story, Journal of Church and State, Spring, 1985, 27:2, p.365.

27. NEA Human and Civil Rights, February 20, 1985, pp.1-3; Hogeboom, "The New Right", pp.78-79.

28. Coalition, Hatch, p.18.

29. The Social Studies Professional, May/June, 1985,
    pp.4-5; NEA, Human and Civil Rights, June, 1985,
    pp.9-10,12.

30. The NEA national office has a sizeable number of
    publications documenting parental involvement;
    Education Week, May 8, 1985; for Department of
    Education implementation see its regulations and
    discussions reprinted in Coalition, Hatch, pp.36-42.

31. Washington Times, November 26, 1985; Forum:The
    Newsletter of People for the American Way, Fall/
    Winter, 1985, p.1; Hogeboom, "The New Right",
    p.79; Moody Monthly, January, 1986, p.110.

32. Swaggart television program, February 3, 1985;
    NEA Fact Sheet, "Pursuing Public Education", 1986,
    passim, and NEA, "Special Edition", February,
    1986, passim; Christian Inquirer, "Freedom Alert"
    booklet, p.6 (1985); 700 Club, October 9, 1985.

33. NEA, "Special Alert", February, 1986, passim;
    NEA Human and Civil Rights, "Preserving Public
    Education", not paginated; see a critique in
    Christianity Today, March 15, 1985, pp.28-32.

34. Available from Eagle Forum; Baptist Joint Committee,
    Report from the Capital, March, 1986, p.9; news
    story, Lutheran Standard, February 7, 1986, p.27;
    NEA, "Special Alert: Preserving Public Education",
    March, 1986, pp.1-6.

35. Jenkinson, The Schoolbook Protest Movement: 40
    Questions and Answers(Bloomington, In., Phi Delta
    Kappa Education Foundation, 1986), pp.10-22.

36. News story on Mel and Norma Gabler, Liberty Report,
    January, 1986, p.12; Carol Flake, Redemptorama:
    Culture, Politics, and the New Evangelicalism
    (Garden City, Doubleday and Company, 1984),
    pp.39-40; Guy Sorman, The Conservative Revolu-
    tion in America (Chicago, Regnery Books, 1985),
    pp.107-08.

37. Jenkinson, Movement, p.55.

38. Ibid., pp.50-54.

39. NEA Human and Civil Rights "Bulletin", September,
    1984, p.7; Falwell Live, TBS program, October 6,
    1985; 700 Club, November 12, 1985.

40. Liberty Journal, January, 1986, pp.3,12,21; The
    Fundamentalist Journal, May, 1986, p.68.

41. News story, New York Times, February 28, 1986,
    p.11; CBS evening News, May 14, 1985 on text-
    books. In this whole area, see Albert J.
    Menendez, ed., School Prayer and Other Religious
    Issues in American Public Education: A Biblio-
    graphy(New York, Garland Publishing, Inc., 1985).
    As this manuscript is being published, the
    Tennessee trial has attracted extensive national
    attention. See the perceptive comments by George
    F. Will in his column of November 11, 1986,
    Boston Globe, p. 19.

Public Morality

Although the major offensives of the New Christian
Right since 1984 centered on politics and public school
education, several old and some new battles emerged
over public morality issues. These were led largely
by religious Rightists not involved in televangelism,
but firmly committed to the triad of fundamentalist
theology, political ideology and conspiracy. This
chapter surveys their activities into the late 1980s,
discussing both specific groups and the battlegrounds
they claimed. Obviously their stories are still being
written, but enough evidence is available to illustrate
their achievements through 1986.

Carrying over from earlier years and now equipped
with an expanded agenda and accumulated organizational
skills was Christian Voice, with offices in California and Washington, D.C. Known largely for its moral
reportcards and its 1984 Presidential Biblical Scorecard, CV leaders now gave extended attention to what
they perceived to be the last chance for righteous
Americans to save their country from the secularists.
To prove their case for their supporters the leaders
pointed to the increased criticism of their program
by such groups as the American Civil Liberties Union
and People for the American Way. Donors received
a letter. "Today, I ask you, who do you wish to
win this battle through the Supreme Court of America?
The ACLU, or Jesus, God's son and our saviour?"[1]
Readers were asked to complete polls stating their
preferences on the social agenda, and being promised
that the Christian Voice "Chairman of the Christian
Advisory Committee to the Reagan/Bush campaign will
hand-deliver the results of the poll to President

Reagan's top advisors as soon as the results are
tabulated." Further evidence of America's last
chance emerged in having the news media controlled
by the secularists, especially McNeil/Lehrer, People
For, Walter Mondale, and associated enemies. CV
leaders argued they needed additional revenue to
pay for radio and television programming where their
case could be brought to the people. "Don't let
the devil stop you! My prayers are with you as you
keep on fighting for God, for America and for our
families."[2]

To emphasize its credibility, CV enumerated
its accomplishments to potential donors. It had
been the first radio program to expose the AIDS
epidemic, and the first to awaken Christians about
child molestation. Stating also it was "the nation's
largest Christian conservative lobby---ready in our
new national headquarters", it announced plans in
1985 to continue the war even though it had never before "been under such persecution, ridicule, and
mockery from such powers, principalities and rulers
of the darkness of this world."[3]

However, by early 1986 Christian Voice faced
serious financial shortages. Readers were informed
"we have had to let go 3/4 of our lobbying staff;
3/4 of our national field and organization staff,
plus having to let go our receptionist, newsletter
editor and most of your mailroom staff!" Later CV
was sued by Wilson Advertising of Glendale, California for unpaid bills estimated at between $300,000
and $400,000.[4] Unquestionably CV had overextended
its resources without having built reliable grassroots support. Yet it had established its own
identity among New Christian Right enterprises,
and in an increasingly crowded field that would be

important. It reminded readers it had organizational
ties to Tim LaHaye and 29 members of the House of
Representatives (including Jack Kemp).

In late 1986 Christian Voice found its place
within the NCR with its report cards and its polemical confrontation with church groups outside its
boundaries. But readers were warned, unless they
sent money America would be lost because the "big
liberal churches" were "busy pouring millions into
the coffers of homosexuals, the abortionists and
communist guerrilla movements!" Such gifts "may
well be the difference between America surviving and
America being destroyed by God's wrath--perhaps
through nuclear fire and brimstone."[5]

II

Among the several battles over public morality,
none engaged the attention of the New Christian Right
more than that of abortion. There the enemy was most
clearly at work. As Walter H. Capps explains, the
pro-choice position was how "secularism comports
itself, so its opponents' attest, when backing away
from acknowledging the reality of the true source
and author of human life. And secularism by definition...is a worldview that has abandoned its
commitment to resilient transcendence."[6]

Throughout the mid-1980s the leading religious
Rightist leaders and supporters increased their
demand that the Supreme Court repeal its 1973 ruling
on legal abortion; they celebrated also the support of
President Reagan. In 1986, after some years of preliminary maneuvering, the militant pro-life organizations made significant inroads into control of the
Republican party. They knew the polls showed the
citizenry was divided on that Supreme Court decision,

45 percent for, 45 percent against, and 10 percent
undecided.[7] Pro-life movements, including every
major NCR organization continued in 1986 to press
for control of the GOP. They claimed legitimacy for
their cause based on their moral absolutist rationale
for defending life and because they had done their
grassroots organizational homework. Along with an
increasing number of Roman Catholics, the religious
Rightists had woven themselves "into the fabric of
Republican politics."[8]

In another domain of public morality, that of homosexual rights, the New Christian Right continued its
offensive started in the early 1980s. Its leaders
saw the demands by gays and lesbians for protective
civil rights measures as part of the humanist conspiracy,
attempting to convince the general public that such
people were fully immoral. Calling on supporters
to love the sinner but hate the sin, religious Rightist
groups conducted extended, often highly emotional
campaigns to convince their supporters the battlelines
must be drawn now or the battle would be lost. Already
the foes had made significant inroads; The _Liberty Re-
port_ detected an alarming increase in legislative
victories for gays seeking protection from "various
forms of discrimination". Some 50 cities, the state
of Wisconsin and some 12 counties by mid-1986 had
enacted such laws.[9] Christian Voice uncovered what
it named "the homosexuals' secret agenda" which, it
claimed, attempted to repeal every kind of law now
on the books restricting homosexual activity; sodomy
laws, prostitution laws, homosexual marriage,
anti-sex education laws, public health controls over
AIDS carriers and discrimination over housing, public
accommodations, employment and public services.[10]

Closely allied to that offensive was the religious
Right battle against the carriers of AIDS. Its rapid
spread in the mid 1980s had created enormous fear and
confusion among the general populace as well as those
affected. Known as a disease rampant among homosexuals, although heterosexuals were afflicted also,
AIDS was considered by the NCR as God's punishment
against homosexuals for their sinful and unrepentant
behavior. Swaggart explained that it was not a plague
sent by God but a "result of the evil, wicked, profli-
gate, life-style of the homosexual community." God
did not create AIDS, "the gays did that."[11] To Professor Edward Dobson God was punishing the sin of
homosexuality, as he had done at Sodom and Gomorrah
and Lot's family; AIDS is "one of the terrible consequences of a chosen lifestyle." "We are obliged
to warn people of the consequences of a sinful
lifestyle."[12]

                              III

      A third arena for increased religious Rightist in-
volvement revolved around the dilemmas of pornography.
Here the leadership was taken by the Rev. Donald
Wildmon, executive director of the National Federation
for Decency, and a veteran NCR leader from earlier
attempts at boycotting objectionable television fare.
Drawing on full support from the celebrity preachers
and from the office of the United States Attorney
General, Edwin Meese, Wildmon in the mid 1980s started
several carefully planned, broadly supported customer
boycotts of convenience stores around the country which
had carried publications the Federation found objectionable. Wildmon identified the crusade with a recent
directive from the Attorney General's office sent to
drugstores and convenience stores informing them they

had been identified as being involved in "the sale
or distribution of pornography" and would be listed
in an upcoming Attorney General's report which would
condemn such publications.[13] After several widely
publicized days of picketing in mid-June, 1986, Wildmon claimed he and his followers had reduced the
number of retail outlets selling magazines such as
Penthouse and Playboy by some 20,000. The head of
Penthouse agreed that some 15,000 outlets had been
lost. On occasion, the NCR found its position being
endorsed by a group usually identified as a part of
the opposition, activist feminists such as Jane Fonda
who also had taken uncompromising stands against pornography in print, on film, or on telephone call-ins.[14]

    In Maine, New Christian Rightists organized as
"The Christian Civic League of Maine" and attempted
in June, 1986, to have written into law a strict definition of pornography that would outlaw what they found
objectionable in its commercial forms. Using the argument that pornogrpahy led directly and documentably
to sexual violence against women, the League quickly
encountered a very stiff counterattack by libertarians;
civil libertarians, some feminist activists
claimed the proposal was censorship by "a small
minority of people...to apply their definitions to
all of us." Both Republicans and Democrats denounced
the proposal. The voters did the same by a 71 to 29
percent margin.[15]

                            IV

    In similar fashion, the religious Right, again
led by Wildmon, launched several programs and boycotts
to rid broadcast and cable television of what it
found to be objectionable sex and violence. As with
pornography, they were joined by another of their
secular humanist enemies, this the National Council

of Churches which was actively organizing supporters
to eliminate the objectionable programming.[16]
Choosing to work apart from the NCC, Wildmon's Federation and Christian Voice specifically targeted several
programs as being objectionable because of the physical violence and explicit sexual behavior: "Falcon
Crest", "Mafia Princess", "Knots Landing", "Scarecrow
and Mrs. King", "Hometown", "St. Elsewhere" and
"Golden Girls".   Christian Voice claimed the chair
of the Federal Communications Commission had given
"the green light to total nudity, homosexuality,
explicit sex and four-letter words on prime TV."
Both Wildmon and Tim LaHaye brought out sharply worded
analyses and calls for action in their books, respective-
ly, The Home Invaders and The Hidden Censors.[17] Their
goal was to force advertisers and production companies
to "change the moral content of programs to include
an accurate portrayal of the Judeo-Christian moral
value system...." Boycotts for non-cooperating advertisers were promised.[18]

                              V

    Throughout the mid 1980s several smaller special
interest groups emerged within New Christian Right
circles. They identified fully with religious Right
teachings, but chose to do battle in their own manner.
This portion of Chapter 12 makes no claims to be
exhaustive in summarizing all of them, but it attempts
to include enough material to illustrate the important
trends.

    The Christian Inquirer of Niagara Falls, New York,
well represents the fortunes of the less highly
funded enterprises. Concentrating largely on print
media, especially its monthly newspaper, the Inquirer
attempted to bring appropriate information, news and

editorial comment as well as compatible advertising
to its readers. Most of its issues contained 32
pages, centering as its masthead stated on being
"A National Voice for Family, Freedom and Our
Christian Heritage." Having started publication in
1968, it found enough support in the 1980s to expand
rapidly as its editor, the Rev. Ron Marr, identified
his ministry with that of other NCR activities. The
newspaper, far more than the other print media journals,
presented considerable information about related topics;
foreign policy, rock and roll music, news about Israel,
Russia, drugs, scriptural prophecy were but a few of
the dozens of subjects discussed, much like the television programs of Bakker and Robertson.[19]

By contrast, however to those national celebrity
preachers, Marr chose to keep alive the older, conspiratorial interpretation that the world's economy
and American politics were dominated not only by the
secular humanists but by the Trilateralists, the
Bilderburgers, members of the Council of Foreign
Relations "all of whom work with the Communists to
destroy our freedom." Marr sharply criticized Falwell
for supporting Vice President George Bush for the
1988 Presidency since Bush himself was a "Trilatera-
list".[20]

Such claims, not a part of standard NCR thinking,
refer to the belief made popular in the 1950s and 1960s
that an intellectual, secret cabal of bankers, journalists, politicians, Ivy League intellectuals, and
other power brokers who had once met in the Bilderburg
Hotel in the Netherlands constituted an underground
conspiracy controlling the world's supply of money
and hence the political power of the western nations
for their own advantage. "Trilateralists" and "CFRer"s

were more sinister. Even though their leaders claimed
their organizations were no more than forums for academic,
business, government and media leaders to pursue
opportunities for international cooperation, conspiracy
aficionados found both were dominated by one-worlder,
procommunists. Marr avoided lengthy discussion of that
familiar conspiracy interpretation, concentrating rather
on warning readers of the pernicious effects of the proposed call for a constitutional convention to revise the
Constitution of 1787.[21]

VI

In a related but distinctly separate arena for battle,
the American Coalition for Traditional Values moved
quickly in 1985 to expand their program. Largely the
work of Tim LaHaye, it had built during the 1984 campaign
a sophisticated list of supporters, including some 300
ministers, for the new campaigns of 1985. The headquarters
were moved from LaHaye's home town of San Diego to
Washington, D.C., with plans for a political lobby to
campaign for the social agenda. Recognizing that its program closely paralleled that of Christian Voice, the
latter's executive director, Colonel V. Doner who had
served on the ACTV director's board announced, "Washington is big enough for both groups". The CV legislative director severed his former affiliations with
ACTV.[22]

LaHaye moved quickly to establish his legitimacy
as a leader in the NCR. To the executive committee of
ACTV he placed Ronald S. Godwin of Moral Majority,
Colonel V. Doner of Christian Voice, and Jimmy
Swaggart. On the Executive Board he placed Jim
Bakker, Bill Bright, Jerry Falwell, Rex Humbard,
D. James Kennedy, James Robison, Cecil Todd, Jack
Van Impe and Don Wildmon, among others. He further

announced the existence of a network of leaders in
the 50 states to bring cohesion and energy to the
cause.[23]

LaHaye found if not a friendly at least a carefully attentive audience when on "The Phil Donahue
Show" in 1985 he debated a highly controversial ACTV
proposal with Representative Patricia Schroeder (D.--
Colo.), an exchange worth probing in detail for what
it revealed about the ACTV agenda. Donahue asked
him, "Did you say that 25 percent of Reagan appointments should be born again Christians? Have I got
that right?" LaHaye replied, "I said that 25 percent
of the people in the United States are Christians and
they ought to have equal representation in government". By Christians LaHaye meant "born again"
Christians, stating the Gallup Polls showed that of
all Christians in America, 25 percent were born again.

Then LaHaye made his point. "What we're concerned about is the born again Christian or fundamental
Christians have for decades taken a stand-off position
of government service and politics, saying we should
never get involved, and so we have self-imposed limita-
tions. As a Christian leader what I'm trying to do is
change that attitude and say, hey, we're American
citizens, we pay taxes, we have qualified people, they
should run for public office and they should be appointed to public office, and, personally, I think we should
work over the next twenty-five years to a point where
an equal number of our percentage in the population
have equal service."

Schroeder suggested that such would be unconstitutional since the Constitution, Article VI forbade any
religious test for persons working in government.
After something close to an hour's wrangling over

definitions and side issues, LaHaye concluded that since
President Reagan had received such a landslide mandate
in his re-election, he deserved to be free of liberals
who where impeding his desire to get the "kind of people he needs" to govern effectively.[24]

Since moving to Washington, LaHaye and ACTV have
concentrated largely on sponsoring large scale conferences to inspire and train volunteer workers for
upcoming political campaigns. On occasion, lobbying
for specific legislation is done, such as the Reagan
proposal for funding the Nicaraguan contras, but
primarily the ACTV mission is educational. In October,
1985, ACTV put on a large conference headed by a speaker's
list of who's who on the religious Right: Robertson,
Kennedy, LaHaye, and Falwell. Lawmakers such as Senators
Jesse Helms and William Armstrong and House members
Newt Gingrich, Vin Weber, and Jack Kemp also participated. All told, some 300 citizens appeared, listening to exhortations, diagnoses of upcoming issue
battles including the social agenda, and participat-
ing in workshops on how to get their people elected.
Specific programs were held for media, for
operating a campaign, raising funds, utilization of
the news media and coordinating volunteers from local
churches. Some weeks later, ACTV announced plans to
raise $3 million for support of some one hundred
Congressional office seekers supportive of its cause.[25]

Bev LaHaye, meanwhile, continued to expand the resources and outreach of the program she directs, Concerned Women for America(CWA). Claiming a membership
of some 500,000, her group in the estimate of _Time_
Religion editor Richard N. Ostling "has replaced the
50,000 member Eagle Forum, run by Illinois Roman Catholic Phyllis Schlafly, at the top of the counterfeminist

women's movement".[26] Created by design to counter
the agenda and activities of NOW (National Organization of Women), its leader, Bev LaHaye has dedicated
the program to strengthen "traditional values" which
include men as head of households, exempting women
from the draft into military service, opposition to
a nuclear freeze and to unisex insurance, opposition
to the ERA, and to gay rights legislation. Having
first been drawn into activist NCR campaigning with
her husband by conducting "Family Life Seminars" around
the nation, and co-hosting with Tim a weekly television
program, Bev in the early 1980s decided to challenge
the NOW feminists when they claimed to speak for
American women. She found enthusiastic support for
her dedication to the NCR social agenda and call for
evangelical women to involve themselves directly
in elective politics.

     Bev LaHaye accepted the internal conspiracy inter-
pretation. America's woe focuses around the "secular
humanist feminists" who were "small in number, but
they have gotten into the key positions--in the government, in education, in those organizations that take
philosophies and mold them into policies regarding
our children and government. We fell asleep and
they took advantage. Now that we are awake again we
have the chance to influence the legislators with
our philosophy and to stay on guard to prevent it
from slipping again."[27] Her specific program included
voter registration, education on the issues, and support
for the social agenda.

     The largest expression of CWA strength and out-
reach occurred in September, 1985. Some 2,200 supporters
met in Washington, D.C. for the annual (this the second)
convention. There they studied the issues of the social

agenda and participated in workshops on fundamentalism,
humanism, pornography, national defense, running for
public office, evolution, the flaws of feminism, fundraising, and public schools. Featured speakers included Norma Gabler, Tim LaHaye, Paul Weyrich and
Congresspersons Kemp and Gingrich. Plans for an expanded convention during the campaign months of 1986
included specific advice on building local CWA chapters,
lobbying, the impact of television, comparable worth,
AIDS, and "how to affect Election Day." CWA also
sponsored religional conferences working often with
other Rightist groups such as The Berean League and
the Rutherford Institute.[28]

VII

The New Christian Right indictment of secular America was specific enough to lead to the creation of major
activist groups such as we have already considered.
It was also general enough to attract a variety of
financially and numerically smaller dedicated interest
groups working outside the boundaries of the largest
organizations. In Milwaukee the National Civil Liberties Legal Foundation appeared in the mid 1980s as
a deliberate response to the programs of the American
Civil Liberties Union. Largely the work of David P.
and Sharan A. Hersh, it identifies with those litigants
searching for legal advice on issues of church and
state and religious freedom. Its newsletter carried
information about its legal services and about struggles
over religious freedom across the country. Its editors endorsed the full social agenda of the religious
Right, using the newsletter's columns to inform readers
about violations of religious freedom by the secular
humanists.[29]

From Stafford, Virginia, would appear occasional
publications and fundraising appeals from the Christian
Family Renewal, headed by Dr. Murray Norris. An old
veteran on the fundamentalist/social agenda trail,
Norris in the mid 1980s concentrated on battling
the homosexuals.[30] Much the same agenda is sponsored
by the Christian Chamber of Commerce, Inc. of Hockley,
Texas.[31]

Mormons, especially in Utah, have been introduced
to the New Christian Right through organizations such
as the Freemen Institute and its President, W. Cleon
Skousan, longtime fundamentalist of the far right.
Largely a printing and educational enterprise, it endorses in terms with which Mormons are familiar the
social agenda and the diagnosis of humanism.[32] From
Manassas, Virginia, the attorney and author, John Whitehead, presides over the newly created Rutherford
Institute. His several books have become basic
reference texts for the religious Right on the impact
of secular humanism. Whitehead speaks frequently
at NCR rallies and acts as a legal advisor to those
seeking his professional services.[33] Other groups,
once prominent in the news media such as "The Roundtable" headed by Ed McAteer, attract attention by
sponsoring prayer breakfasts such as that for the
State of Israel. In February, 1986, the Roundtable
brought to its annual breakfast such celebrities
as Falwell, Swaggart, and Robertson along with lawmakers Jack Kemp and Senator Albert Gore(D.--Tenn.)
and Jeanne J. Kirkpatrick, onetime U.S. Ambassador
to the United Nations. Some 1,250 persons attended.
However, since McAteer's unsuccessful attempt to
be elected U.S. Senator in 1984 representing Tennessee,
the Roundtable carries little clout in the late 1980s
in religious Right circles.[34]

At times, the news media and other watchers of
the New Christian Right attempt to identify that
movement with other groups identified as "rightist".
Such association, however, fails to exist. Those
militarist, often racist vigilante groups which
flourish especially in the frostbelt, and the Pacific
Northwest, stand totally apart from those considered
in this work. To be specific, the news media give
considerable (and justifiable) attention to groups
such as the neo-Nazis, Aryan Nations, National
Socialist Vanguard, The Order, Posse Comitatus,
and the like. These all exist in their own separate
realms.[35]

XII. Notes

1. Christian Voice newletter, "Revive America",
    1985, II:1, p.8; C.V., Colonel V. Doner,
    "Why Christians Must Be Involved", n.d.

2. Letter entitled "ACLU", 1985, p.1; another
    CV publication; "Private White House Poll",
    March 8, 1985; letter from CV, January 30,
    1985; Ibid., letter, "Emergency Reply For",
    1985.

3. Fundraising letter, untitled; it starts "Your
    recent generous...."; fundraising letter,
    September 30, 1985; ibid., August 1, 1985.

4. News letter, February 19, 1986, p.1; news
    story, Christianity Today, April 18, 1986,
    p.44; CNN Television "Crossfire", April 8,
    1986, Gary Jarmin and Anthony Podesta.

5. Letter from Robert Grant "Christian Voice",
    1986.

6. Walter Capps, "A Note on the Rise of the New
    Religious Right", Dialog, Fall, 1985, p.250;
    Ellen Goodman column, Minneapolis Star and
    Tribune, May 5, 1986, p.12A.

7. Gallup Poll, Minneapolis Star and Tribune,
    February 20, 1986, p.18D; Brenda D. Hofman,
    "Political Theology: The Role of Organized
    Religion in the Anti-Abortion Movement",
    Journal of Church and State, Spring, 1986,
    28:2, pp.240-47; Liberty Report, May, 1986,
    pp.16 ff.; The Fundamentalist Journal,
    January, 1986, pp.25-31; Christian Voice,
    "Overnight Pack", January, 16, 1986.

8. New York Times, June 19, 1986, p.11.

9. Liberty Report, May, 1986, pp.26,29.

10. Old-Time Gospel Hour, March 16, 1986; Christian
    Voice, letter from Robert Grant, October 21,
    1985.

11. New York Times, January 21, 1986, p.12;
    opposition to AIDS and sex education from
    Eagle Forum is discussed in New York Times,
    January 9, 1986, p.15; news item, Sojourners,

February, 1986,p.6; Jimmy Swaggart in The
Evangelist, April, 1986, p.55; see also
Joseph Sobran, "The Politics of AIDS",
National Review, May 23, 1986, pp.22 ff.

12. Dobson in The Fundamentalist Journal, October,
    1985, p.14.

13. News story, Minneapolis Star and Tribune, June
    5, 1986, p.32A; New York Times, June 16, 1986,
    p.1; ibid., April 15, 1986, p.12.

14. See all of The Evangelist, Liberty Report, Moral
    Majority Report, and Christian Inquirer, for
    details, issues thorugh 1985 and through June,
    1986; Time, March 10, 1986, p.67; ibid., April
    21, 1986, p.62; Washington Post National
    Weekly Edition, March 24, 1986, p.37; U.S.
    News and World Report, March 10, 1986, p.8;
    Time, June 23, 1986, p.36; ibid., July 21, 1986,
    p.18.

15. News story, Minneapolis Star and Tribune, June
    6, 1986, p.12A; ibid., June 11, 1986, p.14A.

16. The NCC involvement is reported in Christian
    Science Monitor, September 25, 1985, p.7;
    news item, Lutheran Standard, October 18,
    1985, p.33.

17. Moral Majority Report, September, 1984, p.9;
    CV flyer, "Inform Yourself", n.d.; National
    Federation for Decency, "Seven Examples" bro-
    chure; letter from Robert Grant, May 1, 1986;
    Moody Monthly, January, 1986, p.6.

18. A perceptive critique of NCR criticism is
    Guy Sorman, The Conservative Revolution in
    America(Chicago, Regnery Books,1985), pp.
    63-66.

19. See all issues of Christian Inquirer, 1984-86;
    c/o 2002 Main St., Niagra Falls, N.Y. 14305; see
    fundraiser letter from C.I., December, 1985
    starting with "Save Up To...", C.I., "Special
    Bulletin, March, 1985, p.2.

20. George Johnson, Architects of Fear: Conspiracy
    Theories and Paranoia in American Politics (Los
    Angeles, Jeremy P. Tarcher, Inc., 1983); see
    his index for these three; Schlafly in 1964

endorsed the Bilderberger thesis; Lyndon
LaRouche's endorsements are here, pp.22,24,
187-210; Pat Robertson has condemned the
Trilateralists and CFR leaders, ibid., pp.
166-67.

21. C.I., letter of 1985, "God gave me..." and
     pamphlet, "Do We Want Revival?", n.d.

22. Southern Baptist Convention publication,
     Light, January, 1986, p.12; news item,
     Christianity Today, December 14, 1985, p.57.

23. See brochures, "The ACTV Network", 1985, "Has
     the Church Been Deceived"?; and "Who We Are
     And What We Stand for"', see especially
     "Should Ministers Be Involved in Politics?".

24. Multimedia Entertainment, Inc., (P.O. Box
     2111, Cincinnati, Ohio), Donahue Transcript
     number 09065, passim; news story, Time,
     September 2, 1985, p.51.

25. SBC, Light, p.12; ACTV brochure, 1985, "Con-
     ference on How to Win an Election"; Fund-
     raising letter, ibid.; news story, Christian
     Century, December 18, 1985, p. 1164; news
     story, U.S.News and World Report, November
     4, 1985, p.70; news story, Christian Herald,
     December, 1985, p.7, discusses LaHaye's
     support for the Botha government in South
     Africa; see also news item, Inside the
     American Religious Scene, June 20, 1986,
     I:2, p.2.

26. Time, September 2, 1985, p.57; The National
     Education Association estimates 540,000 mem-
     bers, 35,000 of whom are men; see the 1986
     flyer of CWA on NOW.

27. Reprint from CWA for an interview in The
     Fundamentalist Journal, November, 1985.

28. Ibid.,; and NEA, Human and Civil Rights, News-
     letter, December, 1985, pp.10-11; CWA bro-
     chure, "Lake Superior Citizenship Rally",
     October, 1985; see its monthly magazine,
     Concerned Women for America, July, 1986,
     8:7, passim; The Fundamentalist Journal,
     December, 1985, pp.67-69; Christian
     Inquirer, March, 1985, p.23.

29. "The Guardian", National Civil Liberties Legal
     Foundation, Fall, 1984, I;4.

30. See 1985 flyer, "Confidential" from Christian
     Family Review; background is in Erling Jorstad,
     Evangelicals in the White House (New York,
     The Edwin Mellen Press, 1981), pp.111-13.

31. Christian Chamber of Commerce, P.O. Box 117,
     Hockley, Texas, 77447.

32. Anson Shupe and John Heinerman, "Mormonism and
     the New Christian Right": An Emerging Coalition?",
     Review of Religious Research, December, 1985,
     27:2, pp.146-49.

33. "CBS Evening News", May 19, 1986; Liberty
     Report, March, 1986, p.20; The Fundamentalist
     Journal, May, 1986, p.67; Moral Majority
     Report, November, 1985, p.23; Richard V. Pierard,
     "Religion and the New Right in the 1980s",
     James E. Wood, Jr., ed., Religion and the State:
     Essays in Honor of Leo Pfeffer(Waco, Baylor
     University Press, 1985),pp.407-08.

34. Brochures from The Roundtable, P.O. Box 11467,
     Memphis, Tennessee 38111; see the stories in
     Catalyst: A Forum of Jewish and Christian
     Thought, 1985: I;1.

35. See the excellent series by Don Duncan, in
     the Seattle Times, April 20-24, 1986, and the
     bibliography by Laird Wilcox, "Guide to the
     American Right", 1985 rev. ed.

The War Over the Constitution

The landslide victory of President Reagan in Campaign '84 strongly reinforced in Oval Office's eyes the voters' mandate to carry out the social mandate supported by the religious Right. The latter now, according to Martin E. Marty, "had come from apparently nowhere to hold the most visible and assertive political position in American religion."[1] It was at the peak of its political influence at the nation's highest level. Yet by the end of 1986 the agenda remained unfulfilled; abortions were still legal, voluntary school prayer was still prohibited, tuition tax vouchers were not yet approved, and the gay rights movement continued to attract new strength. Despite Reagan's clout, two agencies of the federal government--the Supreme Court and the United States Senate--effectively, if not deliberately, were keeping the agenda in check. This chapter surveys the role of the New Christian Right in its attempt to overcome those institutions in its war to control the Constitution.

The Reagan administration, as discussed above, endorsed two fullscale offensives by the Right, one in 1982 and one in 1984 to adopt a constitutional amendment approving of voluntary school prayer. Now, in 1985 the power seemingly stood overwhelmingly on their side, with a 53-47 margin for the Republicans in the Senate, and with public opinion polls showing the voters favoring some such amendment by a 60 percent for, 31 percent opposed, 8 percent no opinion.[2] In early September Undersecretary of Education Gary Bauer assumed command of the battle for the amendment. He blamed American public schools for much of the perceived decay in the nation's morals and for failing to inculcate sound values in

the curriculum. Bauer connected, in a speech before the
National Consultation on Pornography, the rise in public obscenity to the ban on school prayer, arguing
that to have laws approving pornography but prohibit-
ing school prayer was inconsistent and immoral. Bauer
rejected the argument that the schools strive for a
"value free education", and endorsed Secretary of Education William C. Bennett's call for restoring the three
"C's" of education--character, content, and choice",
the last being a code word for voluntary oral prayer
in public schools.[3]

Such a rationale contributed directly to a new
amendment proposal, this by Senator Jesse Helms. Moving away from the two earlier measures, Helms would
remove the school prayer question from federal court
jurisdiction, turning it over to local and state governments who could decide whether to allow oral prayer.
The television preachers from the New Christian Right
opened a full if brief offensive for its support.
After a very brief debate in the Senate, the amendment
was turned down 62-38 with opponents coming from both
parties and from both conservative and liberal Senators (including Barry Goldwater and Orrin Hatch).[4]

The Republicans decided to make one more attempt,
looking in a rewording of the amendment for the key
which would unlock the two-thirds support required for
passage. In the Spring of 1986 Hatch proposed this
measure

> Nothing in this Constitution shall be construed
> to prohibit individual or group silent prayer
> or reflection in public schools. Neither the
> United States nor any state shall require
> any person to participate in such prayer or
> reflection, nor shall they encourage any parti-
> cular form of silent prayer or reflection.

Again, as with the Helms proposal, this measure
received faint support from the Oval Office; no celebrated, ceremonial armtwisting from President Reagan
was visible. Further, by now the religious groups
opposed to any such amendment were well organized
and experienced enough to mount their counteroffen-
sive quickly and effectively. Within days after
the proposal, vigorous opposition came from the
American Baptists, the Presbyterian Church, the Epis-
cocal Church, the Synagogue Council of America and
the Church of the Brethren, among others. They
interpreted the proposal to mean the government
was attempting to promote religion, and to allowing a local school board or teacher to decide what
proper form of worship for pupils might be. It would
require setting aside school time for group worship,
requiring students to be quiet during the exercise,
and it could trivialize the convictions of those
who think prayer should be audible and spontaneous.
Finally, it would endorse one form of prayer as being more acceptable to some faiths than others.
Within a few days, Senate leaders knew they lacked
enough votes for passage; the measure was turned
down.[5]

II

The post Campaign '84 years found significant
cooperation and agreement among most religious and
civil libertarian groups over another contest in
the battle of religion in the public schools,
that of "equal access"(see ch.4). Clearly some
such measure attracted considerable support beyond
that of the New Christian Right, thus, because such
compromise was so rare during the war over the constitution, we examine in some detail the judicial

background and the unfolding of what became Bender
v. Williamsport.[6]

In Williamsport, Pennsylvania, in 1981 Lisa Bender
and some friends asked permission from school officials
to meet in a classroom where they could read the Bible
and pray. Their meetings would be held on Tuesday and
Thursday mornings from 7:57 to 8:27 during a regular
student activity hour, a time when several other student groups met. Some 45 of the 2,500 students at
that school, in 1981, attended the first meeting; the
group named itself "Petros"("The Rock"). School officials told the group the school attorney had informed
them that activities such as those of Petros violated
the no establishment clause. The program was closed.[7]

The students and their parents in June, 1982, sued
the school district, claiming their rights to free
speech had been violated. A Federal judge upheld
their claim and Petros resumed meeting; the local
school board voted 8-1 not to oppose the ruling. One
year later, however, the one dissenter on the board
took the case to the U.S. Court of Appeals. In July,
in a 2-1, decision that Court ruled to uphold the
ban, arguing that prayer in public schools segregates
students along religious lines. Then in August,
1984, Congress passed the Equal Access Act. The
Williamsport case went before the Supreme Court
late in 1985 where, observers noted, the nine justices "showed a lively interest in arguments for and
against Bible club meetings in public high schools."
In March, 1986, that Court made its ruling, a
complicated decision, which in effect upheld the
first court which had ruled on the case and which
endorsed the student's right to meet. The Court
ruled the one dissenting local schoolboard member

lacked sufficient legal standing to file his appeal;
as an individual he lacked a sufficient stake in
the outcome of the lawsuit to support his appeal to
a higher court. Justice John Paul Stevens wrote for
the majority, "an individual board member cannot in-
voke the board's interest in the case to confer
standing upon himself". Since that member, Michael
Bender, "had no standing to appeal the original pro-
meeting judgment of the district court, that ruling
prevailed even though it now offers no national pre-
cedent."[8] In effect, the Court gave tacit approval
to the Equal Access Act. Hence, the earlier claims
by the New Christian Right that it was dominated by
the secular humanists eager to expunge all religious
influences from American public life found no
support in fact in Bender v.Williamsport.

III

     In post Campaign '84, the new religious Right en-
dorsed one more legislative effort to keep at least
a token expression of religion alive in the public
schools, this the "moment of silence" proposal. By
late 1984 some 23 states had enacted laws allowing
for a fixed time during the school day for silent
reflection, which, of course, could not exclude
the possibility of prayer. The Supreme Court agreed
in 1984 to decide whether this violated the no
establishment clause. The specific case concerned
a law in Alabama which mandated such a moment. The
full spectrum of New Christian Right leadership--
Falwell, Swaggart, Tim LaLaye, Cal Thomas, Robertson and others--called on the Supreme Court to uphold such legislation as evidence that religion
had not become anathema in the public schools, and
as a recognition of the importance of religion in
American public life.

In June, 1985, the Court ruled 6-3 against the Alabama legislation, calling it unconstitutional because
it was designated not for reflection or meditation but
for prayer. That being its sole purpose, the Court
argued, it would foster religious activity in the classroom. Its Alabama sponsors had stated the legislation
had been an "effort to return voluntary prayer" to
the classrooms, which meant the State of Alabama was
endorsing prayer activities. Such endorsement was
clearly a "favored practice" by that government
and hence it violated the constitutional obligation
of that government to remain neutral.[9]

While many religious and civil liberty groups
such as the Americans United for Separation of Church
and State and the Lutheran Council in the U.S.A.
strongly endorsed the decision, the New Christian
Right found it reprehensible. LaHaye stated that
it created a "breakdown in values when we need
recognition of God most." Senator Helms concluded
the ruling was "unwise and unjust", "a slap in the
face of the vast majority of Americans who favor
school prayer". Robert Grant of Christian Voice
called the ruling "stupid, sad and shameful", and
Cal Thomas of Moral Majority concluded that "the
philosophy in our public schools and many other institutions today is that a dose of God is more
hazardous to your health than a dose of herpes or
drugs." Falwell stated, "this is one of the most
severe blows to religious freedom we have sustained
in the history of our nation. In effect, American
public school students shall have no more rights
than students in the Soviet Union, an officially
atheistic state."[10]

IV

At the center of the warfare stood the unresolved
issue, made starkly clear by the end of 1986, that of
the interpretation of the Constitution itself by federal
judges. Specifically, the issue revolved around the
debate over discerning the motives and the convictions
of the Founding Fathers, the "Framers" of that document. The New Christian Right insisted, in the strongest
possible terms, that the secular humanists were wrong
in insisting that the Framers intended a total wall
of separation be maintained between church and state;
the Framers intended no such thing.[11]

The debate, long smoldering in legal, religious
and legislative circles broke out again in post
Campaign '84 days, so much so as to attract the best
intellectual efforts of at least two of the nation's
leading constitutional authorities, Circuit Judge,
U.S. Court of Appeals, District of Columbia, Robert
H. Bork (formerly of the Yale University School of
Law), and Laurence H. Tribe, a member of the Harvard
University School of Law. Specifically, the focus
of the debate centered on (1) could we in the 1980s
determine accurately what the original intent of
the Founding Fathers was towards the permanent,
binding features which they wrote into the Constitution of 1787, and (2) even if we could, should those
interpretations be totally binding on the government
officials, here the federal justices, as they carry
out their constitutional oaths of office?[12]

Justice Bork spoke for the conservatives.[13] He
argued that the justices who today follow what he
called a philosophy of "non-originalism", "according
to which judges should create individualistic rights
that supercede democratic decisions" were in error.

If such justices decided what the law should be, and
in so doing ignored what "the people operating through
the institutions of democracy" convinced to be the
law, then such justices were wrong. Acknowledging
that the debate over "non-originalism" was "just now
receiving public attention", an obvious reference to
the conservative argument, Bork pointed out that many
attorneys and judges "think that judicial power" is
"far greater than anything the Framers intended, and
greater than anything hitherto practiced in the
United States, is desirable and legitimate."

"What is at the heart of the issue", Bork wrote,
is that the non-originalists believe the courts "are
not supposed to follow popular views of the Constitution, but...their own moral, social, and philosophi-
cal predilections in place of the Constitution."
That means, they have usurped authority that properly
belongs to the people and their elected representatives. To Bork, the Constitution is law, "controlling
judges every bit as much as it controls legislators,
executives, bureaucrats, and citizens." "Interpreting the Constitution's general language according
to our best understanding of the original intent of
the Framers is the only way in which the Constitution
can be law in the sense just discussed. No other
method of constitutional adjudication can accomplish
that." To Bork that meant using the method of "original intent" as the only means of applying the Constitution to current litigation.[14]

Why all this is relevant to the New Christian
Right was pointed out explicitly by Professor
Lawrence Tribe, as he rebutted Bork while discussing the 'moment of silence' decision. Tribe focused
on what the Supreme Court justices asked in that

case: Should there be governmental endorsement
of school prayer? He stated

> As Justice Sandra Day O'Conner recognized in
> joining the Supreme Court's recent invalida-
> tion of Alabama's 'moment of silence' statute
> on the ground that its manifest aim was to
> endorse and encourage prayer in the public
> schools, the explication of constitutional
> intent and purpose on issues such as these
> cannot stop with inquiries into what the
> Framers---in whose world free public educa-
> tion was virtually non-existent--had to say,
> or would have said if asked, about the
> challenged practice. Their world was not
> one in which the issue could have been
> framed so as to have the significance
> it properly has today.

Tribe went on to argue that the Framers themselves
never claimed their remarks made at the writing of
the Constitution in 1787 should be "the oracular
guide in expounding the Constitution". The world,
the United States, society itself has changed so
drastically since those days that original intent
simply can no longer be accurately determined
nor bear on today's society.

Tribe emphasized the fact that a judge's interpretation of the Constitution could not help but
be influenced and informed by that justice's life
experiences, his economic and political under-
standings, and "by his sense...of where justice
lies in respect of the great issues of his time."
Tribe stated it bluntly

> The major difference between those who in-
> sist that they are passively discerning and

enforcing the specific intentions of the
Framers, and those who concede that they
are of necessity doing something more, is
likely to come down to this: The originalists
seek to deny their own responsibility for
the choices they are making--and imposing
upon the rest of us--whereas their opponents,
for better or worse, accept such responsibility
as inescapably theirs. Neither side has a
monopoly on candor, insight, or wisdom.[15]

In this writer's estimate, the New Christian Right
endorsed the originalist interpretation because it
purportedly supports their idea that at one time
Americans supported a much greater degree of cooperation between church and state, the "accommodationist"
position. Theirs is a perspective shaped by nostalgia, a conviction that at one time in the history of
the United States, the balance between church and
state, between religion and politics was clear and
compelling; the "American way" prevailed. This interpretation encounters considerable difficulty, however,
in proving that such was the outlook of such Framers
as Madison and Jefferson, neither of whom reflected
anything remotely close to a fundamentalist or
evangelicalist worldview. Yet the NCR faith in
the good intentions of such ancestors compels them
to support the originalist position.

The non-originalists, as Tribe suggests, run the
risk of reading the convictions of each new generation of justices into the words of the Framers. But
they acknowledge, as constitutional historians have
pointed out, that the intentions of those Framers
lack compelling clarity and that they insisted their
words should never be considered as binding in all
situations at all times for the future.[16]

The question, finally, by the end of 1986,
embraced disputes over both legal philosophy and
over practical politics. The New Christian Right
was sophisticated enough by that date to understand
their originalist position could prevail when enough
judges were appointed to their respective benches
by leaders, in this case the President of the
United States, supporting their position. Hence,
they became involved in the full elective process;
registering and educating citizens, getting them
to the polls, lobbying the elected officials for
support and trusting that eventually their candidates for federal judgeships would reflect their
demonstrated strength at the polls. Judges
should be appointed to the bench on the basis
of their demonstrated political ideology. As
frustrating and as cumbersome as that system was
in practice, it constituted in their judgment
the American way.

XIII. Notes

1.   Marty, "Transpositions: American Religion in the
     1980s", Wade Clark Roof, Ed., Religion in
     America Today; The Annuals of the American
     Academy of Political and Social Science, vol.
     480, Beverley Hills, Sage Publications, 1985),
     p.14.

2.   News story, Minneapolis Star and Tribune, January
     3, 1985, p.9A; see the polls in Richard John Neu-
     haus, ed., Unsecular America (Grand Rapids, Wm.
     B.Eerdmans Publishing Co., 1986), pp.149-51.

3.   News story, Journal of Church and State, Winter,
     1986, 28:1, pp.155-56; Bennett's ideas are
     summarized in Washington Post Weekly National
     Edition, September 16, 1985, p.28.

4.   Ibid.; news story, Baptist Joint Committee, Report
     from the Capital, October, 1985, p.8; Minneapolis
     Star and Tribune, September 11, 1985, p.3A.

5.   Minneapolis Star and Tribune, March 29, 1986,
     p.18A; news story, Journal of Church and State,
     Winter, 1986, 28:1, p.156.

6.   A very helpful study is Robert F. Drinan, "Will
     the Supreme Court Permit Prayer Groups in
     Public High Schools?", America, January 11,
     1986, pp.8-10; news story, Christianity
     Today, January 19, 1985, pp.59-60.

7.   News story, Christianity Today, November 22,
     1985, p.56.

8.   New York Times, March 28, 1986, pp.1,13; news
     item, Christianity Today, April 16, 1986, pp.
     45-46; news story, Journal of Church and State,
     Spring, 1986, 28:2, pp.363-64; editorial,
     Baptist Joint Committee, Report, June, 1986,
     p.11; news item, The Fundamentalist Journal,
     June, 1986, p.64.

9.   Newsweek, December 17, 1984, p.57; news item,
     Journal of Church and State, Spring, 1985; 27:2;
     pp.365-66; ibid., Summer, 1985, 27:3, pp.563-64;
     A. James Reichley, Religion in American Public
     Life (Washington, D.C., The Brookings Institu-
     tion, 1985), p.164.

10. Ibid., U.S.News and World Report, June 17, 1985,
     p.9; The Fundamentalist Journal, July/August,
     1985, p.10; news story, Christianity Today,
     August 9, 1985; pp.45-45; ibid., April 19,
     1985,pp.38-42; Lutheran Standard, November
     1, 1985, p.15; Lutheran Council in the U.S.A.,
     Focus on Government Affairs, June, 1985, p.4;
     New York Times, July 10, 1985, p.12.

11. A useful update is Reichley, Religion in
     American Public Life, ch.3.

12. See also a full discussion by Tribe in his
     God Save This Honorable Court (New York,
     Random House, 1985).

13. This section is based on the articles by
     Bork and Tribe in Humanities, February, 1986,
     7:1, pp.22 ff.

14. Ibid.

15. Ibid.

16. See Reichley, ch.3, and William Lee Miller,
     The First Liberty: Religion and the
     American Republic (New York, Alfred A.
     Knopf, 1986), Part Two. Leonard W. Levy,
     The Establishment Clause: Religion and the
     First Amendment (New York: The Macmillan
     Company, 1986).

Campaign '88

The impact of the New Christian Right on American life, while obviously still in process, is best
understood in assessing its role in Presidential
politicing since November, 1984. By late 1986, to
be specific, it no longer stood on the fringes, but
had moved into the electoral power structure.[1] Where
once it lacked elective clout, now following Campaign
'84 every declared Republican Presidential candidate
openly sought its support. In turn, every NCR
leader, except Swaggart, made known his choice
for the Oval Office. Falwell endorsed George Bush,
Gary Jarmin approved of Jack Kemp, and Pat Robertson
was himself running for the position.[2] Such rapid
and carefully orchestrated involvement suggests
that the American citizenry may be in the midst of a
major reassessment of the traditional blend of
religion and politics.

Evidence of the professional vote strategists'
concern for religious Right clout turned up quickly.
The Republican National Committee chose a director
of ACTV, Doug Shaddix, as its representative to NCR
groups. Shaddix explained, "I'm a P.R. man for the
party. I spend a lot of time going to the meetings
of all the social groups like the Freedom Council
and the Heritage Foundation. I try to let them
know how we can help them. I want to see Christians
get involved and be salt and light in every segment of the political sector." "The Lord told us
to occupy until He comes, and that didn't mean
just the pews".[3]

The religious Right offered resources, energy,
and votes for the GOP. The expanded American
Coalition for Traditional Values leadership set a

$3 million budget to support candidates in some 100
districts favorable to the social agenda. Christian
Voice projected a half million budget for the same
general purpose. Before making his announcement
on running for the Presidency, Robertson in 1985
established a political action committee with a
$2 million budget to fund campaign expenses of pro-
Robertson office seekers. He also established a fundraising target of a five dollar gift from a large
number of his regular supporters. Underlying
the program was the understanding that would the
recipient be elected, he would have a friend in
the White House for reciprocal public policy making.[4]

Republicans courted the religious Right after
1984 also because election statistics showed then
what most observers had suspected--a seismic shift
of evangelical and fundamentalist voters from being pro-Democratic to being pro-Republican between
1976 and 1984, a shift of some 22 million voters.
Other polls showed that 69 percent of the voters
describing themselves as "born again" voted for
Reagan and 30 percent for Mondale. In Congressional
races, 60 percent of evangelicals voted for Republicans 34 percent for Democrats. A high Reagan aide
concluded, "You're talking about 10 to 12 million
voters. The evangelical vote for the Republican
Party could be what the Catholic vote was for
the Democrats in the 1940s, 1950s, and 1960s". Falwell's Liberty Federation claimed a membership
of 6.5 million families; Robertson's Freedom Councils
claimed 30,000 churches; ACTV stated it had 100,000
churches on its mailing list.[5]

Republican strategists realized further the potential of this bloc emerging and expanding through

its public relations network; a communications operation that included cable television networks and
direct mail computers, and a political gospel "that
stresses conservative values, patriotism, and social
issues".[6] This gave the NCR a direct, unchallenged
access to millions of potential voters.

Despite these advantages, the presence of the
religious Right within Republican circles also created
certain political risks. First, since NCR leaders
themselves were divided on which candidate to endorse
for the White House, that division could spread into
the ranks of their supporters. Second, both ACTV
and Christian Voice showed a significant decline
in both fundraising and energy during 1986. Third,
Falwell's biographer, Dinesh D'Souza, expressed concern
that "The Christian Right, with a few exceptions,
has so far shown a reluctance to join coalitions, the
clay and mortar of elections, because it seeks theological certainty in what is, after all, only politics."
He along with other observers concluded that although
the 18-to-24 year old group, which so strongly supported
Reagan in 1984, would not be a deliverable bloc of
voters in 1988 because its members were largely pro
choice. That added up to the conclusion that Reagan's
landslide depended upon his charisma, not the social
agenda. Finally, more centrist minded Republicans
feared that the stronger the religious Right became
within the GOP, the greater would be the resistance
to it by GOP moderates.[7]

What everyone within the Republican fold could
agree on was that several well qualified candidates
were going to run, and that what set them all apart
from the Democrats was the issue of abortion. Clearly that controversy had continued to dominate center-

stage in American public life since the 1973 Supreme
Court ruling. So strong had it become that its
pro life activists had by 1986 moved "into the main-
stream of a major political party," the Republican.
Despite polls showing voters, in 1984, opposing a
constitutional amendment to prohibit abortion by
a 77 percent to 23 percent margin, that part embraced
the anti-abortion cause. A New York Times analyst
concluded, "No other single social issue has bonded
Republican conservatives as strongly as abortion.
In recent years, it has become the principal source
of political energy driving the religious Right, which
is emerging as a significant element of the Republican coalition".[8]

Beyond that, consensus among Republicans remained
elusive because for the first time since 1980 the
office of the Presidency was open. A Gallup Poll
of May presented a representative cross-section of
candidates; George Bush, Alexander Haig, Howard Baker,
Jeane Kirkpatrick, Robert Dole, Jesse Helms, Jack
Kemp, Pat Robertson, and a dozen others.[9] Their
candidacies, while obviously in widely varying stages
of readiness, all would have to face an issue largely
unknown even as late as 1980--what each candidate's
recipe would be for mixing religion and politics,
and how those views would be made manifest in the
campaigning for the Oval Office.

This came to a head in the Spring of 1986. Drawing from its experiences with moral reportcards, hit
lists and presidential biblical scorecards, People
for the American Way announced the creation of a new
project to end "religious intolerance" in political
campaigns. Entitled "Election Project", its employees
would monitor and publically report campaign practies

which violated traditional norms and practices.
Specifically, PAW announced the development of a
set of suggested guidelines calling on candidates:
1, not to claim they are best qualified because of
their religious affiliation; 2, not to claim endorsement by God on the issues; 3, not to question the
religious faith of their opponents as based on their
positions on political and legislative issues; 4,
avoid claiming God endorses their aspirations for
public office, and 5, reject support from those who
violated these guidelines.[10]

II

Among the major candidates, this study surveys
the activities of Pat Robertson the most closely.
Observers pointed out he was the first major candidate
for the Presidency ever whose career had been focused
exclusively in television and not in public life.
Television had produced its first, but perhaps not
its last, high office seeker, one taken seriously
by the American public as an electronics medium
personality. While not having run for public office
Robertson had served before 1986 as a director of
a corporation, of the CBN University, and of a bank
and related agencies.

First hints of his Presidential candidacy emerged
in August, 1985, after several other major candidates
had announced their plans. When asked why he wanted
to run against Bush or Dole or Baker or Kemp, he
replied, "George is a wonderful person. We traveled
together to the Sudan this spring. Bob Dole is a
marvelous majority leader of the Senate. Howard Baker
was an   equally skillful majority leader. And
Representative Jack Kemp is a personal friend of mine.
Yet I think the major problem we face is the moral

state of the people. I'm talking about the need for
a spiritual reliance on God, a spirit of patriotism,
a spirit of giving, a spirit, if you will, of self-
sacrifice for noble goals. Unless we reinstate that
spirit in our people, we will continue to look to
Washington for increasingly large handouts, bailouts
and solutions. I believe from a moral and spiritual
standpoint, I would better able to address that
particular point of view and also, perhaps, to build
a national consensus to support that point of view
than maybe the other candidates." Recognizing his
identification with and, perhaps, dependence on other
major NCR leaders, Robertson in January, 1986, met
in a six hour session with Falwell, James Kennedy, Tim
LaHaye, Bill Bright and others. When asked about
their support for him, Robertson stated it was "mixed"
but "I'm amazed at the unanimity..." of evangelical
support. "I am being encouraged from every sector,
from very conservative fundamentalists to centrist
evangelicals to charismatic Pentecostals."[11]

In 1985 Robertson created a political action group,
"The Freedom Council", a tax-exempt political network
with volunteer lobbyists, employing 50 staff, pro-
jecting an annual budget of $5.5 million and a total
of 60,000 dues-paying members in the 50 states. The
Council freely acknowledged its support by the Christian
Broadcast Network system. Each state was to have
its own organization, usually with a newsletter and
information network to coordinate the work of like-
minded supporters. The primary concern, as exemplified by the newsletters for the Minnesota group,
centered on implementing the social agenda.[12]

Throughout that year Robertson talked with a
variety of political consultants but did not declare;

when asked by reporters he replied, "I'm praying about
it." He added a 24 seat jet aircraft, drew plans for
a tax-exempt think tank, "National Perspectives Institute", and renewed ties to such New Right stalwarts
as Richard Vigurie, Paul Weyrich, and Howard Phillips.
He also renewed his attack on secular humanism, calling
on Christians through the political process to win
America "back" from their control. Having earlier called
himself "a prophet of God" he now refrained from such
characterization as the campaign progressed. But
consistently he rejected reporters' charges he was simply
a power broker or stalking horse to get the New Christian
Right a larger voice in Republican policy making.[13]

Robertson's candidacy met with sharp, often unexpected resistance from some conservative religionists. Billy Graham announced in late 1985 that while
Robertson was knowledgeable about foreign affairs, "I've
written Pat and said I wouldn't take part in any partisan politics." Fred Barnes reported on evangelicals
who rejected Robertson's apparent "emergence as the
designated Christian candidate for the White House."
Robertson appeared naive about potential criticism
from those believers who rejected his positions on
faith healing, tongues, and biblical inerrancy. They
worried that his candidacy would in effect be putting
Christianity on trial, that Robertson would be accused
of wanting political power more than wanting to save
souls, and that the candidacy would divide the nation
along religious lines, the godly vs the ungodly.[14]

Not unexpectedly, Robertson's bid met with
very sharp criticism from Paul G. Kirk, Jr., Chair
of the Democratic National Committee. It proved,
if nothing else, Robertson was being taken seriously.
In a fundraising letter to Democrats, Kirk charged

Robertson "openly and aggressively advocates political action to achieve his primary goal--making American a place where everyone has the same extremist
values and views of morality." Kirk argued Robertson
would abolish public education, squelch the ERA,
outlaw abortion, require (as did Tim LaHaye suggest)a
quota of born again Christians in civil service jobs
and increased military spending. Robertson quickly
replied by calling the charges "virulent anti-
Christian bigotry", proof the Democrats were starting
a "full-scale attack on the participation of Christians
in the electoral process. That's bigotry and it's
religious discrimination. If he [Kirk] had written
the same thing about Rabbi Tannenbaum you would have
heard the roof fall in".[15]

Further criticism from other conservatives came
at the same time. Columnist George Will suggested
Robertson "might taint the GOP with peculiarity and
extremism, repelling more voters than he will attract."
Will blamed the Republicans for even taking Robertson's candidacy seriously. From National Review
John McLaughlin acknowledged Robertson's strength
as being his identification with traditional values.
But McLaughlin expressed doubt Robertson could overcome conservative opposition to his proposals for
defense cuts, his reliance on the states to prohibit
abortion, and doubts from Jews because of Robertson's
hard line on church-state issues. McLaughlin suggested
also the "wacko factor", Robertson's involvement
in the charismatic movement, especially regarding tongues
and healing. Other conservatives saw that same identification as a plus for Robertson since the number of
charismatic believers was on the increase.[16]

Throughout the early months of campaigning and
criticism, Robertson reaffirmed his commitment to
the social agenda. When asked by a reporter for
Conservative Digest "what do you see as the most
important issue and what can we do about it?", he
responded, "Ultimately, the social issues are going
to depend on the willingness of people themselves
to live according to Judeo-Christian morality. And
I believe that we need a return to morality in our
country. Now the government obviously can take a
lead..." calling "people to a sense of moral worth,
to a return of the traditional family values, the
dignity of life and these other things that we have
held dear for so many years."[17]

III

During these same months Vice President George Bush
actively cultivated New Christian Right support for
his candidacy. Employing a sizeable and sophisticated
group of political advisers, Bush started clearly
as a frontrunner. That gave him a considerable period
of time to make strategy, recruit followers, raise
funds and, among other things, assess the importance
of the religious Right. The first major outreach for
that constituency came in March, 1985. When planning
an official Vice Presidential visit to the Sudan, regarding famine, Bush announced he would meet there
with Falwell also in the area on his own mission. At
the same time Bush planned to visit Mali and Niger,
there accompanied by Robertson. Whatever the coinci-
dences that existed in planning, observers noted no
other American religious spokesmen were on his
schedule.[18]

By late, 1985, Bush was speaking to a series of
right-wing political associations for which he

acknowledged he was being criticized. The most direct
endorsement of the NCR came in January, 1986. As the
featured speaker of the unveiling by Falwell of the
Liberty Federation, Bush endorsed the social agenda;
abortion, school prayer, anti-pornography, and tax
vouchers. Reporters concluded that Bush had decided,
despite increasing ridicule for so obviously courting
the Right, to continue to do so as to "deny any political rival for the nomination a political base in
that increasingly vocal and influential part of the
GOP spectrum." Within a few weeks, national polls
showed Bush as the first choice among Republicans,
but also that the social agenda did not rank "as
important with most conservatives" as economic issues
and foreign policy."[19]

IV

As it gradually unfolded, Bush's strategy centered
more on winning to his side any potential supporters
for Congressman Jack Kemp more than in stopping any
bandwagon for Robertson. Kemp, identified from his
first days in Congress with economic conservatism,
chose during the 1985-86 months to avoid direct negotiations with Falwell, Robertson, or other NCR leaders.
He had been endorsed already by Gary Jarmin of Christian
Voice, on which he served as a "Congressional Adviser"
director. He was highly esteemed by those Rightists
who cheered his support for the state of Israel. At
a pro-Israel prayer breakfast early in 1986 the group
of 700 evangelicals "made it clear that their choice
for the 1988 Republican nomination was not Mr. Bush,
but Rep. Jack Kemp who was the honored guest at the
breakfast."[20]

New Right spokesmen such as Paul Weyrich noted that
Kemp had high standing among the conservatives. Apparently understanding that he lacked the familiarity

enjoyed by Robertson and Bush with religious Right
voters, Kemp spoke before ACTV audiences in 1985.
There he identified God as the real author of the
Declaration of Independence, and argued God could
not be separated from morality nor morality from
politics in American life. Shortly thereafter he
joined Senators Helms and Hatch to vote to stop some
$142 million in federal funds for family-planning
clinics which provided abortion-counseling services.[21]
Kemp carefully avoided utilizing his family's religious life for elective purposes. Little more was
publicized than the Kemp family membership in an
evangelical Presbyterian congregation where he led a
weekly Bible study; he also conducted prayer breakfasts
with his office staff. By contrast to Robertson and
Bush, Kemp played down his direct involvement with
the social agenda. His strength, in his estimate,
was his leadership on bread and butter economic
issues, and with that cause he identified his candidacy. Yet, for all his well organized and energetic campaigning, he found in the Spring of 1986 he
had slipped in a "first choice" presidential poll
over a year from 9 to 6 percent.[22]

V

     Senate Majority Leader Robert Dole also made known
his albeit low key candidacy for the Presidency.
Having met informally with Rightists, including some
NCR leaders since Campaign '84 ended, Dole increased
and extended his consultations into 1986, citing
to them his consistently conservative voting record
as evidence of good faith with them. By the summer
of 1986 Dole had reaffirmed his support for the social
agenda. Rightists, however, remained skeptical.
Phyllis Schlafly concluded Dole did not have "his

heart in any of the issues that conservatives care
about." Paul Weyrich found Dole not always in the
conservatives' corner, but seemed to be a good
listener to them.[23]

When readers peruse this chapter, they may
well be amused at this writer's attempts to define
by the summer of 1986 the impact of the New Christian
Right on the Republican Presidential aspirants. Bar-
ring any unforeseeable major changes, however, religious Rightists had by then clearly established
their claim to careful consideration by the front-
runners. The all-important test, the one which
would decide their long term clout in Republican
circles would be the extent to which they would influence the selection of President Reagan's successor.
That would be made evident by the time of the
Republican national convention in the summer of
1988.

XIV. Notes

1. The analysis of Kevin Phillips in Bernard Weinraub, "The Reagan Legacy", New York Times
   Magazine, June 22, 1986, p.17.

2. Swaggart's position is in The Evangelist,
   April, 1986, pp.50-51.

3. News item, Christian Life, December, 1985, p.16.

4. U.S.News and World Report, October 21, 1985, p.22;
   Minneapolis Star and Tribune, November 10, 1985,
   p.6B.

5. New York Times, March 17, 1986, p.12; Rob Gurvitt,
   "1986 Elections Generate GOP Power Struggle",
   Congressional Quarterly, April 12, 1986, pp.802-
   07; U.S.News and World Report, November 4, 1985,
   p.70; Ibid., April 21, 1986, p.181.

6. Analysis by Phil Gailey, New York Times, June 2,
   1986, p.16.

7. "Commentary" in Washington Post National Weekly
   Edition, March 10, 1986, p.23; New York Times,
   June 2, 1986, p.16; D'Souza in The American
   Spectator, August, 1985, p.13; Minneapolis
   Star and Tribune, November 12, 1985, p.3A;
   ibid., May 29, 1986,p.3A; Weinraub, "Reagan
   Legacy", p.17; New York Times, April 22, 1986,
   p.13.

8. Gailey, New York Times, June 19, 1986, p.11.

9. Minneapolis Star and Tribune, May 1, 1986, p.6A;
   ibid., March 6, 1986, p.16A; later Senator William
   Armstrong (R.--Colo.) came on this list. Newsweek,
   May 12, 1986, p.7.

10. Baptist Joint Committee, Report from the Capital,
    May, 1986, p.3; news item, Christian Century,
    April 20, 1986, p.432.

11. "Background", Conservative Digest, August, 1985,
    p.8; interview, U.S.News and World Report, Novem-
    ber 4, 1985, p.71; Thomas B. Edsall in Washington
    Post National Weekly Edition, September 2, 1985,
    pp.8-9; The Fundamentalist Journal, February,
    1986, p.64; interview, Christianity Today,
    January 17, 1986, pp.34-38.

12. New York Times, June 2, 1986, p.16; see News-
    letters from Glen Sherwood, May--September, 1985.
    When I sent in a membership check in January,
    1986, I was told "there will be no further
    issues of the Minnesota newsletter" due to a
    cutback in funding from the national office;
    letter to E.J., February 18, 1986.

13. Washington Post National Weekly Edition, Septem-
    ber 2, 1985, pp.8-9; Newsweek, October 14, 1985,
    p.77; Christianity Today, January 17, 1986, pp.
    34-38; Dallas Morning News, December 6, 1985.

14. Christian Life, January, 1986, p.15; Barnes in
    The New Republic, March 17, 1986, p.43.

15. News item, Christianity Today, April 18, 1986,
    p.48; The Arizona Daily Star (column by Bruce
    Buursma), January 12, 1986; New York Times,
    March 2, 1986, p.19; ibid., March 17, 1986,
    p.12; 700 Club Program, March 11, 1986.

16. On faith healing see Robertson's statement in
    Time, February 17, 1986, p.66; George Will,
    Newsweek, March 3, 1986, p.72; McLaughlin in
    National Review, May 23, 1986, p.20; New
    York Times, June 24, 1986, p.8.

17. Conservative Digest, August, 1985, p.5; U.S.
    News and World Report, July 14, 1986, p.24.

18. New York Times, March 1, 1985, p.10; Washington
    Post National Weekly Edition, April 8, 1985,
    p.6; Newsweek, June 24, 1985, p.35; campaign
    funding is covered in the Minneapolis Star
    and Tribune, March 22, 1985, p.3A.

19. Christian Science Monitor, December 6, 1985,
    p.1 ff; New York Times, December 13, 1985, p.11;
    Washington Post National Weekly Edition, Decem-
    ber 23, 1985, p.13; Minneapolis Star and Tri-
    bune, January 25, 1986, p.5A; New York Times,
    January 25, 1986, p.8; ibid., January 27, 1986,
    p.19; comment by Michael Kramer in New York,
    January 6, 1986, p.11; Christian Science
    Monitor, February 3, 1986, pp.1,44.

20. New York Times Magazine, May 23, 1986, pp.28 ff;
    news item, Christian Inquirer, March, p.11;
    New York Times, January 25, 1986, p.8.

21.   Ibid.; Minneapolis Star and Tribune, October 17,
      1985, p.3A; Newsweek, November 4, 1985, p.17;
      Moral Majority Report, May, 1985, p.8; St.
      Paul Pioneer Press and Dispatch, July 7, 1985,
      p.6H; Kemp's case for Israel is in his speech
      in Catalyst, 1985, I;1,pp.9-10.

22.   John M. Barry, "Let the Crusade Begin: The
      Political Ascendency of a Jock Possessed",
      Esquire, January, 1986, p.68; Gregory H.
      Fossedal, "Conservatism after Reagan", Commen-
      tary, January, 1985, pp.29-30; New York Times,
      February 1, 1986, p.10.

23.   Helen DeWar, "Bob Dole's Reach to the Right",
      Washington Post National Weekly Edition,
      June 30, 1986, p.6; George Will column in
      Minneapolis Star and Tribune, May 22, 1986,
      p.18A; Moral Majority Report, March, 1985,
      p.7.   Additional insight on the larger scene
      is furnished by Ernest B. Furgurson, Hard
      Right: The Rise of Jesse Helms (New York,
      W. W. Norton and Company, 1986).

The 1986 Elections

With six years of political campaigning experience
behind them, New Christian Right spokesmen found good
reason early in 1986 to think their cause would be
endorsed by voters in the off-year national Senate
and House elections. Their reasons included: a solid
liaison with a highly popular Chief Executive; high
name recognition throughout the mass media; grassroots
support from such organizations as Liberty Federation,
Christian Voice, American Coalition for Traditional
Values, and The Freedom Council; the popularity of the
coat tails of Marion G. (Pat) Robertson for the
Republican Presidential nomination; and confidence
they plus other voters could turn out even more liberal Democratic Senators and Representatives as they
had done starting in November, 1980. Their cause
was clear and compelling, summarized by Christian
Voice, "Our future hangs in the balance."[1]

Jerry Falwell, among others, provided specific
detail for religious Right optimism. He claimed "over
a hundred thousand Bible-believing and soulwinning
local churches" along with 30,000 Christian day
schools made up the strength of the movement. Some
82 percent "of all religious broadcasting in America
is controlled" by fundamentalist ministers. Para-
church ministries such as Campus Crusade and the
Gideons "are impacting our society in an unbeliev-
able way." America was indeed moving rapidly towards
a "great spiritual awakening." All these people were
turning America around at the grassroots level. The
news columnist, S. J. Masty, writing for Liberty
Report, claimed much the same strength for the NCR;
America was moving lastingly towards conservatism;
the Republican party was gratefully welcoming the
religious Right involvement in party matters, knowing

from there came "thoughtful and popular policies...."
Finally, Professor Ed Hindson, historian from
Liberty University of American fundamentalism con-
cluded

> The facts cannot be ignored. Liberalism is
> in reverse and shows no signs of changing
> gears. In the meantime Fundamentalism has
> been in overdrive putting its dynamic force
> into the political and social arena. Committed
> to the absolute authority of Scripture and
> undaunted by criticism and public opinion, the
> resurgence of Fundamentalism into the main-
> stream of American life could well change the
> course of history by the end of this century.[2]

Within New Christian Right leadership ranks, however, this appearance of momentum and strength failed
to reveal some serious problems for the crusade.
Being accustomed to directing their own empires, the
major spokesmen could find little common ground
among themselves. For example, before September,
1986, Christian Voice had endorsed Congressman
Kemp, Jimmy Swaggart had stayed neutral, ACTV
remained quiet, Falwell had endorsed Bush, and Robertson continued to pursue his own course. Beyond that,
the top leadership of the Republican Party had shown
something less than full enthusiasm for the energetic,
often divisive maneuvers of religious Rightists to
control the party at local and state levels. Among
NCR leaders, matters of personality and rivalry
for viewer and donor support kept the movement from
unifying. At various Republican headquarters,
spokespersons found demands by the religious Right
to give the highest party priority to the social
agenda was less than what the full part envisioned

as the course for legislation for the next two
years.[3]

Christian Voice, slowed down but not defunct from
its financial crises of 1985, moved boldly in early
1986 to claim leadership for the full New Christian
Right. Using 17 field directors in some 25 states
primarily to organize churchgoers, CV leaders turned
again to their format of moral report cards and target lists for incumbent and challenger liberals. Its
Campaign '86 instrument, "Candidates Biblical Scorecard", identified 19 "family-moral-freedom" issues
used to evaluate lawmakers' loyalty to its cause.
These included abortion, AIDS, a balanced budget,
child abuse, comparable worth, education, ERA,
euthanasia, faith and morality, freedom fighters
(Nicaragua), homosexuality, infanticide, national
defense, parental rights, pornography, religious
freedom, sanctions (South Africa), school prayer,
and secular humanism. Expanding from its earlier
scope of ratings, CV now evaluated close to 3,000
candidates for national and state offices. Some 10
to 20 million copies of the document were sent to
some 350,000 readers including 50,000 ministers; its
mailing list had been constructed from direct-mail
recruiting, grassroots campaigning, and television
fundraising.[4]

Other evangelical public affairs organizations
rejected the CV claim that it was the premier religious Right enterprise. The director of the Washington office of the National Association of Evangelicals, Robert P. Dugan, Jr., claimed some gullible
people may have believed that Christian Voice, was
as claimed, representative of that cause. But it
was, in fact, ruled by a handful of activists, account-

able only to themselves. Falwell, Swaggart, and
Robertson made no attempt to identify their programs with Christian Voice. Further, NCR supporters
could see on the "Scorecard" the printed disclaimer
that the office seeker's record was not to be taken
to be a judgmental reflection on her or his personal faith or morality. But those same readers could
also remember that in the 1984 Scorecard Senator
Mark O. Hatfield (R.--Ore.) received only a 20 percent favorable rating from CV. Known over the
years as a strong and clear voice for evangelical
Christian witness, Hatfield had achieved a legislative record warmly endorsed by many evangelical
organizations.[5]

     Falwell's organization, Liberty Federation, pre-
sented before the November elections a more modest
"Voting Record" of the national lawmakers. After
listing, with pictures, the "Ten Worst" and "Ten
Best" in the House, the organization's Liberty Report
ranked every Senator and Representative according
to these issues; the Gramm-Rudman budget amendment,
the Smith Amendment to ban federal or D.C. funds
for abortions, funding for third world abortions,
a cut in funding of printing Playboy in braille,
funding for 12 MX missiles, and contra aid.

     Not all of these issues received the same evalua-
tion weight; the contra "weighted factor" was 25.0
percent, those matters on abortion only had weighted
factors of 12.0 percent. This was done, the Report
stated, because the readers had placed a greater
importance on those issues which were weighted
higher. Also, although more than 10 lawmakers
achieved either a 100 percent favorable or unfavorable

rating, the Report editors decided to hold to a list
of 10. They thus introduced more subjective factors,
such as aggressiveness on the issues, years spent in
Congress, the extent given by national media to the
lawmaker and his (no woman made either list) leadership in introducing appropriate legislation.[6]

Other New Christian Rightists, in various ways,
announced their choices of Senators and Representatives
whom they wanted returned to office or to replace the
errant incumbent. Those states given the most religious Right attention were Alabama, Arkansas, Georgia,
Florida, Nevada, California, Nevada, Maryland, and
South Dakota. Falwell, alone among NCR leaders, endorsed Ed Zschau of California running against incumbent Alan Cranston. All the other leaders rejected
Zschau, finding Falwell's support "incomprehensible"
because the candidate was pro-choice on abortion. The
ACTV Chairman, Curtis Maynard, stated, "I can't understand why the Falwell people are doing that." Another
prominent religious Right activist commented to reporter John B. Judis, "We achieve no good if we continue to support people who are not with us. Why should
we cast our jewels before swine, when we are going
to get taken for granted?"[7]

Meanwhile, all through 1986 Pat Robertson moved
to the brink of becoming a formal candidate for the
Presidency. His activities, his strength, and his
persona all reflected both the confidence that the
New Christian Right had in its mission, and its weak-
nesses created by personalities and power contests.

Robertson's first major invasion of professional
political territory came in his challenging of Bush
and Kemp for candidates to be delegates to the Michigan Republican party nominating convention. The

campaign, such as it was, focused largely on personalities through media blitzes, with Robertson investing
some $340,000 in the race. Pro-Robertson clergy would,
on the advice of the campaign's national leaders, call
fellow fundamentalist pastors who would give them the
names of members of their respective churches who were
known to be politically active. The selected leaders
then enlisted those parishioners for involvement
on why and how to enter elective politics. One of these
told the   Washington   Post, "It was like mining gold."
Beyond those policies, Robertson's Freedom Council, its
leaders estimated, registered some 400 Democratic
delegates and 4,500 Republican delegates in Michigan.[8]
That Council also announced it had branches in all 50
states, and a dues paying membership of 60,000. As to
budget, one half came from corporate and individiual
gifts and the other from the Christian Broadcast Network, a tax exempt enterprise.[9]

Robertson claimed the vote in Michigan constituted
a great victory--he sent a letter to supporters stating,
"THE CHRISTIANS HAVE WON!...What a breakthrough for
the Kingdom."[10] Most non-aligned observers, however,
found evidence pointing to other conclusions. The
vote count procedures were extremely complicated, not
a simple listing of candidates in 1,2,3 order. A
Detroit Free Press survey concluded that while Robertson received 21 percent of the total vote, Bush received 45 percent. A Wall St. Journal/NBC poll in
July discovered that, nationwide, only nine percent
of the voters wanted Robertson to run, 32 percent
did not, and 54 percent had not heard of him. Some
weeks later, 40 percent of those polled held an unfavorable view of him, while 20 percent supported
him.[11] Other analysts found that Robertson, despite

his campaigning, failed to recruit large numbers of
new voters into the Republican party. The turnout,
across the state, was rather low, less than 600,000
of which only nine percent were first-time voters.
Another NBC poll showed Robertson was supported by
23 percent of those stating they were born again,
but only one percent of other registered Republicans.
In response, Robertson stated he was not disputing
the polls but believed they had been unduly influenced
by Democratic leaflets.[12]

In his most bold and well orchestrated penetration into elective politics, Robertson on September 17
told some 150,000 viewers attending closed circuit
video presentations in 216 sites "that God wants him
to run for President, and he is waiting to see if at
least 3 million Americans agree." Those 3 million were
asked to send in a minimum contribution of $100 for
the potential campaign. Speaking in Constitution Hall,
Washington, D.C., the televangelist stated that when
that goal had been reached, he would make his official
announcement for the White House, on or about September 17, 1987. Drawing on the full range of New
Christian Right concerns over humanism and related
symptoms of major decay within American life, Robertson pledged to provide a Presidency dedicated to restore
the primacy of family, morality, and national pride.
The audiences, in many locations, responded as they
would to a church service. At last, a real born
again leader had taken his stand.[13]

Robertson's bid received impressive endorsement
from several leading conservative Christian leaders.
Former Presidents of the Southern Baptist Convention,
Charles Stanley and Jimmy Draper, gave their public
approval as did Evangelist Oral Roberts, Bishop J. O.

Patterson, presiding bishop of the Church of God in
America, Beverly LaHaye of Concerned Women of America
and, in a decided reversal of position, Jimmy Swaggart.[14]

Swaggart's support, given before the television
program, summarized in superb religious Right fashion,
just what the issues were. He stated

> I believe the tide is running today in a way
> that mankind has never before known. It will
> affect the entire planet. And in a few months
> a hand is going to be laid on a Bible and take
> an oath of office for the highest position in
> mankind. And for the first time in human history
> the possibility definitely exists that the hand
> that lies on the Bible to take the oath of
> the highest office of the land will be joined
> to a shoulder and a hand and a heart that's
> saved by the blood of Jesus and baptized in
> the Holy Spirit.

A New Republic reporter commented, "That was the preacher
talk for: I endorse Pat for president." Swaggart went
on, "But if God be in it, it doesn't matter what the
world says."[15]

The other dominant televangelist, Jerry Falwell,
also reversed his well-known position on involvement
in politics. Just before the Robertson announcement
he told Cal Thomas, news columnist and former vice
president of Moral Majority, he would "not stick
his neck out for another political candidate the way
he did for Reagan" because "it is too polarizing
to unbelievers. I will no longer allow in my pulpit
anything but a miniscule amount of politics. We
are going back to where we were before Moral Majority
when we had a clear purpose, but did not have a
major emphasis on politics." Liberty Federation,

he stated, would remain involved in such issues as
gay rights and drug abuse.[16]

Such as announcement, catching most close observers by surprise, emerged from two considerations
by Falwell. Early in September, in a meeting with
Robertson, he agreed not to campaign for Bush, but
pledged to remain involved in political education.
In fact, Liberty Report in November, 1986, carried
detailed, non-partisan stories on each of the leading
Republican candidates: Bush, Dole, Kemp, and Robertson. Further, "sources close to the Falwell campaign",
according to Malcolm Caldwell, suggested that Falwell's
break with Bush emerged from the fact that his contributions had declined as much as $20 million or 25
percent of his revenue intake in 1985. Then, when
Robertson chose to run, thus challenging for the
first time another celebrity evangelist, "Falwell
had to deal with Robertson or watch his organization
slowly bleed to death."[17]

These major changes occurred all in the space of
a few weeks. The disarray by the leaders that the
total picture suggested was accented further by
unexpected comments from other major spokesmen highly regarded by New Christian Right supporters. Just
as Robertson announced, Secretary of Education
William J. Bennett, long a favorite on the Right,
warned in a speech at the University of Missouri
against "zealots" who wanted to "promote their own
particular brand of religion into a favored position
in public life." "There are real dangers from
religious activists in politics."[18] Also, fellow
fundamentalist and prominent Republican U.S. Senator
William L. Armstrong of Colorado, sharply criticized
Robertson for claiming that Christians "feel more

strongly than others do" about love of God and country.
The Coloradan, something of a dark horse Presidential
candidate himself, stated publicly that an evangelical Christian "should never, never, never give the
impression that in pressing their opinion...they are
somehow speaking with the authority of Scripture
or church or God." They make "a horrible mistake"
if they do. Armstrong added, "For Christians to
step across the line and try to assume for the church
a role of being power brokers or power bloc is not
only being untruthful to the faith, but invites a
backlash and properly so."[19] Robertson later apologized for his remarks. Still another major evangelical, Billy Graham, at this point made clear his position. Speaking of Robertson, he said, "I wrote and
told him that I would not support him in this running
for president, because I was not going to take sides
in partisan politics."[20]

Robertson also created considerable disputation
for views on whether the Supreme Court rulings are
the final authority for the American government, for
his televised views on faith healing, his belief
that prayers he offered were able to change the course
of an imminent storm, on whether he distorted his
record of service in the American military, and in
general, whether preachers as such were even qualified
to serve in so important a position as President.[21]

In all the controversy, voters could easily lose
track of the fact that they had been given the
responsibility by New Christian Right leaders of saving America through their voting in November. Falwell sensed this and sent a telegram to supporters
to underline the urgency of having ministers supportive
of his cause to speak to the 30 to 40 million Americans

attending church the Sunday before the November 4
elections. "We will encourage these pastors to
urge every member of their congregations to go to
the polls November 4th and vote their convictions."
This would help ensure a moral victory for America.
"Mr. Jorstad, so much rests on your gift of $15
today." "The success of our last minute 'Eleventh
Hour Blitz' to bring Americans to the polls November 4th--and, with it, the future of America."[22]
Moral Majority sent out extensive mailings calling
on supporters to fund their program for ending drug
abuse and for combatting pro-gay rights legislation.
Swaggart continued his program for support of those
legislators who would put an end to legal abortion.[23]

Just prior, then, to the November 4 elections,
the New Christian Right found itself sharply divided
within its own ranks, with its most powerful leaders
shifting their endorsements, and with little direct
encouragement from the Republican party to continue
on its designated programs of political involvement.
Further, directors of the chief critic of the religious
Right, People for the American Way, were not knowledgeable and affluent enough to be ready by the time
of Robertson's announcement for the White House to have
prepared an extensive, twenty minute tape for television highly critical of many of Robertson's religious, moral, and political ideas. Even as a rebuttal
of its major criticisms came from Robertson's Virginia
headquarters, the film stood as a vivid reminder to
NCR supporters that they would continue to face sharp,
highly sophisticated media opposition to their agenda.

Careful observers also detected additional compli-
cations for the crusade. They noted that by supporting
Robertson, Swaggart and Falwell followers were leaving

the Bush or Dole or Kemp or Baker camps, thus taking
themselves out of the political arena where horse
trading was essential. They were, Thomas B. Edsall
concluded, locking themselves into non-compromisable
positions on the social agenda (abortion, school
prayer, tuition tax credits), thus cutting themselves
off from having maneuvering power on such larger
issues as taxation and foreign policy. Beyond that,
since both Swaggart, with his sharp criticisms of
the Roman Catholic Church, and Falwell, with his
criticisms of Bishop Tutu, for instance, had become
so unpopular with voters that the two would furnish
"ideal ammunition for Democrats seeking to undermine the growing success of the Republican party in
winning over substantial blocs of support among
working and middle-class Catholics". In sum, the
New Christian Right had taken its stand within the
Republican organization for its social agenda without
thinking through the long term implications of its
positions in the arena where only one outcome
mattered: who was elected.[24]

II

That court of final appeal was convened on November
4 with the religious Right clearly lacking the commanding position it held at the time of President Reagan's
re-election. Perhaps sensing, among other things,
that Republican control of the Senate and NCR credibility were being severely tested, the President himself
spent much of October and early November crossing the
country to personally endorse party candidates for
election or re-election, including those targeted by
the New Christian Right. While political analysts
were making no firm predictions on how the Republican majority of three in the Senate would survive, the

White House apparently sensed that the President must
make his leadership and his agenda the major issues.
Repeatedly, while endorsing Republicans, Reagan
told voters that if they wanted to vote for his program, they should vote GOP. Across the nation they
voters heard the President say, "The next couple of
years will decide whether all our progress since 1980
will be set in concrete or only written in sand. If
we don't keep control of the U.S. Senate we're going
to wake up one morning and find it all gone with the
wind."[25]

Then, on Election Day, as the results started to
reach the public it became clear, as one news magazine put it, "The Gipper stumbles". By the end of
the tallying, the Republicans had lost their majority
in the Senate; the Democrats had been given a commanding majority of 55 to 45. In an unusually low voter
turnout, only some 37.3 percent eligible went to
the polls, the Democrats made a net gain of eight
seats, including winning each one targeted in the
Senate by the New Christian Right.

For that movement, that outcome was the overwhelmingly significant feature of Campaign '86. In
Florida Governor Bob Graham had defeated Senator Paula
Hawkins. Much to the great surprise of the White
House, Senator Jeremiah Denton of Alabama was replaced
by Richard Shelby. In North Carolina, former governor Terry Sanford replaced James Broyhill in a state
which had sent two far Right senators to Capitol Hill,
Jesse Helms and John East (Broyhill replaced East
after the latter's death in 1986). In South Dakota
Tom Daschle turned out Senator James Abnor, who had
a 100 percent rating from Liberty Federation. In
Georgia Wyche Fowler upset Mack Mattingly, the candidate

of the Right. In California, the liberal Democrat
incumbent, Alan Cranston, turned down the Falwell-
endorsed Ed Zshau. In Arkansas the fundamentalist
challenger, Asa Hutchinson, lost to incumbent Dale
Bumpers. In Maryland the criticism by former White
House staff member Linda Chavez that her rival
Barbara Mikulski was "anti-male" and "a San Francis-
co candidate" (i.e., pro homosexual) failed to
convince the voters. In Nevada the endorsement by
retiring Senator Paul Laxalt, a favorite of the new
religious Right, of Republican James Santini could
not stop his defeat by Harry Reid. Every new
Christian Right candidate representing Southern states
was defeated, a major reversal of form for the Bible
Belt. In all, at the very least, the Senate turn-
around was a stunning setback for all conservatives.[26]

Exit polls by ABC News helped point to the reasons
for the outcome. Voters expressed their concern over
the issues most needing legislative solutions; federal
budget deficits, keeping the United States out of
war, reducing unemployment, protecting social security,
and illegal drugs.[27] Further, the polls suggested
that a large number of those voters identifying themselves as "born again Christians" did vote; some 47
percent of the Democrats and 53 percent of Republicans gave themselves that classification when polled.
But large numbers of those naming themselves as
"strong feminists" and "strong environmentalists",
"farmers" and "retired people" also voted. Also,
the large support for President Reagan in 1984
among the 18 to 24 year old voters failed to repeat
in 1986; the majority in that class who voted now
went Democratic.[28]

However, analysts pointed out the Senate victory
meant no sweeping revision of Reagan Republicanism.
The victorious Democrats had not called in their
campaigning for major overhauls of existing legislation, but emphasized the need for continuing biparti-
san support on the key economic and foreign policy
issues.[29]

For the New Christian Right, the election results
failed to confirm their earlier claims of growing
strength. Beyond the Senate, such religious Right
candidates as Representative Bill Cobey of North
Carolina, State Senator James Butcher of Indiana,
and gubernatorial candidate Cal Ludeman of Minnesota,
all identified as supportive of the NCR, lost in
their races. Nationally, Pat Robertson attributed
the setbacks to local issues, personalities, and the
heavy voter registration of Democrats.[30] People
for the American Way, however, stated the reversals
were signs the voters were rejecting the way the
Republicans were trying to align themselves with
the religious Right. In more guarded terms, other
Republicans stated they were resentful of the manner
in which the NCR leaders were demanding their social
agenda be enacted. Those spokesmen, in turn,
claimed the national party had scuttled their issues
and office seekers.[31]

In concrete terms, the 1986 Senatorial elections
especially pointed to the difficulty the New Christian
Right would have in implementing its program before November, 1988, with both houses of Congress now
controlled by the Democrats. Leaders there could
bottle up any proposals for a new voluntary school
prayer amendment or restrictive gay rights legislation.
The Senate Judiciary Committee could seriously compli-

cate plans of the White House to appoint a new
Justice to the Supreme Court who would be pro life.
Tuition tax credit legislation would have a serious
uphill struggle in both Houses. Further, shortly
after the elections, the Attorney General's office
announced it would not put forward any controversial ultraconservative candidates for federal judgeships. With the Democrats controlling the Judiciary
committee, Republicans would not want to give
them controversial candidates whom the Democrats
could turn into media victories.[32]

The losses at the polls would mean that NCR fund
raisers would probably have increasingly difficult
times in attracting money for their programs and
for their political action committees (PACs). Even
before the November elections, some leading religious
right groups such as Christian Voice were seriously
considering abandoning that form of fund raising.
Other right wing political activist groups submitted
reports showing their revenue already was in decline.[33]

Finally, those Republican presidential candidates
who had been seeking New Christian Right support by
winning the endorsements of the latter's leaders would
need to reconsider that strategy. For instance, Vice
President Bush had gone to considerable trouble and
encountered enormous ridicule for courting Jerry
Falwell's approval, and then Falwell went on to drop
him. Those religious leaders who support Robertson
have risked alienating their churchgoing followers.
As Malcolm Glaswell concludes, "There is no evidence
that the people will follow their leaders' endorsements".[34] Everyone involved could see that President
Reagan's coattails popularity failed to extend to
those candidates he endorsed. So, suddenly after the

euphoria (especially among the Bush strategists) of President Reagan's landslide victory in 1984, the trophy of Campaign '88, the occupancy of the White House, seemed now to be accessible only to those who were willing to start their quest over again from Square One.

1. Fundraiser letter, October 6, 1986, signed by
    Colonel V. Doner, p.2.

2. Falwell in The Fundamentalist Journal, September,
    1986, p.10; Masty, "Commentary", Liberty Report,
    November, 1986, p.6; Ed Hindson, "Perspective",
    Fundamentalist Journal, November, 1985, p.14;
    see also the view that the NCR was gaining
    strength in 1986, by Jeffrey K. Hadden, "News
    Analysis", Christianity Today, June 13, 1986,
    pp.38-39.

3. John B. Judis, "The Charge of the Light Brigade",
    The New Republic, September 29, 1986, pp.16-19;
    Houston Post, May 15, 1986; News story, New York
    Times, October 26, 1986, p.16; "News" column,
    Christianity Today, October 17, 1986, p.40; "News
    Analysis", ibid., November 7, 1986, pp.46-48.

4. It advertised itself to be "nonpartisan" and "non-
    sectarian"; Candidates Biblical Scorecard (Washing-
    ton, D.C., 1986); Christianity Today, November 7,
    1986, pp.46-48.

5. Ibid.

6. Liberty Report, August, 1986, pp.16-18.

7. Judis, "Charge", p.17; Miami Herald, April 16,
    1986; Liberty Report, September, 1986, p.9.

8. Quoted in a news story in Sojourners, August/
    September, 1986, pp.10-11.

9. Ibid.

10. Fred Barnes, "Rarin' to Go", The New Republic,
    September 29, 1986, p.15; Los Angeles Times,
    September 18, 1986, p.25.

11. Ibid.

12. Carl P. Leubsdorf, "Viewpoints", Dallas Daily
    News, August 14, 1986; a helpful, extended
    critique is Remer Tyson, "Pat Robertson",
    Detroit Free Press, September 14, 1986, pp.
    B1 ff.

13. News story, Christianity Today, October 17,
     1986, p.39; see a background story by Steve
     Berg, correspondent for the Minneapolis Star
     and Tribune, September 16, 1986, pp.1A,9A,
     12A; Sandy Grady, Knight-Ridder Newspapers, in
     the Arizona Daily Star, September 21, 1986,
     p.4; Dallas Morning Star, September 19,
     1986, p.7A.

14. Christianity Today, November 17, 1986, pp.41 ff.

15. Quoted in Barnes, "Rarin' to Go", New Republic,
     September 29, 1986, p.14.

16. "News", Christianity Today, October 17, 1986,
     p.55; Washington Post National Weekly Edition,
     November 10, 1986, p.28.

17. Malcolm Caldwell in The New Republic, November
     24, 1986, p.15; U.S.News and World Report,
     August 4, 1986, p.13.

18. Los Angeles Times, September 18, 1986, p.26.

19. Washington Post National Weekly Edition,
     August 18, 1986, p.15.

20. See the full interview in U.S.A.Today, September
     30, 1986, p.9A.

21. See the Washington Post National Weekly
     Edition for July 14, 1986, p.16; and ibid.,
     October 20, 1986, p.28; Arizona Daily Star,
     October 2, 1986; Newsweek, October 13, 1986,
     p.48; Michael Kramer in New York, September
     29, 1986, pp.20-22; William Buckley in Dallas
     Morning News, August 21, 1986, p.31A; Russell
     Baker in The Denver Post, September 24, 1986;
     see also the monthly "Inside the American
     Religious Scene", Religious News Service,
     I:17, October 23, 1986, pp.1-2.

22. "Telegram to Mr. Jorstad", October 22, 1986.

23. Moral Majority, "National Task Force on Drug
     Abuse" letter to supporters, 1986; Liberty
     Report, August, 1986, p.19; The Evangelist,
     July, 1986, p.44.

24. Thomas B. Edsall, Washington Post National
     Weekly Edition, November 10, 1986, p.28.

25. Washington Times, September 10, 1986; David
     Broder in Washington Post National Weekly
     Edition, November 17, 1986, p.4; Broder,
     Seattle Times, November 6, 1986, p.A14.

26. U.S.News and World Report, November 17, 1986,
     pp.16-21; U.S.A.Today, November 5, 1986, pp.
     3A-5A; Christian Science Monitor, November
     6, 1986, pp.20-21.

27. U.S.A.Today, November 5, 1986, p.3A.

29. Ibid.; Washington Post National Weekly Edition,
     November 17, 1986, p.8.

30. "Op-Ed", Michael Barone; ibid., November 17,
     1986, p.29; ibid., p.37; New York Times, Novem-
     ber 9, 1986, p.1E,sect.4; Newsweek, November
     17, 1986, pp.28-31; Time, November 17, 1986,
     pp.38-41; Minneapolis Star and Tribune, Novem-
     ber 6, 1986, p.B2; Christian Science Monitor,
     November 6, 1986, pp.1,40; Newsweek claims the
     fundamentalists voted for economic issues; see
     November 17, 1986, p.37; U.S.News and World
     Report, November 17, 1986, p.13.

31. Ibid.

32. Story, Robert E. Norton, "Reagan's Impact on
     the Courts", Fortune, November 24, 1986, pp.
     121-28; U.S.News and World Report, November
     17, 1986, p.13.

33. Edsall in Washington Post National Weekly
     Edition, November 10, 1986, p.12.

34. New Republic, November 24, 1986, p.16.

The Continuing Struggle: Critics and Estimates

By choice, New Christian Right leaders have confronted their adversaries with aggressive, polemical
criticism and judgement. In turn, they have become
the targets of those they selected for intensive
scrutiny. This chapter summarizes the major criticisms
and critics of the religious Right, and its response
to that commentary. Such information helps illuminate the manner in which the general public perceived
the movement in its first seven years of existence.

Clearly the most influential and controversial
of the critics has been People for the American Way.
Had not the NCR entered into politics so obviously,
PAW would never have come to life. After its initial
founding by television producer Norman Lear in 1980,
it expanded rapidly over the next six years. One
commentator noted it "has become a major force in
the national debate on religious liberty, censorship, church-state relations and judicial independence...a preeminent spokesman on the left, fueled
in part by a $5 million budget that dwarfs those of
most liberal advocacy groups."[1]

Its prominence emerged from its energetic and
comprehensive use of both news and print media,
and its financial support form some 200,000 contributors who were kept informed by PAW leaders about
their victories, defeats, and current agenda. They
found a ready national market by serving as rebuttal
on popular talk shows to NCR spokesmen. Lear,
John Buchanan and Anthony Podesta proved capable
adversaries to Falwell, Jarmin, LaHaye, et.al,
on shows such as that of Phil Donahue, CrossFire, CBS
Morning News, The McNeil/Lehrer Report, and Take Two.
Such exposures brought the new organization instant
and national publicity, a prerequisite for increasing
its base of supporters.

On television and in their tapes, radio and television spots, brochures, pamphlets and books, they engaged the religious Right on the most controversial
of the agenda items: school prayer, gay rights,
creationism, schoolbook protest movements, controversial appointments by Reagan to high federal positions
including the bench. Some 300 radio talk shows received
regular taped material. PAW also produced brief, pri-
mer form publications replete with brief summaries of
major controversies such as religion in American life,
education, public policy questions and book censorship. These contained information on the involvement
of the NCR in such controversies, information on why
the PAW rejected that involvement, information on
the many Rightist groups involved in the battles,
and suggestions for further study.[2]

Beyond that, the organization has utilized members
in specific regions and cities to speak on the social
agenda issues at local meetings and on the lecture
circuit. Such formats gave PAW considerable flexibi-
lity and often strong credibility by using speakers
familiar with local situations and hence more acceptable to local citizens.

As noted earlier, PAW sponsored legal counsel for
parents and schoolboards facing legal action by New
Christian Right groups over the selection of textbooks and related curriculum issues. PAW claimed
a major victory over the Gablers when the Texas State
Board of Education voted to repeal that state's ten-
year old anti-evolution textbook rules. Further,
PAW leaders created what they called the "Freedom
Network", a program of training members in how to
resist what they perceived to be censorship programs
in local schools. A letter explained that "The 'Network' concept works because it teaches people, in

their own communities, to fight for themselves. We
give the tools and the know-how and they produce results."[3] PAW sponsored on March 31, 1986, a four
page ad in the national daily newspaper, USA Today,
explaining its program and asking for financial
support. On issues concerning Congress or the
Presidency, PAW used the same format as the NCR
in sending its members information petitions with
the member's name printed on it, and addressed to the
officials in Washington responsible for taking action
on the controversy. Finally, as NCR criticism of
their program increased, PAW leaders responded by
producing two minute radio and television rebuttals
sent to local news outlets.[4]

　　All of this, observers noted, was made possible
because PAW had the funds and the know-how to use "a
time-honored technique: painting the opposition
in fearsome colors".[5] That opposition wasted no
time in returning the favor. Calling Norman Lear the
man who gave American television such "sleaze" as
"Mary Hartman! Mary Hartman!" and "All in the Family"
Falwell and other leaders used the programs of the
PAW as further proof of how deeply the secular humanist
conspiracy had permeated the broadcast media.
Swaggart devoted considerable time in his April, 1986,
issue of The Evangelist for rebuttal. He renamed
it "People for the Atheist Way"--since, in his judgement, Lear considered himself an atheist. PAW, to
Swaggart, was pro homosexuality, pro Feminist movement, pro choice, and wanted "to close every church
door in the land because their real argument is
with the Bible and the morality it represents."
"These people for the atheist way are doing their
very best to sweep clean every influence of true

Christianity, and if they had their way, every vestige
of freedom this nation knows would be lost forever."
"They want to espouse socialism and communism over
the true American way of life...their philosophy is
much more attuned to communism via the road of socialism
than it is the free enterprise system."[6]

Falwell's Liberty Report in February, 1986, gave
extended attention to People For. Falwell especially
resented what he perceived as the attempt by the
group to exclude religious people from political
activity and public life. It claimed PAW wanted religious tolerance only for its position, but not for
fundamentalists. "People For is less interested in
preserving the Constitution than it is in eviscerat-
ing fundamentalists. And while it objects to the
fundamentalists involving themselves in politics
and education, it is appalled at what men like
Jerry Falwell actually believe."

Falwell in his Sunday worship service made his
objections even clearer. He claimed Lear "decided
to attack all the Gospel preachers"; "John Buchanan,
a Christian preacher, a Southern Baptist preacher
who didn't make it in the ministry, became a Congressman, didn't make it there, they voted him out, I
suppose he drove an Edsel at one time or another
and then he joined this t.v.mogul..." and Podesta,
"A Kennedy staffer...who worked for Ms Ferarro in
her quest for the Vice Presidency and then he
joined the same group, it's a group of losers."
Falwell concluded that PAW wanted "to shut down
the Jerry Falwells and Billy Grahams and Pat
Robertsons and you name it, the Gospel preachers."[7]

II

Alongside People For, other church-related and

civil libertarian organizations increased their
criticisms of the New Christian Right after 1984.
Americans for Religious Liberty, with headquarters
near Washington, D.C. devoted much of its program
to sponsoring lectures, offering information,
and making extended criticism of the social agenda.
It found Reagan, with full endorsement from the
Right, "shamelessly" using religious piety for political purposes. By nominating an Ambassador to Vatican
City, by using tax support for sectarian schools,
by sponsoring amendments for school prayers and by
standing for pro life, Reagan was in ARL judgement
subjecting "all women to the dictates of Rome and
Lynchburg on reproductive matters."[8]

Equally opposed, along with having a wider range
of programs for its members was Americans United for
Separation of Church and State, also located near
Washington. It found the NCR leaders had launched
a "go-for-broke campaign to rewrite the Constitution." Sharply criticizing Falwell, LaHaye and
Robertson, AU spokesmen found those leaders ready
"to take the law into their own hands. They have
launched the most dangerous attack on the United
States Constitution that I have ever seen--perhaps
the worst in our nation's history." AU was especially
concerned over the call for a new constitutional
convention in which delegates could write into the
fundamental law of the land their social agenda.
Pointing out that since its founding in 1947 AU
had fought to protect religious liberty, it identified its mission with the defeat of the school
prayer amendment, the defeat of tuition tax vouchers, the defeat of the creationists, and the defeat
of unqualified appointees to high federal government

positions. This, of course, was much the same agenda
as People For. Lacking that group's resources, AU
leaders appeared nonetheless frequently on radio
and television talk shows promoting their cause
and continuing to search for more support. It also
provided resources for further study such as extensive bibliographies by its Director of Research,
Albert J. Menendez.[9]

Other groups, such as Americans for Democratic
Action, and various local chapters of the American
Civil Liberties Union carried out much the same
activities. In a decade when the older political
liberalism seemed at best quaint and to many irrelevant, activists started to rebuild anti-Right
coalitions in local, decentralized ways. Think
tanks such as the Institute for Policy Studies promoted extended study programs on "The Rise of the
American Right". Others such as that calling itself
"New Directions" brought together in May, 1986, a
conference featuring Jesse Jackson, Michael Harring-
ton, Gloria Steinem, Julian Bond and Congressman Ron
Dellums to find ways to rebuild liberal opposition
to the social agenda.[10]

III

Of considerable importance for an understanding
of how the New Christian Right claimed legitimacy for
its blend of religion and politics was the increasing criticism made of that by conservative and
evangelical leaders. Among the several prominent
spokesmen, we examine here the views of three; the
editors of Sojourners, Charles Colson, and Professor
Richard V. Pierard, the bibliographer of the New
Christian Right.

Dedicated to a disciplined, community form of

political activism and evangelical theology, Sojourners found the religious Right leaders to be
seriously deficient on several matters. Editor Jim
Wallis sharply criticized easy and fulsome identification of Christianity with the domestic and foreign
policies of the White House, thus eliminating any
prophetic distancing from the powers and principalities of this world. The televangelists, Wallis
argued, gave the right-wing politicians a "reliqious
and moral credibility" they had not earned. That in
turn, narrowed the range of discussion and dissent
on key issues. In a key sentence, he wrote, "Through
effective religious oratory, extreme right-wing political views can be made to sound like the things that
made this country great and the good old-fashioned
values that most Americans believe". Wallis added,
the celebrity preachers, in the name of evangelical
values, are peddling "a nationalist, exclusivist,
materialist, militaristic, and repressive world view
that is decidedly un-evangelical." The preachers had
sold out to the politicians. And by claiming their
critics were "left-wing" or "communist" the preachers
had discredited genuine religious dissent. Finally,
the gospel they preached was not the Gospel of Jesus
Christ, "not good news to the poor, to the margin-
alized and disenfranchised, to racial minorities and
women, to the starving millions..." Sojourners
dedicated its energies to resist the attack by "the
most powerful political forces in the world...the
wolves in sheep's clothing."[11]

Charles Colson, best known for his participation
in the Watergate debacle, produced what in some observer's evaluations were the most searching criticisms
of all; "no one's criticisms carry the weight of

Colson's."[12] A dedicated and influential evangelicalist after his born again experience, Colson found
cause to enter into the battle after listening to
some television preachers who "sound like they've
just hung up from a private session with Him before
going on the air..." As to Robertson, Colson stated,
"the presidency would not be something a Christian
leader could run for, but something he'd be drafted
for, and there is only one Person who could do the
drafting."

In brief summary here, Colson criticized the
idea he found within the NCR that something close
to the Kingdom would be ushered in when the social
agenda became law. Politics, to Colson, simply by
necessity had to wrestle with the weighty but secular issues of the secular world. Religious faith
must be kept isolated from that enough to stand in
prophetic judgement of its pretensions. One observer
summarized Colson's comments that "there is simply
too much eagerness in fundamentalist political
activism--the exploitation of direct mail, the pro-
liferation of PACs, the slick and lavish promotional
efforts. They may have been pushed into politics,
but now they like the game an awful lot." Pat
Robertson had spoken on that, stating God used oak
trees, not mushrooms, i.e., the meek and lowly. La-
Haye claimed a Christian had a birthright to political power. For Colson, it was all too much.[13]

Finally, from the evangelical community also
came far reaching criticism from one of the New
Christian Right's most careful trackers, Richard
V. Pierard. He interpreted the increasing political power of that movement as placing Americans
"on the brink of a Kirchenkampf of monumental

proportions"; he called on believers to fight back.
The religious Right had erred in several regards, in
his estimate for several reasons. First, they
created attractive personality cults where leaders
aspired to fame and greatness with "empires with
churches, schools, TV studios, modernistic buildings,
and outreach divisions which employ hundreds of people and consume untold sums of money." Such leaders
enjoyed the company of the President, riding high
in the saddle. Second, they interpreted America's
woes as being caused by the internal conspiracy,
a theme very attractive to millions, but which simply
was wrong. Third, the leaders placed an excessive
emphasis on "absolutes" being injected into public
life which in turn blurred the need for everyone
to understand how ambiguity and paradox contribute
to public life. These absolutes, Pierard concluded,
were highly selective, based on their own preferences,
such as Falwell's belief that capitalism was endorsed
in the Old Testament. Next, they often created among
supporters a weakening loyalty to the latter's local
church or denomination by insisting on support for
their national programs. They are celebrities,
"electronic church personalities, organizational
entrepreneurs...not loyal churchmen." They fall
short of the biblical way in achieving their objectives, as did Falwell who once lied about homosexual influences on Jimmy Carter. They lack "humili-
ty, deference, and self-denial", all qualities
Jesus taught his disciples. Theirs was not a religious gospel but a different one, a political gospel,
an American gospel bound by time and culture.[14]
     Obviously what was at stake in this debate,
among other things, was a conflict of seismic propor-

tions over what constituted the essence of the expression of Christian faith in a secular world.

IV

As this is written in late 1986 the appearance
of the New Christian Right is the dominant theme,
among many significant developments, in American
religious history in the 1980s. It spread quickly
and powerfully because of its skills in fundraising,
utilization of the several media, and its legitimization by the President of the nation. Its appearance
and obviously secure position along the religious
spectrum stands as an unmistakeable reminder of its
being a reappearance of the older, traditional division within American Christendom between liberal
and conservative, or modernist and fundamentalist.
What was original in this new movement was its
adroit management of the political process for its
agenda. Never before had it enjoyed such power and
never before had it been so bitterly and thoroughly
resisted by secularists and believers alike.

The New Christian Right leaders are best evaluated
in terms of their successes and failures in their
newly chosen arena of activity--elective politics.
For all of their consciousness raising about the obligations of believer to participate in politics,
they chose to accept the criteria of success, the
"reward system" of elective politics: Did it work?

Was the social agenda implemented? The answer
obviously that when using the short list, only the
opposition to the Equal Rights Amendment was success-
fully carried out by the end of 1986. Legal abortions
continued on, gay rights civil legislation increased
slowly but persistently; no voluntary school prayer
amendment was on the statute books; no tuition tax

credits were legalized. The secular humanists, as
such, stood in their positions of power by this
time just as they had in years before. Some significant inroads were made in eliminating printed pornography from convenience stores, but this was accomplished outside the political arena. Clearly, the
general public endorsed the NCR enthusiasm for demonstrations of flagwaving patriotism, but within their
own ranks conservatives expressed serious doubts
about whether this constituted what Jesus had in
mind about rendering to Caesar what was his.

What the New Christian Right had not been able
to prove, or convince the electorate, was that its
particular agenda would save America. Knowing of
that society's tribalization and its endorsement of
religious and moral pluralism, the religious Right
offered a series of legislative and constitutional
proposals aimed at restoring what it considered
had once been America's rightful place in God's
providence. They assumed their consensus was the
only one stamped with God's approval and fit for a
society such as ours.

But, as observers such as Martin E. Marty stated,
they were wrong. In writing about the death of the
Challenger astronauts, he stated, "No legislation
privileging 'Judeo-Christians' in an imposed 'consensus' is needed to hold us together. As the
nation mourns we relearn the boundaries of our
circle--nationwise, they are--to match the bound-
less grieving and new hope. What holds the circle
together is what we have together. We share time
and space, the land whose earth we kiss when we
return home, and the few short years we have to
mess it up together. We own a shared memory, in

myth and symbol, in narrative and proposition, that
the newest Asian boat children cherish alongside us--
from ghetto blacks who were denied centrality in
earlier chapters. We share failures, and there are
shared problems, of awesome kind, often recognized
and sometimes faced and, in rare cases, met and
transcended. We share intentions and projects,
and these often acquire a sacral glow "under God";
they do so best when no law would program them."
Marty concluded, "we are all kindred with affection
for one another. Kin do argue and they must in a
lively republic."[15]

The New Christian Right has served Americans well
in this regard--as a reminder of our civic responsibilities. But it often overlooked the dangers result-
ing "when religion and power got too cozy", when
its truths "were the truths it sought to enforce."
John Garvey reminds us that religion "betrays its
nature and its deepest helpfulness when it is token
of belonging to the crowd of good citizens and
respectable people. It may indeed have served well
as a social control at certain points in the past,
but that isn't what the prophets or the gospels
are about."[16]

Does this suggest that the more things change,
the more they stay the same? This writer would
say no; the appearance of the New Christian Right
marks a significant new development in the history
of the nation, and the history of the church. How
well that blend of religion and politics to find
the American way results in an improvement in the
general welfare of everyone of us concerned is an
event which makes our immediate future a memorable
time in which to be alive.

XV. Notes

1. Howard Kurtz in the Washington Post, February 3,
    1986.

2. See, for instance David Bollier, Liberty and
    Justice for Some (New York, Frederick Ungar
    Publishing Co., 1982), and Barbara Parker and
    Stefanie Weiss, Protecting the Freedom to Learn:
    A Citizen's Guide (Washington, D.C., People for
    the American Way, 1983).

3. Fundraising letter, 1986, starting with "Wednes-
    day morning..."; Kurtz, op.cit.

4. Letters to members, November 27, 1985, February
    13, 1986, June 4, 1986; News item, Christianity
    Today, September 20, 1985, p.44.

5. See the PAW quarterly newspaper, Forum; Kurtz,
    op cit.; a good summary of its activities is
    in the March 31, 1986, issue of USA Today, insert.

6. The Evangelist, April, 1986, pp.42,43,44,52.

7. Liberty Report, February, 1986, pp.11,22,23; Old-
    Time Gospel Hour, March 16, 1986; a thoughtful
    critique of some of Podesta's positions is David
    Wagner, "The New Right and the New Pluralism",
    National Review, May 23, 1986, pp.28,29,32,52.

8. Ed Doerr, Executive Director of the ARL, comment
    in The Humanist, January/February, 1986, p.37;
    see the ARL newsletter, Voice of Reason,
    1983 to the present.

9. A letter in 1986 from Dr. Robert L. Maddox, p.2;
    Albert J. Menendez, ed., Religious Conflict in
    America(New York, Garland Reference Library,
    1985); ibid., Religion and the U.S. Presidency
    (Garland, N.Y., Reference Library, 1986).

10. The Nation, March 22, 1986, p.436; Washington
    Post National Weekly Edition, June 24, 1985, p.11.

11. Wallis, "A Wolf in Sheep's Clothing", Sojourners,
    May, 1986, pp.20-23; see also the critique by
    S.R. Shearer, "The Evangelical-Jewish Coalition",
    Catalyst, I;1, 1985, pp.59-77; Shearer is with
    the TAV Evangelical Ministries.

12.   Malcolm Gladwell, "Chuck. Colson vs. The
      Fundamentalists", The American Spectator,
      February, 1986, pp.21-23.

13.   Ibid.; see also the evaluation by Richard John
      Neuhaus, "What the Fundamentalists Want",
      Commentary, May, 1985, pp.41-46.

14.   Richard V. Pierard, "The Christian Right
      Threat to Evangelical Christianity", Baptist
      Joint Committee, Report from the Capitol,
      November/December, 1985, pp.4-5; See the
      Pierard bibliography, "Bibliography on the
      Religious Right in America", 1986: ISSN
      0193-970X; P1852; Vance Bibliographies,
      P.O.Box 229, Monticello, Il., 61856; see
      also David Basinger, "Voting One's Christian
      Conscience", Christian Scholar's Review,
      1986, XV:2, pp.141-56.

15.   Martin E. Marty, "Commentary", Minneapolis
      Star and Tribune, February 5, 1986, pp.11A.

16.   Comment by John Garvey in Commonweal, Novem-
      ber 2-16, 1984, p.585.

TOPIC INDEX

NAME INDEX

STUDIES IN AMERICAN RELIGION